WHY AMERICA'S PUBLIC SCHOOLS ARE THE BEST PLACE FOR KIDS

Reality vs. Negative Perceptions

Dave F. Brown

ROWMAN & LITTLEFIELD EDUCATION
A DIVISION OF
ROWMAN & LITTLEFIELD PUBLISHERS, INC.
Lanham • New York • Toronto • Plymouth, UK

KH

Published by Rowman & Littlefield Education
A division of Rowman & Littlefield Publishers, Inc.
A wholly owned subsidary of The Rowman & Littlefield Publishing Group, Inc.
4501 Forbes Boulevard, Suite 200, Lanham, Maryland 20706
www.rowmaneducation.com

Estover Road, Plymouth PL6 7PY, United Kingdom

British Library Cataloguing in Publication Information Available

Library of Congress Cataloging-in-Publication Data

Brown, Dave F.
  Why America's public schools are the best place for kids : reality vs. negative perceptions / Dave F. Brown.
      p. cm.
  Includes bibliographical references and index.
  ISBN 978-1-61048-357-5 (hardback) — ISBN 978-1-61048-358-2 (paper) — ISBN 978-1-61048-359-9 (electronic)
  1. Public schools—United States. 2. Education—United States. 3. Academic achievement—United States. I. Title.
  LA217.2.B78 2011
  371.010973—dc23
                                                      2011040904

Printed in the United States of America.

5/1/13

WHY AMERICA'S PUBLIC SCHOOLS ARE THE BEST PLACE FOR KIDS

To
Jerry J. Bellon,

who leads by example, and in the process, teaches so
many of us to think critically, question authority, and
make research-based decisions for the good of children

CONTENTS

Foreword by Richard L. Allington, Ph.D.   ix

Preface   xiii

Acknowledgments   xvii

1 Public Schools: Successful Graduates   1

2 Is the Public School in Your Community a "Good" School?   11

3 How America's Schools Outshine Other Nations' Schools   25

4 The Value of Public School Teachers   53

5 Inaccuracies and Absurdities Delivered by the Press, Pundits,
and Politicians   89

6 When Government and Big Business Get Cozy: More Lies
and an Expensive Agenda   113

7 Advantages of Attending Public Schools   139

8 Charter Schools and Vouchers: Tax Dollars Down the Drain   159

9 No Child Left Behind: Damaging Public Education   179

10 Urban Schools: More Successful Than We Hear   217

Afterword 245

Notes 247

Index 263

About the Author 269

FOREWORD

As I read Dave Brown's new book, *Why America's Public Schools Are the Best Place for Kids*, I kept thinking about Gerald Bracey. Bracey, before his early and untimely death, was the consummate critic of various sorts of official "truths." I also thought of David Berliner, the past-president of the American Educational Research Association and another vocal critic of federal education policies. Finally, I thought of Susan Ohanian, whose books and website present highly critical analyses of conservative educational policies and practices.

The book had me thinking of these icons of educational comment and criticism because Brown, like these critics, has managed to pull together powerful arguments for just why American public education deserves almost none of the criticisms most often leveled at it. Public schools work as well as or better than private schools, charter schools, and voucher-based reforms. Nonetheless, the public rarely hears about the positive aspects of public schools. The federal and state governments, regardless of which political party is in charge, are just as likely as any other group to criticize American public schools while demonstrating support for private schooling, charter schools, and voucher-based alternatives to attending public schools.

What Brown has managed to accomplish is a spirited defense of public education by relying on data—that's right, by sticking to the facts about public education, often facts gathered by federal and state education agencies. He describes just how education "news" has shifted from primarily positive to primarily negative, even as public schools have dramatically expanded the number of students who complete high school and the number who complete college degrees. While this feat was accomplished, student achievement on the National Assessment of Educational Progress (NAEP) remained at least stable or improved.

As Bracey notes, Simpson's paradox provides an explanation of how even though there has been large growth in minority reading achievement, there has been less growth in national reading-achievement trend data on the NAEP.[1] Take the case of Hispanic students in American schools. When the NAEP began in 1971, there were so few Hispanic children enrolled in American schools that their scores were not broken out by ethnic group. Back then, a few states (e.g., CA, TX, FL) had a substantial proportion of Hispanic students, but Hispanic students were almost unknown in many if not most states (e.g., KS, NE, ME, LA, MS, TN, MN, OR). In the most recent NAEP report, 20 percent of the students participating were Hispanic students, and Hispanic-student population growth is now a nationwide trend, with states as diverse as NE and TN showing surging enrollments of Hispanic students. Many, if not most, of these Hispanic students are English-language learners from poor families headed by parents with substantially lower levels of educational attainment than the general population of American parents. Yet, even with this influx of Hispanic students from low-income families, NAEP reading achievement continues to rise when compared to the outcomes obtained in 1971.

Similarly, the gap in reading achievement between economically advantaged and economically disadvantaged students has been narrowing over the years; but that gap may be better described as opportunity gaps. The evidence that this reading-achievement gap results almost entirely from disparities in what children know when they enter kindergarten and whether they read voluntarily during the summer months[2] indicates that "ineffective" schools and teachers are as likely to simply be unlucky teachers as ineffective teachers. "Unlucky" because the students they teach simply lack the opportunities more advantaged children have. It is clear we can close this achievement gap, but not without addressing the opportunity gaps. Still, federal and state educational policies and programs rarely, if ever, address unequal opportunities.

Brown presents his arguments in clear and plain language. Personally, I will be sending a copy of the book to my elected state and federal representatives. Perhaps superintendents should purchase copies for every member of the school board, if not for every teacher. I hope the book attracts attention and is widely read. I worry, though, that the book's upbeat message may undermine its popularity. Bracey (2003) wrote, "Good news about public schools serves no one's political education reform agenda" (59). Perhaps, but what of "fair and balanced" news about American education? Fair and balanced is how I would describe the central messages in Brown's book. I think he was too hard on some people and programs and went too easy on others. But that, to me, is what it means to be fair and balanced.

Readers will become informed about the general state of American public schooling. They will learn of some of the most egregious examples of news distortion and disinformation. Readers will learn a bit about how money has influenced the arguments made and the reforms advanced over the last few years. All of this will help readers understand that while public education can certainly be improved, too many of the reforms so popular among politicians today advance only a very narrow agenda, reducing the cost of public education.

So, sit back, relax, and read Brown's book. Then pass it along so that others will benefit from the solid arguments Brown makes in defense of public education.

Richard L. Allington, Ph.D.
University of Tennessee

PREFACE

We all recall educators who made a difference in our lives, who helped us learn something we never thought we'd be able to comprehend. The teachers in my life who helped me grow deserve my respect. In all my years as a student, I can only remember two teachers I disliked—and, despite that, they probably helped me grow even though I didn't realize it. Millions of acts of kindness, sincere concern for children's and adolescents' personal lives, hours of careful planning, and delivery of perfect lessons occur in public classrooms all across America every day of the school year.

We have all probably used the phrase "It's not rocket science" in referring to a task that anyone should be able to do. If it is rocket science, then it's complicated, and it takes a highly skilled and educated person to make sense of it. After years as an elementary and middle school teacher, and many more as an educational researcher, I now know this for a fact: teaching *is* rocket science!

Those who haven't been trained as educators won't likely succeed in this profession. Not everyone has it in him or her to be a teacher—it's not innate. The work is intense, and the results are often unpredictable. It takes a tough interior and exterior to survive a week of teaching—imagine 180 days of it!

Educational researchers used to debate whether teaching was a profession or merely a job. The debate is over—teaching is a profession, because educational research continues to accumulate and informs those in the profession on a daily basis. Every year educators learn more about how the brain works and how that knowledge can be used to better meet students' needs.

Researchers are constantly making discoveries about which educational practices have the most influential impact on student learning. Teaching is a profession for lifelong learners because educators must develop a different set of innovative strategies for teaching every year, based merely on the fact that they'll be meeting 30–130 new students each September about whom they know nothing.

Teaching is not for those who prefer to relax during the day. There's no such thing as a coffee break when you're a teacher; you don't have an opportunity to stand at the watercooler and discuss last night's game; and you won't spend 30 minutes with your colleagues deciding where to go to lunch, because you have a lunch date with 33 seven-year-olds every day of the week.

I don't understand how an entire nation can stand on the sidelines and watch the media, politicians, and businesspersons say over and over again how bad public schools and teachers are in the United States. The public as a whole and professional educators seem to be paralyzed whenever another disparaging comment is made about our public schools. The tenor in America is as if no one wants to admit to knowing or valuing any public school teachers. When will we awake from our coma and start supporting the one avenue to a better chance at happiness as adults that we are all entitled to receive—a public school education?

When will Americans begin to explicitly support their public schools with the pride that they deserve? When will public school teachers receive the respect and recognition that other nations' teachers receive? When will education in America actually be a priority rather than a popular rallying cry by politicians who offer empty promises? It's time for the media, politicians, and businesspersons to start talking to teachers, the education professionals, instead of ignoring them as new state and federal policies are created and implemented—it's actually past time. America's children make the most academic gains when educational decisions are made by educational professionals—not businesspersons or politicians.

I wrote this book to provide evidence for the unmatched success of America's public schools. U.S. education is the best in the world because we educate everyone for an entire 13 years. Our technology is unparalleled; our military is above all others; and we continue to garner Nobel Prizes in the sciences and medicine. International patients come to the United States for medical care—we don't leave here for better medical care somewhere else.

None of these advances occurs without one central principle holding our civilization together—equal opportunity for everyone to receive an education until adulthood. Attacks on schools and teachers are eroding the democratic philosophies and resultant structures that support and unite us as Americans, as embodied in a public school education that is proudly delivered to every hamlet in America.

This book provides volumes of evidence that anyone can make note of, share, and brag about to families, friends, enemies, elected representatives, and anyone else who disparages our public schools. The words within are the source of energy needed to awaken our spirits and change the attitudes and mind-sets of those who can't "see" how public education is responsible for every success this nation can claim. Wake up, America—this may be your last chance to make a difference in the continuance of our successful public school system and, in the process, preserve democracy for all Americans.

ACKNOWLEDGMENTS

The idea of writing about the value of public schools developed through my day-to-day conversations with family, friends, and colleagues. The frustration I've experienced is often soothed by sharing it with others who value the power and significance of public schools as much as I. But, as is often said, "Talk is cheap."

When it came time to put pen to paper, I needed some guidance. Realtors aren't generally known for solving all the world's problems, but my realtor, Charna Satnick, listened to me long enough to introduce me to a family friend in the publishing world, Scott Miller. Scott politely accepted my e-mails and provided me with some leads that eventually opened the door to a contract. Many thanks to Charna and Scott, whose interest in this project led to this book being published.

Monthly conversations about public school ideas with family members were essential to clarifying what I wanted to say as the writing continued. Sandy and Bill Shusta share the passion for public schooling that I do, and they added to my thoughts each time we engaged in conversations. Thank you both for sharing the ideas and the fun along the way.

I needed help explaining "educationese," the language of teachers, as I wrote about topics that are so familiar to those of us in the profession. Sharing first drafts with my brother Bob and my sister Carol Ann helped me understand when I wasn't connecting with the rest of the world. Every comment they made was right on the mark, and this is a much better book because of them. When I thought I was finished with the book, my brother Brian provided some valuable details in the nick of time—a real lifesaver. I thank my brother Ken for providing his expertise in advising me on marketing design and creating the webpage. Thank you, Fred Gerleve and John Canning, for helping me understand how those first drafts sounded.

As months passed, and the writing became more urgent, I needed more advice and assistance from other educators. My close friends and former fellow coaches listened and found some answers for me. Thanks to Tom Fey and Gaylord Schelling, who have always shared my passion as public school teachers, coaches, and advocates for what's right for students at every level.

Speaking to my editor, Tom Koerner, is like an evening around the campfire—it's always relaxing and jovial. Because we've both spent our fair share of time in the Chicago area, it's a joy to talk about the places we've been. Thank you, Tom, for believing in me and guiding me through the process of getting this right.

I look forward to sharing this book and life's other stories with my daughter, Lindsay, her husband, Dan, and my grandchildren. My younger daughter is always supportive of my need to voice opinions on the injustices of the world—especially those surrounding this issue of public education. Thank you, Taylor, for understanding my need to write when I'd rather be spending time with you. I hope you'll continue to use your talents throughout your life as a writer—you have so much potential.

Dana could almost be considered a cowriter of this book through her patience in listening to my concerns, expressing her valuable and accurate insights, and sharing stories from her teaching experiences with me. Her editing and revising are as professional as it gets. I owe Dana more than I can ever repay for her understanding of my need to spend time writing about and sharing my passion for the value of public education in America.

PUBLIC SCHOOLS

Successful Graduates

> When will our governors, presidents, legislators—and public school teachers themselves—understand that the humble public school is one of the greatest democratic inventions in the world?[1]

Do you ever feel guilty that you attended and graduated from a public high school? Do you feel angry when you hear another newscast of negative comments about the public schools in America? Gerald Bracey notes that "Americans never hear anything positive about the nation's schools and haven't since the years just before Sputnik in 1957."[2]

Do you ever get tired of hearing the mantra that Americans fall behind other nations in education? Are you spending thousands of dollars a year to send your children to private K–12 schools thinking that your local public schools are hopeless? Does the new charter school sound appealing to you? Hearing the truth about public schools is difficult. Everyone from comedians to politicians has a sound bite—and it isn't a good one. All the negative rhetoric probably has you asking, "Why bother to support public schools if they're not any good?"

This nation has provided the opportunity for every person to attend school for 13 years of his or her life. Some of our founding fathers insisted upon public education for everyone. If you visit the Thomas Jefferson Memorial on your next trip to Washington, DC, you can read his words on the walls that surround his statue: "Self-government is not possible unless the citizens are educated sufficiently to enable them to exercise oversight. It is therefore imperative that the nation see to it that a suitable education be provided for *all its citizens*" (my emphasis).[3]

Jefferson further supported a free public education by introducing to the Virginia legislature in 1779 a bill in which he proposed that schools be established in every county "so that all children could receive three years of reading, writing, and computation."[4] Of course, at the time, Jefferson only intended this education be provided for White males who owned land.

Public education in America has come a long way since that time, so that for decades now, all citizens are permitted to attend school. Every state has a minimum age at which students are permitted to officially drop out of school—usually at either 16 or 17 years of age. Some state departments of education have recently amended the dropout age to 18.

Educating all the citizens is a tall order for any country—especially when that guarantee is for a full 12 or 13 years of schooling at the public's expense. There are many countries that make little attempt to educate the masses for as many years as Americans are required to attend school. Many other countries in Europe (e.g., the United Kingdom, Germany) and Asia (e.g., Japan, China) cease their financial responsibility for educating all their citizens upon students reaching the age of 14 or 15.[5] At that point, in several European and Asian countries, adolescents are required to take examinations in which their scores determine their future educational career paths. Some go on to a high school for college preparation, but many others do not.

The objective of American teachers is to provide the incentive, motivation, and learning experiences to engage all young people until they graduate from 12 or 13 years of schooling—usually at the age of 17 or 18. You can see that in the United States we have a different educational mission than other countries. A free education is a commitment to our youth and our communities that the populace shouldn't take for granted—because without this commitment, the nation as a whole loses much of its international prestige and respect. Familiarity with America's education system may tempt people to grow complacent in the areas of preserving, honoring, and supporting public education—but that would be a mistake.

America's public educational system is an avenue for all Americans to better their lives. Education provides opportunities for overall individual growth that are immeasurable on any scale. When one considers the mission of educating every American for so many years, it becomes quite clear that the United States has an amazing rate of educational success considering all the factors that affect a child's academic ability, attitudes toward learning, and opportunities for some kind of academic success.

Parents who have children and adolescents with special needs also benefit from the required services offered by public schools. As early as 1975 the U.S. Congress passed a law currently known as the Individuals with Disabilities Education Act (IDEA), which entitles all children with special needs to a free, appropriate public education.[6] Prior to that time, many students with special needs were forced to leave public schools and find assistance elsewhere—a dilemma that left many parents without the resources to handle their children's various needs.

Public schools are required to educate all, including students all along the spectrum of autism; those with mental retardation; those with physical disabilities (e.g., asthma, AIDS, cystic fibrosis, multiple sclerosis); those with learning disabilities; and those with Down syndrome. Helping these students requires many resources: physical, professional, and monetary. IDEA also protects and provides specific learning environments that meet the needs of students who are gifted and talented, as defined separately by each state's education laws.

WHO GOES TO PUBLIC SCHOOLS?

Public schools are the education choice of an overwhelming majority of American parents. You may be one of millions of adults who graduated from a public high school. Take a guess at the percentage of Americans who attend public schools. What was your guess? Fifty percent? Sixty-five percent? Seventy-five percent? You're off by a number of percentage points if you guessed 75 percent.

The answer is that just under 90 percent of American children and adolescents attend public schools in America. That may sound astounding to you, especially based on where you live. In some geographic locations, especially near or in large cities, there is a higher percentage of private schools available than one would find in rural or suburban areas. Despite that possibility, even in cities, an overwhelming majority of students attend public schools. Data collected from the National Center for Education Statistics (NCES) reveal that public school enrollment rose 26 percent from 1985 to 2008, from 39.4 million to 49.8 million students.[7]

If 89 percent of students attend public schools, that means only 11 percent of students are receiving schooling at a private, parochial, cyber, or charter school. Children and adolescents can also be homeschooled, according to each state's regulations for that process. By 2003, the proportion of students in private schools had dropped to only 11.5 percent of the total population of school-age students.

Among private schools, Catholic schools enroll only about 5 percent of the population of students, according to a report written in 2000. That means the other 6–7 percent of students are attending other types of private schools (i.e., nonsectarian, charter). The other alternative, homeschooling, includes less than one percent of the student population.

Since almost 90 percent of children and adolescents are attending public schools in America, that means that for every 10,000 students, approximately 9,000 of them are attending public schools. According to the NCES, the enrollment figures for public schools are expected to rise, so that the projected enrollment for the fall of 2013 is 5 percent higher than the 2003 enrollment figures.[8]

More students are in public schools now in the United States than there have ever been over its entire history. Parents have many reasons to believe that the public schools in their communities are the best place for their children. There are also many facts that the general public is unaware of that shed light on the effectiveness of the U.S. public school system.

WHAT DO PUBLIC SCHOOL GRADUATES MAKE OF THEMSELVES?

In determining just how successful a public school education is, it may be appropriate to look at some famous public school graduates. What type of success would adults deem significant in one's life? Some might value those who have received our highest honors, such as Nobel Prize winners, Pulitzer Prize recipients, or those who have received an Academy Award for best actress or actor.

In a few autobiographies and biographies of the Nobel Prize winners, the authors mention the winners' basic K–12 educational experiences. Of those accounts, 94 refer to winners with public school educations—including Sinclair Lewis, Cordell Hull, Ernest Hemingway, John Steinbeck, and Martin Luther King, Jr. (who, of course, attended segregated schools during his childhood years in Georgia).

Among Pulitzer Prize winners for literature who recorded their educational backgrounds, 30 of 72 winners received public school educations, while there were only 10 noted as having attended private schools. The public school authors include James Michener, William Faulkner, James Agee, Alison Lurie, John Updike, Harper Lee, and Philip Roth.

More famous actors with public school educations include Bruce Willis, Will Smith, and George Clooney. Among Oscar winners who graduated from public schools are Meryl Streep, Tom Hanks, Jack Nicholson, Halle Berry, Dustin Hoffman, and Hilary Swank. Among comedians with public high school degrees are Jon Stewart of Comedy Central fame and David Letterman.

What about politicians? A few who have succeeded and graduated from public schools include these former Speakers of the House: Tom Foley, Denny Hastert, and Newt Gingrich. The recent presidents who were public high school grads include Jimmy Carter, Ronald Reagan, and Bill Clinton.

Some readers may value athletes, and they may be curious if any succeeded via their public school backgrounds. Professional football players with public educations include Brett Favre, Walter Peyton, and the lovable Terrell Owens. Baseball players include Mickey Mantle, Roger Clemens, and Derek Jeter.

Successful musicians and singers graduating from public schools include Carrie Underwood, Wynton Marsalis, and Madonna. It appears that attending public schools can lead to success in many fields and across many disciplines. No one has been denied access to any particular endeavor or possible fame and fortune due to his or her attendance and graduation from a public school.

HOW MANY PUBLIC SCHOOL GRADUATES GO TO THE "BEST" COLLEGES?

It seems that every college graduate knows which institutions of higher learning are the best. Often a graduate exclaims with pride that his or her own alma mater is the single most appropriate university for every high school graduate to attend. Many people often hail certain universities as the "best" schools in the country.

Ivy League schools are certainly valued as some of the best institutions in the United States. Most admit that acceptance at one of these institutions is prestigious and entitles one to certain advantages over those who attend the hundreds of other colleges and universities. So, what percentage of those admitted to Ivy League colleges are public high school graduates? Sixty-one percent of those admitted to Princeton University in its 2006 entering class were public school graduates, and 55 percent of students admitted to Yale that same year were public-school graduates. Princeton and Yale don't have admissions counselors who proclaim, "Your application will not be accepted, nor will you be considered for acceptance, due to your diploma being from a public high school."

The Ohio State University, a notable midwestern university, admitted 87 percent public school graduates in the fall of 2009; and perhaps the most prestigious university worldwide, the University of California at Berkeley, admitted 74 percent public school graduates in its last freshman class.[9]

WHAT DO *YOU* WANT FROM PUBLIC SCHOOLS?

What do you want for your children? Many prioritize the following: children being happy, enjoying life, acting responsibly, developing a comfortable and healthy economic life, learning to communicate well, becoming socially adept in many circumstances, being skeptical at the appropriate time (especially during election years), and eventually learning to be effective parents.

Some parents want their children to learn English well, since they immigrated to America and don't speak the language very well. Some parents want their children to engage in social activities with other children from the community. Other parents want their children to have the experience of being with students from different cultural and ethnic backgrounds or different religions, so they come to understand more about others' family heritage. And probably many parents just want their children to learn how to make money and to be able to eventually live independently.

Do you think your children are progressing toward some of these critical outcomes by attending the local public school? If not, what are they missing by attending public schools every day? What did you get from your public school education? If you are satisfied with your K–12 public school education, and most of your family and friends are too, who is it that keeps the rumor going that the public schools are such terrible places to receive an education or to send our children each year?

Many in the media are responsible for spreading inaccurate rumors about the public schools, while failing to mention the many successes that occur daily in local schools. Politicians are often just as guilty as the media of spreading inaccurate rumors about what's occurring in public schools. You'll read some of the inaccuracies told about public schools throughout this book, but particularly in chapters 5 and 6.

WHAT DO PEOPLE THINK OF AMERICAN PUBLIC SCHOOLS?

Believe it or not, most of your friends and family members agree that the public schools in their neighborhoods *are* doing an effective job. The *Kappan*, a publication of the Phi Delta Kappa educational organization, has been conducting a survey of approximately 3,000 adults every year for the past 42 years about public education in America.

One of the questions respondents are asked is, "Suppose the public schools themselves, in your community, were graded in the same way. What grade would you give the public schools here?"[10] The answer from year to year is consistently near the response given by those surveyed in 2010: 49 percent of those surveyed gave their schools either an A or a B. In the past five years, 57 to 67 percent of those surveyed *who are parents of public school students* have given the public schools in their communities an A or a B, with an overwhelming majority of 77 percent noting in 2010 that they would give the public school that their eldest child attended an A or B.[11]

Some states and cities have approved the use of taxpayers' monies to be spent on vouchers. A *voucher* is a check written to a family by the state or local government to send their children to a private or parochial school. A clear majority of those surveyed believe that public dollars should *not* be spent sending students to private schools. To prove this point: among respondents in the 2007 *Kappan* survey, 60 percent surveyed were *opposed* to "allowing students and parents to choose a private school to attend at the public's expense."[12]

Conclusions from the *Kappan* Survey

The authors of the study made some conclusions based on data collected over the past three years:

- Conclusion III. The closer people get to the schools in the community, the higher the grades they give them.
- Conclusion VI. There has been no decline in public support for public schools. Approval ratings remain high and remarkably stable.
- Conclusion VII. Support for vouchers is declining and stands in the mid-30 percent range.[13]
- Conclusion IX. There is near consensus support for the belief that the problems the public schools face result from societal issues and not from the quality of schooling.
- Conclusion from the 2008 survey: "Americans support an increased use of federal funds to maintain local public schools."[14]

It's impractical, of course, to make broad generalizations from one survey. These results, however, reveal a considerable level of support for what occurs in most people's local public schools. It's surprising that these survey results are never heard on national or local TV broadcasts. Perhaps the real answer to how satisfied Americans are about public schools is found in the overwhelming majority of parents who continue to send their children and adolescents to public schools every day: 89 percent!

Any Advantages to Avoiding Public Schools?

Those who graduated from public schools must have many horrific stories to tell about their experiences for the media to deliver such a dismal perspective. Frequent attacks by the media and politicians may lead much of the public to actually accept the opinion that America's public schools are ineffective. Would these views make others conclude that public school graduates

- are forced to sit through mediocre teaching for 13 years?
- have limited opportunities available after graduating, due to attending public high schools?
- would have better jobs if they had attended private schools?
- would gain admission to better colleges with private school educations?
- might have better marriages if they had received private school educations?
- would have more money as adults if only they'd attended private schools?
- would have a vastly improved quality of life by having attended private schools?

The answers to these questions are obvious to a majority of the public. Reading this book will provide the truth about what Americans, their parents and grandparents, and their children and grandchildren have benefited from and will benefit from as a result of attending public schools. Perhaps the best reason to read this book is so that one can make accurate statements to others about what the public schools offer, and about how attending one is and has been an advantage for most Americans, and will continue to be for their children.

This book is filled with information from accurate and research-based sources (rather than hearsay) on a number of topics, as the individual chapter titles suggest. Hopefully, reading a few of these chapters will help dispel many of the negative attitudes that exist in the United States about public schools. This book provides evidence to defend and support local public schools in every community.

2

IS THE PUBLIC SCHOOL IN YOUR COMMUNITY A "GOOD" SCHOOL?

We have made the point repeatedly that there is no such thing as the "nation's" schools. Every school in the nation is someone's community school.[1]

It is common for people to make statements such as "My friend teaches in a *good* school district," "I went to a *good* high school," or "I hear that district is a *good* school district." What does it mean when someone says a "good" school district or a "good" school? It's as if there is a common understanding of the phrase without any explanation ever provided by those who speak these words.

Many admit, when asked, that they attended a "good" school. They believe, with evidence, that their teachers provided them with the strategies and skills needed to succeed in college and in life. Most adults admit that their children or grandchildren attend good schools.

But how does one actually know for a fact that the school is a "good" school? What does it take for a school to be considered an effective school?

HOW IS A "GOOD" SCHOOL DEFINED?

Is It Safe?

In exploring the possible definitions of a good school, first and foremost is the idea that the school is a place where children are happy and secure each day. That includes schools in places like New York City, Los Angeles, Wichita, Minneapolis, Helena, Knoxville, Las Vegas, and even the town of Lost Nation in Iowa. The first test, and perhaps the most significant one, of a good school is the safety of the children and adolescents who attend that school.

Safety refers to both physical and psychological safety. When students are safe at school it affects the quality of their academic growth. This concept is supported by educational researcher Robert Marzano. He has summarized several studies and reports that overall school factors such as "a safe and orderly environment," "productive climate and culture," and "pupil rights and expectations" all have a positive impact on student achievement.[2]

Many public schools are in need of physical repair, as evidenced by visiting some urban schools, but also schools in the suburbs and rural areas in which community members may not have voted to build or renovate new schools. In fairness, though, private, parochial, and some charter schools are usually in greater disrepair than the public schools because these schools can't rely on public dollars or support for new building projects.

Do Teachers Care about the Students?

All parents want to know that their children's teachers actually care about them—not merely in words, but actually demonstrating care for each child in various ways throughout the day. Parents can tell by the events they hear about in their children's descriptions of a day at school whether their teachers care about them.

How important is care? According to educational researchers, extremely important. One particular study stands out as evidence of the value of care to students, as the researchers reported that "showing care and respect for students 'promoted learning and overpowered the comparative effects of instructional methodologies."[3] In essence, teachers who demonstrate care for children are more likely to have a positive impact on children's learning in that fashion than through their planning of and delivery of great lesson plans.

Students interviewed by one researcher noted specifically that caring means that teachers perform actions such as

- walking around the room talking to everybody to see how they were doing [and] to answer questions
- helping students with school work
- noticing and inquiring about changes in behavior
- seeking to know students as unique human beings
- encouraging students to improve.[4]

Additional evidence of how much it matters that teachers "care" was presented by the annual *Phi Delta Kappan* poll conducted in 2010. Researchers asked 3,000 respondents which words they would use to "describe a teacher who had the most positive influence in their life." The most frequently mentioned word was "*caring* followed by, *encouraging, interesting, personable*, and of *high quality*."[5] Many people share the perspective that caring teachers make effective educators.

Determining whether *all* the teachers in the building care about every child is rather challenging. An entire school wouldn't be considered a "bad" school unless a majority of the teachers could be identified as uncaring. This scenario is highly unlikely, because caring for children is one of the primary reasons that adults choose the profession.

Most parents recognize when their children have teachers who don't demonstrate enough care to positively influence their children's attitudes and efforts toward learning. This effective trait is not actually a *school* trait at all, but rather a separate *teacher* trait. Caring would therefore not be used as a criterion for identifying a school as either a "good" or "bad" one.

Will Students Succeed Academically?

A third criterion for judging whether a school is effective is its status as a place where every child frequently succeeds academically. *Success* has many different definitions. For some parents, academic success may mean that their children learn to speak conversational English; complete most homework assignments; start to read chapter books by the end of second grade; get straight As; or actually begin asking questions at school.

Everyone has definitions of academic success, but most would probably agree that children should be capable of successfully learning and completing most of the academic work required of them. That may mean that adults believe their children should receive at least passing grades, and hopefully grow academically from year to year.

Academic success for many adults is only measured by good grades, but teachers must have varied definitions of academic success if they hope to see *every* student grow cognitively during an academic year. Educational researcher James Stronge provides this research-based definition of effective teachers: "Effective teachers offer all students opportunities to participate and succeed."[6]

This trait shouldn't be too difficult for most schools to exhibit; but this too is actually more of a *teacher* trait than an entire-school characteristic. Who's responsible for ensuring a student's success? Individual teachers are responsible for identifying children's learning needs, finding appropriate instructional materials or curricula for their students, and then choosing appropriate ways of delivering instruction to them so that they succeed.

Children have a better chance of succeeding if the teacher also chooses effective means of providing them with feedback about their learning. When students know what mistakes they are making, they have the opportunity to improve their academic performance. Many educational researchers have identified that high-quality, specific, detailed feedback to students demonstrates high-quality teaching and leads to meaningful learning.[7] Providing effective feedback to students also refers to *teacher* effectiveness, so we cannot assign this trait to an entire school as a designation of a "good school."

Are Teachers Effective?

Among elements such as a well-articulated curriculum and a safe and orderly environment, the one factor that surfaced as the single most influential component of an effective school is the individual teachers within that school.[8]

No one factor has a greater impact on a student's learning than being with an effective teacher. In chapter 4, specific details will be provided about what effective teachers do. One of the traits of a good school is that it's a place that has genuinely effective teachers. But wait—that's also obviously *not* a school trait, but instead a personal and professional trait controlled only by the individual competence of each teacher.

An essential component of effectiveness is that teachers must be officially certified by their state education departments, an issue addressed in chapter 4. Certification is rarely discussed in social gatherings, yet the value of certified teachers is well supported by educational research. It's evident that the *school* itself is not what primarily determines whether children will receive a good education—instead, it is the resources that determine a majority of the relative value of a child's education.

Good Schools Are More Than Merely "the School"

Few if any criteria are actually used for evaluating a school based only on the school itself. Use of the word *school* makes it sound as if someone is referring to the building, which should be a comfortable space, physically, for a school to be considered good. Many American schools are in need of physical repair, as mentioned earlier in this chapter. It is often difficult to get a building repaired or replaced, especially when it affects precious tax dollars.

When most speak of a good school, the physical condition of the school is not generally a concern, as long as the building is clean and safe. It's primarily the people inside the building and the materials and programs available to students that determine the effectiveness of a school—teachers, principals, support personnel, available technology, challenging curricula, programs, and services.

It is inaccurate and faulty thinking to believe that a school is either "bad" or "good" based on its location or the socioeconomic community that surrounds the school. It's the resources (including educators) inside the building that define a "good" school. One poor teacher or administrator isn't enough to label a school as "bad."

Available Services

Understanding that those involved in designing and delivering educational programs for students are what really matters leads to another characteristic of an effective school: the services they offer for children. Services offered to students can be attributed to the *school*, not merely a teacher. Children should have many varied learning experiences during the school day; that includes opportunities to engage in activities in art, music, and physical education.

Diverse learning opportunities have been standard in schools for a long time. Schools should have support services such as nurses, guidance counselors, and school psychologists available when needed. Again, these are basic services that are available at almost every public school in America.

The proliferation of these services since the inception of public schooling in America has been amazing. Nurses and guidance counselors were rare in many schools even as late as the 1960s, when millions of baby boomers were attending school. Today, approximately 75 percent of public schools have at least a part-time nurse available daily; and the ratio of students to guidance counselors ranges anywhere from 400 to 1,200 students per counselor.[9]

One critical guarantee in public schools is the availability of services and programs for students with special needs. These services range from reading specialists to a variety of special-education teachers who provide learning experiences for many students with all types of cognitive and physical challenges.

Extracurricular Opportunities for Learning

Another criterion of a good school is a large number of extracurricular activities. Schools should provide a multitude and variety of opportunities for learning that can't be provided by parents. Education is not merely about academics in U.S. public schools.

The priorities of any local community are obvious when one visits its schools and observes the programs that are offered and the facilities that exist within the physical structure of the buildings. Students are engaged in many extracurricular activities when a school building has facilities available for these opportunities.

Many schools advertise their priorities through their athletic facilities, such as the building of a new 2,000-seat basketball gymnasium, a renovated weight room built especially for football players, or a new soccer field. Other schools may prioritize other extracurricular programs, such as their music programs, through expenditures on musical equipment or the building of a new school theater. These facilities and the ensuing opportunities they provide matter to Americans. The evidence for their value exists in the fact that public school students have these facilities available to them. Local taxes provide the revenue to build these structures, with approval from the community.

Shared Values

When people speak of a *good* school, they also mean that the students who attend the school share some of the values that their families believe in—especially the values related to the importance of being academically successful. Most parents explain to their children how education can improve their circumstances in life—from the advantages of future financial earnings to the opportunity for personal growth and happiness.

Perhaps what people really mean by a *good* school is that it's in a community where the majority of the families share a passion for and value education. The opposite is a school where a majority of students may not be interested in being academically successful or earning the grades needed to extend their education deep into high school.

The value of education may be a problem in communities if the residents who live there do not believe that schooling can improve their life circumstances. The dropout rate may be high in these areas, and this can be an indication of whether community members believe that education can improve their lives.

The question, "What is a good school?" elicits the following answers:

1. A safe place for children and adolescents.
2. A place with caring teachers.
3. A place where students regularly experience academic success.

4. A place with teachers who use effective strategies to engage learners.
5. A place with support services available to meet the learning needs of *all* students.
6. A place with a broad array of curricular and extracurricular opportunities.
7. A place benefiting from community members and caregivers who value education.
8. A place benefiting from parents and caregivers who hold reasonable expectations for their children to achieve some measure of academic success.

These specific components of successful schools are not merely people's opinions; these principles are supported by educational research—a body of common research findings that have been revealed over decades. Those responsible for establishing and regulating public school policies can and do have an impact on the first six criteria.

However, neither educators nor policy makers can control how much emphasis or value community members place on education. How does your public school measure up if you use these eight criteria to judge the schools in your community?

An important question to ask now is, "Does the private school in my town/city offer these same services and opportunities?" Some private schools do offer a few similar services and extracurricular activities. In many circumstances, though, private schools of all kinds fail to provide equal opportunities and services for the students who attend.

The reason they fail is that they are not required by the state education departments to provide these services, because they are not public entities. The second reason they may not provide many of these services is that they prevent many students with special learning needs from attending by requiring prospective students to pass entry-level achievement tests. Therefore, in most situations, only those students who are academically successful are permitted to attend private and parochial schools.

One last significant criterion for attending many private or parochial schools is a student's behavior. Private and parochial schools can expel students with inappropriate behavior whenever they like. Choosing which students attend is not a public school's option.

A REALITY CHECK FOR TWO STUDENTS

A Tale of Two Schools

The following is an example of the differences that might exist between a private and a public school. I was asked by a local county-court judge in the mid-1990s to evaluate two schools for a divorced couple's children. One parent wanted her two children to attend a local private school, and the other parent wanted the children to attend the public school. I was asked by the two attorneys representing each of the parents to provide an evaluation of the two schools.

I proceeded with the evaluation based on two overarching significant, yet simple, questions: What services did the two children need? and Which of the two schools provided those services? I interviewed the principals of each school to uncover the essential services each school offered. I discovered some striking differences between the two schools in conducting those interviews.

The public school teachers were all certified; the private school did not have a full set of certified teachers, nor was it required to have them. The significance of this factor is discussed in chapter 4. The public school offered both a reading specialist and a remedial reading program; the private school had neither. The public school had a special program for students identified as gifted; the private school did not offer this service.

The public school offered many curricular opportunities that were not available at the private school, such as a regular music program, both choral and instrumental; an art program; and regular physical-education classes. The private school did not offer these opportunities for learning.

The reason to focus on these public school attributes is that in conversations with one of the parents, it was revealed that one of the children had been identified by a psychologist as gifted, and the other as having difficulties with reading. You might be able to see which school has the edge based on these students' learning needs. Remember that in the selection criteria for an effective school, the services offered, especially as they are related to the learning needs of the child, are a critical element in a school being considered *good*.

I was never called into court to provide testimony, and about eight months after filing my written report with the court, I received a phone call from one of the parents. The parent noted that the children were both currently attending the public school. There's no gloating necessary—this story is about a school that meets the academic needs of these two children. The basic need for, and U.S. citizen's right to, a comprehensive and quality education should never be politicized—not in any arena. I'll discuss later, in chapter 9, how the No Child Left Behind (NCLB) federal policies have politicized children's rights to an appropriate and equal education.

But Which School Had Better Test Scores?

As an interesting side note, prior to my conducting the interviews with the two school administrators, one of the attorneys asked if I was going to cite each school's summary of students' test scores as evidence of the better school. Perhaps you're also thinking these data should have been presented. This idea, however, represents faulty thinking, no matter how many people believe that test scores should be the primary criterion for judging a school's success.

The assumption one operates under to believe that students' test scores reveal the effectiveness of a school is this: that teachers are primarily responsible for a child's performance on standardized-test measures. The honest response is a simple "No, teachers are not primarily responsible for students' standardized-test scores." There are too many variables that exist in children's and adolescents' lives for teachers to alter the previous and numerous influences on students' test scores.

Variables are the experiences children have prior to schooling, each evening at home, and during the summers, which have a much greater impact on their test scores than what teachers can do for students for a mere seven hours a day for 185 days of the year. Alfie Kohn notes, as have many educational researchers, that the best test scores in America belong, in almost all cases, to students whose families are not living in poverty.[10] Kohn insists that if one drives through any neighborhood and checks out the house prices, one will be able to predict with amazing accuracy how well students do on standardized tests. This is no surprise to educators at any level.

Much research recognizes the importance of parental involvement in children's academic success.[11] It's certainly no secret to most that those parents/caregivers who provide meaningful and frequent support to their children's education significantly increase their children's opportunities for success. In chapter 10, on concerns about urban education, I provide details concerning the external factors that affect children's learning.

Another thing that reveals the faulty thinking about a school's test scores as a determining factor in every child's success in school is this essential question: How does every other child's test-score data relate to a student's success at school? Unless the very presence of smart children in a classroom makes other children smarter, those other students' test scores are completely insignificant to each child's daily cognitive growth. Each teacher must identify, recognize, and then respond to each child's academic needs in order for every child to succeed academically.

Every family produces diverse children; and thus, their needs are quite different from one another's. Meaningful learning is ensured when educators recognize the differences among students and alter their teaching methods to meet each child's learning needs.

TEACHERS' LIMITED INFLUENCE ON CHILDREN'S TEST SCORES

The influence of teachers on students' test-score performances is a contentious issue that, if not based on a research perspective, may lead to poor educational programs and policies across the nation. A study conducted by researchers Angela Duckworth and Martin Seligman, "Self-Discipline Outdoes I.Q. in Predicting Academic Performance of Adolescents," revealed something teachers and students have known all along. Their findings were that self-discipline among adolescents has a greater impact on academic success and reaching full intellectual potential than "inadequate teachers, boring textbooks, and large class sizes."[12] That's a significant finding that must be understood by parents, the media, and policy makers.

Kathy Christie, who reported Duckworth and Seligman's study, describes the researchers as revealing that "correlations between self-discipline and most academic performance variables were considerably higher (at least twice as large) as correlations between I. Q. and the same academic variables (final grades, high school selection, school attendance, hours spent doing homework, hours spent watching television, and the time of day students began their homework)."[13] This is more evidence that schools, teachers, administrators, and school board members have little, if anything, to do with children's and adolescents' test scores. Many other variables exist that also inhibit the efforts of teachers to improve students' test scores (see chapters 9 and 10).

The good news is that you, as a parent, have the greatest impact on your child's test scores. That impact starts in utero and continues throughout a child's life. It's critical to recognize the faulty thinking that a good school is one in which students' test scores are high. Students' test scores are more of a reflection of community members' views and attitudes about learning and the importance of succeeding in school. More emphasis on blaming teachers for students' scores on external standardized tests will continue to erode the kind of learning that matters at school.

Another significant negative effect of valuing tests will be a decline, as is currently occurring, in the number of adults who choose to become teachers. Fewer teachers can only be bad news for the United States, as the enrollment rate continues to rise among students of all ages, thus increasing class sizes in many U.S. classrooms. Many teachers are baby boomers and thus near the end of their careers. A huge exodus of experienced teachers and the concurrent rise in student population will lead to a considerable teacher shortage within the next 10 years. Negative factors such as tying test scores to teacher evaluation will only exacerbate a teacher shortage.

Unfortunately, most of the policies associated with the NCLB legislation are founded on the premise that teachers are the only or the primary factor responsible for students' test scores (see chapter 9). This premise is a dangerous philosophy that erodes exemplary teaching, and the development and implementation of challenging curricula, and destroys the creativity and authority that teachers need to help students become lifelong learners.

WHAT SERVICES DO PRIVATE SCHOOLS OFFER?

Some specialty private schools in America offer some services to their students that meet their learning needs. But keep in mind that private schools under any umbrella are not required to offer any special services—from specific testing to ascertain students' specific needs to the resultant special programs that are provided to help every student succeed academically. These types of services are required in every public school in America. If you know or even suspect that your children have special learning needs, the public schools must respond to your concerns.

If you know parents who send their children to private schools, you may want to ask them what services their children receive. Do their children receive services if they are gifted, struggle with reading, or have a learning disability? The answer is generally no in every circumstance.

Your definition of a good school may differ from others', but not by much. Take a closer look at what the students in your community are offered in the local public school—you may be surprised. You may even think that the public school around you is a *good* place. Most adults realize that the public schools in their communities are good schools. The reality is that public schools in *every* U.S. community are good schools.

3

HOW AMERICA'S SCHOOLS OUTSHINE OTHER NATIONS' SCHOOLS

China is determined to transform from a labor-intensive, low-level manufacturing economy into an innovation-driven knowledge society. Thus China decided to change its "test-oriented education" into "talent-oriented education." To engineer this change, China made a conscious, global search for models—education systems that are good at producing innovative talents. As a country with the most Nobel laureates, most original patents, most scientific discoveries in the 20th century, and the largest economy in the world, the United States of America seems a reasonable candidate.[1]

In January of 1991 when the United States decided to attack Iraq, a large group of undergraduate students were parading around the University of Tennessee campus chanting "We're number one!" while waving American flags. They were obviously referring to U.S. superiority as the top military might in the world.

They were probably accurate about the U.S. military—it is number one militarily across the globe. Many adults don't know or don't understand that the United States is number one in many categories of desired traits that a country should possess. The fact that America is number one in so many categories is due to U.S. development of, insistence on, and support for a public education system. The advantages of living in the United States exist in part because so many Americans are educated for so much of their lives—until the age of 17 or 18.

The advantages that exist in the U.S. lifestyle can't occur without equity of educational opportunity (every resident is entitled to an education), and a great deal of success in educating so many adolescents until they reach adulthood. All high school seniors eventually feel the exhaustion of years of schooling—*senioritis*—and who can blame them?—but the rewards of successfully encouraging a huge majority of students to hang around school for 13 years benefit all Americans.

OUR STRENGTHS AS U.S. CITIZENS

Newsweek magazine ran a story on "The Best Country in the World Is . . ." during the summer of 2010.[2] The criteria for determining the best country included rankings in the categories of quality of life, economic dynamism, education, and health. The author ranked the United States first in the category of economic dynamism among populous nations, and second in the categories of quality of life and overall ranking among populous nations. That's a promising starting point—a high quality of life. One specific the author doesn't mention is the fact that the World Economic Forum Global Competitiveness Report ranked the United States first in creativity among 131 countries in 2008.[3] Being creative seems to be a valued trait in the United States, so it's good to know that we're number one in that category.

Another reason the United States deserves a high ranking is the way in which U.S. schools promote critical thinking. Gerald Bracey reports the following comment from a *Wall Street Journal* editorial-board member: "Comparing his American school days with his rigid school life in his native Poland, Kaminski [the board member] wrote, 'From primary school through America's unparalleled universities, our schools teach children to think critically better than almost any other [country's].'"[4]

Another strength that defines the power of the United States over other countries is Americans' competitive spirit and efforts. Bracey notes that a management firm in Switzerland has ranked the United States first in the world in competitiveness since 1994, when the United States jumped ahead of Japan.[5] Among the factors used to determine competitiveness were economic performance, government efficiency, business efficiency, productivity, scientific infrastructure, and health and the environment. Among the "Golden Rules of Competitiveness" the Institute for Management Development mentioned was "Invest heavily in education, especially at the secondary level, and in the life-long training of the labor force."[6] Do you suppose the *Wall Street Journal* carried that story and emphasized the investment in education?

One more first-place finish for Americans comes from U.S. productivity. A report from 2008 revealed that U.S. workers were the most productive among G7 countries.[7] Americans work longer each week and throughout more days per year than citizens in any other nation. Those statistics should be mentioned when pundits speak about the strength of American public education; but these findings are never publicized or associated with the quality of the public education system.

HOW PUBLIC EDUCATION HELPS MAKE US NUMBER ONE

What We Value in U.S. Graduates

A few years ago Alfie Kohn, a frequent contributor to meaningful education research, asked a group of parents of students from an elite independent school in Texas what their future goals were for their children. Kohn reported that the parents wanted their children to be "happy, balanced, independent, fulfilled, productive, self-reliant, responsible, functioning, kind, thoughtful, loving, inquisitive, and confident."[8] Later that year he asked the same question of parents in a Minneapolis suburb and received similar responses. Graduates of America's high schools should represent what U.S. citizens value. It is clear what Americans value from what they experience in their communities.

U.S. graduates should reflect what adults spend their time doing each day of their lives, in both their spare time and as productive adults. High school graduates should mirror the way the United States organizes and conducts its government. They should reflect the work ethos that defines Americans and honor U.S. economic values. In other words, as adults, Americans want their children to grow to be just like them—only more successful.

Being Creative and Inventive   If graduates reflect who American adults are, just what product do citizens want for a U.S. graduate? Primary traits of a well-trained high school graduate are creativity, inventiveness, and resourcefulness. This matters because U.S. citizens value ingenuity.

The excitement that ensues from the release of a new electronic device is amazing in this country—witness the lines around the Apple store when their next new product is released. Honoring the creative spirit isn't a recent phenomenon in this country. Listen to people in their eighties talk about when their parents purchased their first family automobiles. Some baby boomers are willing to speak about the excitement of their first televisions—or, even better, their first color televisions. Following World War II, the number of innovations that flooded local communities was amazing—from toasters to transistor radios to the hula hoop. These inventions define the people of the United States. Innovation is what the global community expects from the United States.

These innovations don't just satisfy the general public as buyers; innovations in the way things are built also make an imprint on people's lives. Medical devices and procedures have improved health, and machines have made manufacturing a more efficient process. Some call it "Yankee ingenuity," and many are often proud to see that label, *Made in America*, because they know Americans invented and produced it.

It's not just inventing something that drives the American spirit; it's thinking of a better way to make something, or a faster way to solve a problem or create a more convenient way of living. Think about microwave ovens, cell phones, and pooper-scoopers! Our successes in space are evidence of U.S. global superiority in technological advances, as are our military weapons. You may remember the "smart bombs" of the Persian Gulf War from 1991, or *drones* that fly unmanned and deliver bombs via remote control, created by Americans and used by U.S. forces—not other countries.

A creative mind and spirit are essential aspects of becoming a successful adult. Researchers in the late 1950s studied creative children and discovered that those who scored high on a creativity scale "grew up to be entrepreneurs, inventors, college presidents, authors, doctors, diplomats, and software developers."[9] If someone is particularly inventive, he or she wins the Nobel Prize for an invention and perhaps the development of a subsequent product that significantly affects the lives of others globally. Few honors mean as much to the American spirit as winning a Nobel Prize.

How can teachers help produce Nobel Prize winners? When schools' programs and courses and teachers' instructional processes encourage students' creative spirit and innovative thinking, schools produce Nobel Prize winners. A Chinese-born U.S. university professor describes the importance of valuing the creative spirit: "An innovation-driven society is driven by innovative people. Innovative people cannot come from schools that force students to memorize correct answers on standardized tests or reward students who excel at regurgitating dictated spoonfed knowledge."[10] Thinking about, designing, building, and producing a better mousetrap defines truly educated Americans.

It takes curious, imaginative, and well-educated teachers to encourage youth to be creative and innovative. With the emphasis on testing that currently exists, it takes *creatively insubordinate* teachers who realize that they can't sacrifice genuine student growth by narrowly focusing on preparing students for standardized tests. Required teacher certification within states and the universities across the United States helps produce teachers who are savvy enough to use their critical analyses to make the "right" decision on how and what to teach American children.

Capitalism: Its Influences in Our Classrooms A second valued trait for U.S. children to learn is the importance of capitalism to the American spirit. It's difficult to speak about the importance of capitalism without noting the emphasis Americans place on seeking and obtaining gainful employment. It is woven into the fabric of almost every classroom teacher. Teachers ask regularly of their charges—no matter what the grade level—"How do you expect to get a job with that attitude and lack of effort?"

Another common statement is, "You can't act so irresponsibly when you get into the real world, where your boss will expect more." Many educational ideas, programs, and lessons center on preparing students to enter the world of work: to become capitalists who love work, and thus are entitled to receive the many benefits of their labor.

Competition may be the driving force behind a capitalist spirit. Competition is valued in every classroom. It is the reason teachers assign grades, group students by ability, and administer tests: to sort students by categories so as to encourage them to choose "appropriate" career paths as they work diligently to better themselves to create solid career paths. Some adults mention to children, "Everyone can't be doctors," or "Maybe college isn't the best fit for you." It sounds cruel, but the system is in place to guarantee that our children find jobs commensurate with their abilities or efforts. The role of competition in American life seems to be the driving force for capitalism.

To ensure that children and adolescents understand these rules of life, and that teachers enforce them, we have the Business Round Table hounding schools with their agenda of more standards, more tests, and more accountability for students and teachers (see chapter 6). These measures, standards, and tests don't actually prepare our children for a lifetime of work. The effects of testing and the accompanying restrictive teaching and curricula discourage the development of inventive minds. Teachers are drawn into a constant dilemma of either preparing students to become creative inventors or having them memorize a mile-wide, inch-deep set of insignificant pieces of information.

Teachers can encourage hard work and persuade their students to become successful entrepreneurs without the tests and without the constant list of content standards, that is, more topics to teach every child. If all those facts learned in school were so important, why can't college students recall them two years after leaving high school? Teaching the thinking processes—creative and critical thinking, problem-solving strategies, research skills, communication abilities—is much more essential to promoting future success than those infinite facts students are barraged with throughout their schooling careers.

The Importance of Extracurricular Activities   One can always tell what a community really values by touring a high school campus. A drive around the outside of the building reveals a recently built, huge football stadium that seats 6,000 people. At least three other athletic fields exist—two with the latest artificial turf. The inside of the building reveals a band room twice the size of those from earlier times, adjacent to an auditorium that seats 2,500 with a full stage complete with Broadway-style lighting. Like many schools, this one has two full-size basketball gyms, a separate swimming facility, and separate locker rooms for each.

It's clear what this community values for its children: extracurricular activities of every possible kind. These athletic, drama, and music experiences are of great value to Americans; the expenditures on these activities reveal this fact. Other countries don't go quite as far as the U.S. schooling system to ensure that children have so many opportunities beyond academics and spend so much time engaged in these pastimes. Many high school students define themselves by their interest and participation in extracurricular events; and, for some, initial experiences lead to careers in the arts or professional athletics.

These meaningful activities make us who we are as Americans. Even when economic times are tough, Americans find the money to pay for new uniforms, more athletic equipment, and a better tuba. What do Americans get as a result of the extracurriculars? Well-rounded, competitive, hardworking capitalists. Students also develop unique personalities, which leads us to the value of individualism and its meaning to Americans—"You can be whatever you want to be in the United States!"

Opportunities for Different Career Paths Another defining characteristic of U.S. schools is the development of alternate paths for those not interested in college. High schools offer auto-repair classes, training for careers in hair salons, and opportunities to learn beginning carpentry, to name a few examples. Since states mandate attendance in school until the age of 17 or 18, schools have a responsibility to offer adolescents a chance to discover their interests and begin to pursue them during high school.

Many adolescents work part-time during their high school years. Some participate in going to school for half a day while working during their afternoons, as part of their training for future employment. Even those students who aren't in work-study programs take jobs during their high school years, thus developing responsibility and learning time-management strategies needed for future employment.[11]

When Americans choose to prioritize these opportunities through school programs and tax expenditures, they create a philosophy of schooling that differs from a traditional college-bound preparation. Some might propose that we aren't helping students unless we prepare them all to eventually complete college. That's a lofty goal, and it sounds laudable, but those kinds of goals ignore many high school students' needs. That view ignores those students who are searching for a productive and satisfying adult life while realizing that college won't create for them the challenge that they envision for *their* further learning.

Critical Thinking: Its Meaning for a Democratic Society   In the wake of a historic midterm election in 2010, a new group on the political horizon won a few seats in the U.S. Congress—people calling themselves *Tea Party* candidates. These candidates were trying to compare themselves to the cynics from the original 13 colonies who were disgusted with the King of England, so dropped a few pounds of the King's tea in the brink to irritate him.

The original group of tea partiers became American heroes—real role models. Disagreeing with the king in the 1700s was punishable by death; but if those brave souls hadn't followed the tea party with a revolution that created the United States, perhaps Americans wouldn't value critical thinking and the right to question authority as much as they do.

The result is the belief that as citizens, Americans have a responsibility to be critical of the government, leaders, and all authority. This sentiment is so imperative to our culture that we purposely encourage children to begin questioning authority at an early age. Schools sanction critical thinking by offering social studies at every grade level. By the time students have completed kindergarten they've been taught about George Washington—a man who led an entire army against the king's authority, represented by the British military.

Children are taught about elections, the role of government in everyday life, and how they can participate as members of the government. Parents take them into the voting booth with them and teachers hold mock elections at elementary schools. Americans love to say terrible things about political leaders, and they say them in front of their kids so that children begin to comprehend the way democracy works in the United States. Every child has an opportunity to receive an entire year of U.S.-government content during their 5th, 8th, and 11th grades of school.

It isn't merely by chance that Americans focus so much of the curriculum, that is, what children learn, on issues of government—from the Bill of Rights to Martin Luther King's "I Have a Dream" speech on the steps of the Lincoln Memorial. Americans live it, and news events reveal these rights through video footage of U.S. citizens exercising their rights of free speech every week. These constitutional rights matter to Americans, so educators and parents formally and informally teach them with pride.

Defining U.S. Public Education: We Are Who We Want to Be

These five emphases—teaching to encourage creative thought; helping some students develop trade skills rather than attending college; ensuring the questioning of authority through criticism; training students to develop effective work habits so they can contribute to the U.S. economic system; and offering extracurricular activities—are critical facets that Americans ensure every K–12 student is exposed to and understands before graduating from high school.

These unique qualities are prioritized in our public schools through state laws that require these concepts and principles become a part of what teachers focus on each year. Local school boards and superintendents sanction the use of these practices so that public schools ensure the inculcation of the American philosophy for future generations.

In the past 30–40 years of public school bashing, there have been few disagreements with or complaints against these programs or content. Often a local community will have a few parents who press for a change in the curriculum, but these battles generally yield very little, if any, substantial change in what gets taught regarding these philosophies.

If these principles are so critical to us, though, why do we often hear of how we should be more like other countries in our educational practices and content? There are several pundits who proclaim we have an inferior educational system compared to other countries; but these "experts" lack full comprehension of what they are saying, and also are not aware of the American values that actually drive our educational practice.

The U.S. educational system has certainly been influenced by other countries. This occurs when some U.S. citizens, for instance, make attempts to suggest that the public school system should mirror other nations' schools. These errant suggestions reveal an ignorance about why U.S. schools have different priorities from other countries' schools—ignorance concerning what the genuine American educational mission is. Making some of these suggested changes would detract from our mission.

INFLUENCES FROM OTHER NATIONS ON OUR EDUCATIONAL SYSTEM

Fostering a *creative spirit* is a strength of our public schools, and it's prioritized because in the United States, creative energy and production of useful ideas and inventions are critical to who we are. The United States' education has been influenced by foreign countries' technological advances throughout the years—but not always in positive ways. When the Soviet satellite Sputnik flew into space in 1957, the United States altered its mathematics and science curricula in significant ways—not necessarily for the better.

After the Japanese had begun making appealing, fuel-efficient automobiles during the late 1970s and early 1980s, someone in the Reagan administration surmised (inaccurately; see chapter 6) that the American schooling system was to blame for the U.S. auto industry's lagging behind. Teachers were asked to "go back to teaching the basics" better than they had been before. Was the fact that executives in Detroit were stuck on producing large, gas-guzzling vehicles the fault of American public school children or their teachers?

When China began making headway as a producer of many products used in the United States, American businesspersons began to suggest that we needed rigorous standards and more tests. Now, we've almost institutionalized a testing culture in U.S. public schools. Testing occupies weeks of preparation in classrooms across the United States, thereby eliminating the kind of learning that leads to—you guessed it—creative thinking.

If you're following the story line, you might respond, "Oh, no! What's going to happen to our creative spirit, our inventiveness, our Yankee ingenuity?" You've guessed correctly—it will no longer exist with the testing emphasis legislated in every state in America through the No Child Left Behind (NCLB) federal law. NCLB's emphasis on testing is unprecedented in U.S. education policy, whether one is looking at state- or federal-level policies.

Evidence already exists that U.S. children are beginning to suffer as a result of emphasis on standardized tests. Researchers discovered that students' creativity scores rose for years until 1990. Since that time, scores have steadily fallen each year.[12] The drop in creativity scores was six years after the release of the ill-written government document *A Nation at Risk*, which created negative teaching practices associated with narrowing what gets taught (curricula) to match standardized-test preparation. The United States won't be number one in creative thinking for long if the testing culture remains as prominent as it is now.

Should We Try to Emulate the Chinese System?

On two occasions, I led groups of visiting Chinese educators on field trips to visit two local schools that offered progressive educational practices to their students. "Why are they visiting our schools?" you might ask. Because they want *their* schools to produce what we produce in our public schools—Nobel Prize winners. (See chapter 1: U.S. public schools have produced many winners.)

On both occasions, the Chinese visitors visited a public middle and high school from two local districts. The middle school offers a nationally famous curriculum-integration program in which students choose what they will learn based on their questions. Students determine the curriculum, how they will learn it, and how they will present what they learn to fellow students and the public.

The local high school uses a block-scheduling program for all of its students. In block scheduling, instead of the traditional seven-to-nine periods a day of 42 minutes each, students only attend four classes a day, each lasting approximately 90 minutes. As in college, after a semester of these four classes, students start four new classes halfway through the year.

Researchers studying both of these programs have found considerable advantages for students and teachers. The middle school class improves students' thinking skills much better than traditional curricula do, as students problem solve, analyze data, and create presentations and projects to represent their learning. Students are more motivated, work more cooperatively, assume more responsibility, and become better readers and writers.[13] The most significant advantage for students in this program comes in the form of the decision-making opportunities that mirror democratic processes.

Block scheduling at the high school provides numerous advantages for teachers. They enjoy having additional time to provide more hands-on, direct learning experiences; helping struggling students; seeing more opportunities for student-to-student conversations during lessons that improve their learning; seeing greater occurrences of student questioning; and benefiting from the development of better relationships with students, which leads to more cooperative classrooms.[14] These innovative practices occur in public schools in your neighborhoods.

The Chinese are visiting American public schools to see educational innovation, and to try to imitate it in their country. Who can blame them for searching for solutions to their stifling educational system? They have been visiting us for many years, searching for solutions to their challenge of developing Nobel Prize winners.

Yong Zhao, a professor at Michigan State University who was the founding director of the US-China Center for Research on Educational Excellence, describes his initial interest in writing his book, *Catching Up or Leading the Way?*:

> I was going to write about China's efforts to decentralize curriculum and textbooks, diversify assessment and testing, and encourage local autonomy and innovations in order to cultivate creativity and well-rounded talents. I was also going to write about China's repeated failures and unwavering desire to undo the damages of testing and standardization.
>
> But while I was going through the reform policies, scholarly writings, and online discussion forums and blogs about education in China, I realized that what China wants is what America is eager to throw away—an education that respects individual talents, supports divergent thinking, tolerates deviation, and encourages creativity; a system in which the government does not dictate what children learn or how teachers teach; and culture that does not rank or judge success of a school, a teacher, or a child based on only test scores in a few subjects determined by the government.[15]

Based on these findings from an expert on Chinese and U.S. educational systems, Americans are certainly ahead of China when it comes to educating the masses. Why would anyone suggest America should emulate the Chinese education system?

China's limitations on personal expression alone are completely archaic for someone from a democratic world. Then there are the limits on the number of children couples can have, prohibitions on Internet use, a smog in Beijing that cripples the city, and an infrastructure of buildings that crumble under minor stressors. China's educational system is not creating what the U.S. system is creating—healthy, psychologically happy, productive, innovative adults.

Many schools in China have 50 to 80 students in each class. Every educational researcher and classroom teacher can explain the detriment to genuine learning that having so many students creates. CNN recently announced that 68% of America's high school students go on to higher education, whereas only 40% of Chinese students attend some form of postsecondary educational institution.[16] The Chinese can have their high test scores and the communities they've created with them. Their education system and philosophy don't reflect American ideals.

Should We Emulate Singapore, Finland, Canada, or Japan?

Maybe you'd like for us to exceed the high test scores of students from Singapore, who have done well on international comparisons. CNN journalist Fareed Zakaria revealed that the *high-scoring Singapore students who reached adulthood weren't as productive* and "faded as they moved into real life 10 or 20 years down the road while Americans who trailed Singapore badly on the tests outdid them in every aspect of life."[17]

Another country Americans used to be envious of was Japan, during the 1980s. That was then: Japan's economy *diminished* three times as much as the U.S. economy in 2008.[18] After sixth grade, Japanese students take a highly competitive test to get into high schools. Up until that time, all children stay together in the same class and move at the same pace. There are no special reading groups determined by ability—they're all equal in Japan. Maybe we shouldn't look to the Far East for educational advice.

When pundits refer to the success of other nations' schools, they seldom mention the geographic size of those countries compared to the

United States. Singapore is the size of the state of Kentucky. Finland, whose educational system Americans frequently praise, is the size of Colorado. Educational systems that small can't possibly be as challenging to manage as the U.S. system.

If pundits are anxious to compare Finland's and Singapore's educational systems with ours, then the United States must consider adopting some of their educational strategies. The entire cost, for instance, of training teachers at the universities in Finland and Singapore are paid for by the government—absolutely no tuition or other educational costs exist for education majors in those countries. Even in neighboring Ontario, the government pays about 66 percent of students' college costs if they are education majors.[19]

Finnish students have scored well on some international tests. In examining the possible reasons for their success, researchers note,

> Schools are equitably funded, well stocked, and uniformly well supported; class sizes are fairly small; students receive food and health care as well as educational supports. In addition, teachers' instructional hours are short by U.S. standards (about 60 percent of the time U.S. teachers teach), so teachers have time for fashioning strong instruction, planning, meeting with students and parents, and grading papers, while also maintaining a reasonable family life.[20]

Small class size, "food and health care," more time for teachers to plan lessons and grade papers, and "a reasonable family life" are amazing advantages for students and teachers. It's a wonder anyone would choose to teach in the United States considering the lack of resources for students and the additional hours American teachers put in after school compared to Finnish teachers.

Unlike U.S. students, who are tested almost every year they're in school, Finnish students take no external standardized tests *except for a college admissions test designed by teachers*. Finnish students do well academically without testing companies' intrusions into their learning experiences.

U.S. teachers used to be trusted to conduct their own assessments too, until the standards and testing movement started in the mid-1980s. The test-prep business now controls the work of educators in this country. Experienced Finnish teachers also make much more money than experienced U.S. teachers, meaning a commitment to the profession by the public through taxes.

A positive domino effect exists in countries' educational systems when substantial resources are provided. It starts with respect for the profession, which leads to trusting and permitting professional educators to do their jobs without outside interference. The affective components lead to financial support for students and teachers, which leads to providing teachers with structural support through a school day designed for more professional time for teachers, balanced with leadership responsibilities.

Ultimately, the greatest reward is student-centered learning, with teachers ensuring motivational learning activities rather than a back-to-the-basics approach that demeans students and teachers. The reason it works:

> Because Finland does not have a standardized assessment for evaluating students, there is no formal consideration of student learning outcomes in the evaluation. Teacher and leader effectiveness are defined using a broader meaning of student learning than just test scores in mathematics and reading literacy . . . . A good teacher [in Finland] is one who is able to help all children progress and grow in a holistic way.[21]

Finnish educators value and prioritize personalized learning and creativity. These two processes don't develop when test scores are the measuring tool of meaningful learning and effective teaching, as they often are in the United States.

The Canadian province of Ontario's educational leaders had an awakening in the early 1990s. The province chose to end teacher testing to determine entry into the profession. Since that time, teachers have received a great deal of support during their professional years, and the most positive result is a much lower turnover rate among teachers. The testing movement intruded on the certification process of U.S. teachers. Many states require their teachers to take a test for initial certification—again, a process that wasn't institutionalized until after the 1980s.

The overwhelming advantage to the educational environments in Finland, Singapore, and Ontario is the emphasis placed on teaching as a profession. Certification in these countries is dictated and regulated by the universities, who set the standards for certification and teach researched-based strategies that support effective learning.

No one can become a teacher in these countries without passing through the university gates. That's how certification began in the United States; and it continues to be the most appropriate way to ensure effective teacher development. Alternative certification routes, such as Teach for America, reduce the effectiveness of the profession (see chapter 4).

The Value of American Education in Their World

Thomas Friedman, who wrote *The World Is Flat* and later *Hot, Flat, and Crowded*, notes in the latter that in 1968 the United States established a Department of Defense high school based on American education principles in Bahrain, a small island nation off the coast of Saudi Arabia in the Persian Gulf.[22] The school was primarily intended for navy dependents, but 70 percent of the students who attended were high-socioeconomic-status Bahraini adolescents, including the crown prince when he was high school age.

Not long after 9/11, the United States decided to close the school for security reasons. According to Friedman, the Bahraini elite desperately wanted and urged the Pentagon to keep the school there, primarily because most of them had been educated in that school.

One graduate remarked to Friedman,

> Once you walked into that school, who you were did not matter—you were always judged on merit, which was different from other schools in Bahrain, where you were judged on your wealth or family connections. Until today, the people in Bahrain who graduated from that school are different—you got discipline, you were encouraged to take risks and fail . . . It was run according to the American value system.[23]

Friedman's Bahraini, *American-educated* friend knows what we often fail to recognize here in the states: American public education has many advantages that exceed the absurdity that exists in many other nations—the pressures of high test scores, children who study for hours on end, or the use of Saturday school for additional instruction. The values that arise from a level playing field at public schools represent the hope of the population. That equalizing factor created by public schooling for all is the reason that thousands of immigrant families flock to the United

States, just as most of our ancestors did. Public education defines our global success on every front.

WHAT ABOUT INTERNATIONAL COMPARISONS ON STANDARDIZED TESTS?

Pundits frequently cry about how U.S. students score considerably lower than international students on standardized tests. U.S. children have never been at the top of international comparisons on some tests. The reasons for lower scores have to do with the priorities in our society—priorities that don't include having our children study for five hours every evening.

Mathematics and reading are not "life" in America. But they are in other nations, where nothing else is a priority in children's lives. Insuring that *every* child receives an education is also a U. S. priority that affects students' nationwide test scores.

Education in the United States is supposed to be driven by the principle of *equity*—all are entitled to an equal opportunity to receive an appropriate education in order to eliminate poverty, poor health, and dysfunctional family living conditions in their lives to become happy, productive adults. Many believe that equity actually exists, but the forces of politics and tradition won't permit that to occur in every U.S. community. (See chapter 10, on urban education.)

In the United States, equity means everyone receives an education until he or she is 17 or 18 years old. It means that everyone is entitled to the services, from bus rides to special-education services to all the extracurricular activities—*everyone* is entitled to a comprehensive education until he or she finishes high school. Most countries don't require students to go to school for that long.

Developed European countries—France, Spain, Portugal, Italy, Greece, the United Kingdom, Ireland, Norway, Sweden—force their students to choose a career path that siphons some of them from the college track long before the age of 17. The career path is determined by scores on tests that will determine their future educational opportunities at 14 or 15 years of age. If you think that makes sense, try to recall how ready you were for a lifetime decision about a career at that age.

The impact of such a decision means that when you read about an international test comparison, those countries' students that usually do better than U.S. students are destined for college. When our students take an international-comparison test, all of them take it—not merely the college bound. A high percentage of students from other countries taking the test are the best the country has to offer.

We in the United States insist on comparing our *total population* to a few of the other countries' students—the higher-echelon few! The huge number of students we test and the varying academic abilities of our students explain why American students often finish lower than some European and Asian countries on international high school comparisons.

Younger European students—children from countries such as Norway, Switzerland, and Sweden—often score higher than U.S. students of same age on international comparisons. Across all grades, when the total American population is compared with their populations, there is much more poverty that exists within U.S. borders. Many pundits say that blaming *poverty* for lower U.S. student test scores is inexcusable—comments that demonstrate considerable ignorance on the effects of poverty.

The effects of poverty on a child's learning ability are well documented. Eric Jensen, a long-time researcher on learning and the brain, reports the following effects of poverty on the brain:

> Socioeconomic status is strongly associated with a number of indices of children's cognitive ability, including I.Q., achievement tests, grade retention rates, and literacy. There is a gulf between poor and well-off children's performance on just about every measure of cognitive development from the Bayley Infant Behavior Scales to standardized achievement tests.
>
> The correlations between socioeconomic status and cognitive ability and performance are typically quite significant and persist throughout the stages of development, from infancy through adolescence and into adulthood.[24]

Countries like Sweden and Norway have little poverty, and they have higher student test scores than almost all nations—not merely the United States. On one international test comparison, the Progress in International Reading Literacy Study (PIRLS), the highest scores in 2001 were among nations with the lowest percentages of poverty.

U.S. public schools with more than half of students living in poverty had scores on the PIRLS from 70 to 100 points lower than those U.S. students living in less poverty. The signs are pretty clear—reduce poverty and increase chances tenfold to improve students' academic success.

As a nation, politically, U.S. citizens don't do much to reduce poverty, but many are willing to disparage teachers for using it as an excuse for not having high student test scores. If politicians want to punish teachers and school districts for not having high student test scores, then citizens from these cities out of necessity must hold federal and state politicians responsible for erasing some of the conditions that cause poverty.

Politicians can begin by actually taxing the businesses in their states and cities as much as they tax private citizens (see chapter 6 for an explanation of business tax breaks). There will be no "we're number one" in international student-test-score comparisons as long as the extent of poverty in this country continues, and corporations maintain such gigantic tax breaks for moving into many communities.

Just Who Is Proficient?

Designers (primarily politicians—not educators) of the federal NCLB legislation in 2001 utilized a term to describe a level of having learned enough: *proficiency*. Educational researchers, school administrators, teachers, and parents have no idea what *proficient* actually means. Each of the 50 states' education-department personnel choose or design a test, then establish a cutoff score that is used to determine who is and is not proficient. Those cutoff scores for proficiency have been lowered each year in many states since NCLB became law in 2002.

When enough students are proficient a school district receives praise and even more money to continue doing what they had little to no control over in the first place: raising students' test scores. A student who reaches a high enough score on the state tests to be considered proficient is not necessarily a good student, is not necessarily well educated, and may have not grown any during the academic year. It's often easy, therefore, to comprehend how worthless the *proficiency* label is to teachers and students.

Shortly before President Barack Obama took office, a pundit complained that it was "unconscionable" that not one state in the United States had a majority of fourth or eighth graders proficient in math and reading. It's doubtful that most U.S. adults would have been proficient in their childhoods, because there is plenty of evidence that each succeeding generation is intellectually smarter than the last.

How about the rest of the world's students—do you suppose they're proficient? According to the commissioner of the National Center for Education Statistics, the following countries were the only ones with a majority of students proficient in mathematics: Singapore, South Korea, Hong Kong, Japan, and Taiwan. Who wants to move there and place their children in their public schools? Not one country had even one half their students proficient in reading, with Sweden having the most proficient at 33 percent (the United States was at 31 percent that year, 2007).[25] *Proficiency* also has no significance for many parents concerned about their children's futures.

The many international tests that U.S. children take rarely match what Americans teach children and adolescents. A test is called *valid* if it measures what is says it measures. When you take a driving test, it should measure how well you drive, and there shouldn't be any trick questions on the written test that aren't in the driver's manual for your state. That indicates a positive *content validity*—it measures what it tests, your driving knowledge and ability to drive.

Educational researchers use content validity to determine whether the content on a test—the questions—mirrors the content taught in a school. When the army tests recruits on how to use their weapons, those recruits know exactly what's on the test, because they're taught on the exact weaponry that they'll be tested on. That represents a strong content validity.

U.S. test companies don't provide that same courtesy to public school teachers with the tests given to their students. For many standardized tests, teachers have no idea what will be tested. No one is monitoring the international tests U.S. students take for content validity—tests like the Trends in International Math and Science Study (TIMSS), the Program of International Student Assessment (PISA), and the PIRLS. If the tests don't measure what is taught, why use them as valid indicators of how U.S. students are doing compared to other countries?

If we know that our children aren't faring as well as South Koreans in mathematics, do we need to panic if we aren't teaching the same concepts that the Korean children are learning? Will South Korea eventually surpass the U.S. in economic development, creating new products, solving challenging problems, or resolving conflict across the globe? Americans shouldn't be feeling any stress about this possibility.

The statistics indicate that the connection between students' test scores and a country's economic success are not significant. In 2007, one researcher reported, *"The higher a nation's test score 40 years ago, the worse its economic performance."*[26] After hearing of those findings, Zhao added, "If test scores are *not* such reliable indicators of the quality of education or good predictors of a nation's or an individual's success, how did the United States come to accept the general notion that its public education system is broken and to support the reform efforts to put more standards and tests in schools?"[27]

Using these tests as a way of evaluating America's public schools seems absurd. If you also question the value of using these tests, you should contact your Congresspersons and let them know that you'd rather not spend your money on purchasing and scoring these tests. The PIRLS alone costs $120,000 for four years per state; the TIMSS would cost $15 million if every state participated; and it costs $25 million to cover the PISA assessment for every state.

At a time when many are concerned about huge federal and state budget deficits, do we need to know how our children stack up against South Korea and Sweden at a cost of $40 million a year? Wouldn't you rather use U.S. advanced technology and part of that tax money to repair the aging bridges in your state?

If politicians want the U.S. education system to be more like Japan's, then taxpayers will need to shell out much more money for teachers' salaries. Japanese educators make as much as engineers there, while here in the states, teachers make about 60 percent of an engineer's pay. Once again, the playing field is not equitable among nations' educational circumstances.

Education Expenditures—Who's on Top?

One might believe that if Americans value educating their children, then they would lead the world in education expenditures. Data presented by the National Center for Education Statistics (NCES) in 2006 showed a rank of *ninth* for the U.S. among all industrialized countries on education expenditures for elementary and secondary education, based on percentage of gross domestic product spent on education.[28]

Ninth place—can you believe it? When politicians speak, they always say that we want to be number one in the world in education. How can we be number one when we only place ninth among industrialized nations in our spending? This is embarrassing, considering our alleged economic superiority among other nations.

If IBM, Bill Gates's Microsoft business, pharmaceutical companies, and the oil corporations would begin paying the same taxes that private citizens pay, we might make some hay toward getting to the top of education expenditures globally. Until that time, we'll continue within our state governments to permit corporations to pay little to no taxes for years as a reward for their promise to build their plants in our state (see chapter 6 for details).

An education researcher reported that in the mid-1990s, the state of South Carolina legislature "awarded BMW $150,000,000 in tax breaks and other incentives in order to secure the construction of its new production plant within the state."[29] U.S. government officials revealed in the early 1990s that local property-tax revenues from corporations dropped from 45% in 1957 to 16% by 1990. When examining the expenditures for education, it is important to recognize that most education funding comes from state revenues—not federal tax dollars. State taxes on corporations are essential to improving U.S. global-educational standing.

Politicians who say they want a first-class education system with the highest test scores in the world are going to have to find a way to fund a first-class "Mercedes" education, as opposed to a much less expensive "Yugo" education. I haven't heard any politicians, even the Tea Partiers, requesting this kind of a change in state tax practices.

The politicians' and businesspersons' voices are loud on the subject of improving education in the states; but what's more obvious is the 800-pound gorilla in the room breathing quietly, so no one will notice how the corporations are clearly avoiding paying their share of the taxes while complaining that they're not getting enough of an educational advantage for their money. We're still driving a Yugo when it comes to funding education in the states, thanks primarily to big-business money influencing elections.

The *our-kids-are-not-as-smart-as-other-countries'-kids* debate is a worthless conversation because American adults are not willing to change the profile of educated U.S. citizens. Americans like what they are, and they continue to value their current identity more than just test scores and intelligent people. Some people suggested during the 2000 and 2004 presidential elections that they liked George W. Bush because he was someone "just like me, someone who I feel like I can sit down with and enjoy a beer."

On the other hand, fewer adults likely announce, "I'll always vote for the smartest presidential candidate." Being *smart* in America is just one of the possible traits that makes someone likable, and not the most important one.

There exists a significant difference in American philosophy, which permeates our schools: climbing the social, economic, and happiness ladders is not dependent on extended hours of daily studying in mathematics and reading. Most Americans believe that their opportunity for future economic happiness can be met by merely participating in the educational game, not by excelling at it.

If so many of our millionaires hadn't attained that status *without* a high-school or college education, then perhaps this wouldn't be our view of education. Bill Gates, as a college dropout, often inadvertently espouses philosophies and accompanying education policies that often reflect that America doesn't really want to be number one in education. Many Americans have other goals in mind, and making money is probably at the top of the list. Did the smartest people in your high school eventually become the highest money earners? Perhaps the people at the lower end of the academic realm from your high school are also quite happy and successful. Americans should give up the "brain race" and choose other, more agreeable, goals. It's obvious they're already doing that.

THE AMAZING PROGRESS OF PUBLIC EDUCATION IN AMERICA

When I was born, the majority of young people in the United States never attended high school, and what they learned from formal schooling was a very small part of what counted for getting on in the world.[30] [from Deborah Meier, born in 1931]

Each semester, a few students at the university, who are 22 years old, will complain about how terrible kids are today compared to when they were kids. Other students complain that today's children are less intelligent than they were as children. Every successive generation of adults has this belief that they are more polite, better behaved, and much smarter than the next generation.

If only this were true. Education in the United States has grown immensely over the past 100 years. The phenomenal progress of U.S. education is a story that is never realized by the public and certainly not addressed in the media.

Look How Far We've Come: Dropout Rates Then . . . And Now

What was the school-dropout rate when your grandparents graduated from high school? In 1950, only 34 percent of 25-year-olds had completed at least four years of high school. That means two of every three adults had *not* completed high school.[31] Those who graduated from high school at the age of 18 in 1950 would be 79 years old in 2011. Do you suppose these adults are saying to you how academically talented their generation is compared to later generations! Compare the 1950 figure with the fact that in 1977 the high school dropout rate was only 14 percent.

How about when you graduated from high school? Let's check another year. By 1985, during the Ronald Reagan presidency, when many politicians and U.S. Department of Education personnel were decrying the state of public education, 74 percent of the American population 25 years or older had completed at least four years of high school.[32] These were far greater graduation rates than the older generation of people that these politicians represented.

Perhaps times were worse during the 1990s. Think again: five years after 1985, in 1990, according to the NCES, the proportion of adults over the age of 25 who had completed high school stood at 78 percent. In 2001, in another revealing statistic about the effectiveness of public schools in America, the dropout rate was at only 11 percent.

How many students are graduating from high school each year now? It is critical to look at the past to discover whether as a whole public education in America is making gains in the "war on ignorance," as educators sometimes refer to their task. Looking at the gains in the number of graduates from high school certainly indicates success in American public schooling.

Although compulsory schooling for adolescents originated in the late 1800s, it wasn't until the 1930s that a majority of adolescents even attended school in America.[33] In 1930, 73 percent of 14- to 17-year-olds were enrolled in school, and by 1940 that figure had risen to almost 80 percent. It's important to note that *less than one half* of students attending school in those years was graduating from high school.

My father, born in 1925, received a high school diploma after only 11 years of schooling. He is from "the greatest generation" that Tom Brokaw mentioned in his 1998 book.[34] You can see that it was a few decades before 12 years of compulsory attendance had a significant impact on Americans' graduation rates.

Why Are They "The Greatest Generation"?

In Brokaw's book *The Greatest Generation*, the author describes those adults who lived from approximately 1920 and are now in their eighties and nineties:

> They succeeded on every front. They won the war; they saved the world. They came home to joyous and short-lived celebrations and immediately began the task of rebuilding their lives and the world they wanted. They married in record numbers and gave birth to another distinctive generation, the Baby Boomers. A grateful nation made it possible for more of them to attend college than society had ever educated, anywhere. They gave the world a new science, literature, art, industry, and economic strength unparalleled in the long course of history.[35]

Were they the greatest generation because they were the first to be provided with an opportunity to complete a high school education through the public schools? Did they use their public education to provide the services needed to improve the quality of life for all Americans?

Think about all the technological advances that have been made in our quality of life by those who were educated in America's public schools from 1927 to 1950, when less than half of Americans were successfully completing high school. So many more adolescents are now completing high school than ever before; this is a success that other countries don't even attempt to provide for their 17- and 18-year-olds.

Other significant findings show how well Americans have contributed to U.S. economic success since the 1960s. U.S. workers educated during the 1970s and 1980s have improved productivity considerably, increasing the productivity rate to "unprecedented levels . . . rising faster than in other industrialized nations during the mid-1990s."[36]

Why Doesn't Everyone Graduate from High School?

Many hardworking adults believe that through their effort and energy they are responsible for their personal and family success. Perhaps your family is no exception to the lessons from our parents: go to school, work hard, and you'll meet your needs financially as an adult when you get a job. The advantages many U.S. families had are many:

- Their ancestors arrived in the states from northern Europe hundreds of years ago.
- Poor treatment of many families' ancestors ended decades ago— for instance, there has been no more mistreatment of or prejudice against Irish, Welsh, or Scottish immigrants for at least the last 85 years.
- Most Americans are currently Caucasian, an advantage that many Whites never recognize.
- Millions are fortunate enough to be free of learning disabilities, brain injuries, autism, and behavioral disorders.
- As preschoolers, many academically successful adults were exposed to reading materials, many play activities, and national travel that helped them build a knowledge of the world, prior to entering school.
- Many peoples' parents believed in the value of education, and set an example by reading at home and encouraging children to do homework.
- Many baby boomers' parents had enough money to start college.
- Many parents always insisted that their children attend college for at least a year or two.

- Some have been fortunate enough to grow up in healthy neighborhoods where the water was clean, healthy food was readily available, one could exercise outside daily, and the crime rate was minimal.
- Many parents received medical benefits at their jobs as a result of union victories to support their children's medical needs (e.g., visits to the dentist, doctor, and optometrist).

It is no accident many adults managed to succeed academically; all the supports were in place. Millions of children have been fortunate enough to grow up in similar circumstances. Some families have had difficult times, struggling financially, but still managed to achieve academic success, graduating from high school and college. Each successive generation of U.S. immigrant families has received multiple opportunities to reach success as adults. A free and appropriate public education is the reason for that success for the 89 percent of U.S. citizens who attend public schools.

It's often difficult for many adults to believe that every child doesn't have the same chance for success that they had. That perspective demonstrates an ignorance about the thousands of children and adolescents who experience much more challenging circumstances. Considering all the possible physical, social, emotional, ethnic, and cognitive factors that are necessary for a child to move successfully through 13 years of schooling, it is indeed a success story that 89 percent of our adolescents make it through successfully.

Speak to any public school teacher, and you'll hear about the students who are constantly challenged in school. Students with learning disabilities, reading difficulties, autism, and behavioral disorders are just a few of the challenges teachers experience daily. Those are the obvious situations that teachers see. Other challenges include

- children who enter kindergarten who have never seen a book;
- children and parents who don't speak English;
- family poverty that prevents parents from being home due to their second jobs each evening;
- family traditions or expectations that adolescents begin working at age 16 or become married and have children by the age of 17 or 18, thus dropping out of school early;

- unidentified learning difficulties that exist for years before being discovered;
- absent parents who have neither the time nor the desire to help their children with school or in developing appropriate socialization skills;
- children and adolescents in constant hunger as a result of poverty;
- poor environmental conditions within communities, such as lead in drinking water that causes brain deficiencies;
- stressful emotional lives that cause brain deficiencies and mental-health challenges;
- funding inequities that result in fewer resources being available for students and teachers in schools affected by low tax bases (which is common in most major U.S. cities).

The factors beyond the control of teachers far exceed the ones they can control within their classrooms each day—in every classroom in America, urban, rural, and suburban. In urban schools, the struggles for teachers are magnified due to the environmental and economic problems that exist, which affect families in ways that many of us have never experienced and cannot imagine (see chapter 10).

Many rural schools face similar challenges. The determining factor for many adolescents regarding graduating from high school is the influence of past family practice: if no one in their families has completed school yet, it is unlikely that they'll feel a compulsion to graduate.

It's likely that pundits, politicians, businesspersons, and the media will continue to make disparaging remarks about the quality of public education in America, with indications that the U.S. is falling behind several nations in its educational efforts and endeavors. Blaming teachers and their unions for a less than perfect graduation rate ignores the multitude of social and economic ills that are the true culprits affecting further public-school success.

Despite the purposeful ignoring of these social problems by Congressional bodies, public school teachers continue to educate all who enter their buildings with an amazing rate of success. If we want this trend to continue, we'll have to start supporting public schools, armed with the facts of our success, rather than destroying them with ignorant rhetoric.

THE VALUE OF
PUBLIC SCHOOL TEACHERS

As parents, we entrust our most precious assets to this system. . . .
We leave our darling child with this person [teacher]. That person
has to be very worthy, and has to be deeply moral. I don't mean to
be fuzzy about that; they have to have a real commitment to acting
in a humane, honest way, intellectually and in a person-to-person
fashion, all the time.[1]

That charter schools are not substantially more effective, on average, than other public schools calls into question the view that
bureaucracy and union contracts are major impediments to school
improvement.[2]

It is time that policy makers recognize that teaching, which is at
the very core of education, involves complex tasks that require spe-
cialized skills and knowledge. It is not enough, for example, for a
teacher of mathematics to know mathematics.[3]

Teachers are often as verbally assaulted publicly as the schools themselves because, let's face it, you can't say something about the public
schools without actually directing your comments at the professionals
who teach in them. Foolhardy pundits, newscasters, and politicians may

not realize how their negative comments about public schools impact those teachers who truly make a difference in the lives of their students.

Educators are often the brunt of offensive comments and highly erroneous information about their professional abilities and their academic qualifications. Kenneth Kastle, the deputy executive director of the Middle States Association's Commission on Secondary Schools, notes that for more than 20 years, "public educators have developed an inferiority complex and a strong sense of hopelessness," due to sustained inaccurate attacks on the teaching profession.[4] Those in the profession have their own ammunition to lob at their attackers, as evidenced by this written scenario that recently made the rounds in teacher lounges around the country.

What Do You Make?

The dinner guests were sitting around the table discussing life. One man, a CEO of a company, decided to explain the problem with education. He argued, "What's a kid going to learn from someone who decided his or her best option in life was to become a teacher?"

He reminded the other dinner guests that it's true what they say about teachers, "Those who can—do. Those who can't—teach."

To corroborate, he said to another guest: "You're a teacher, Dana. Be honest. What do you make?"

Dana, who had a reputation of honesty and frankness, replied, "You want to know what I make? I make kids work harder than they ever thought they could. I can make a 'C+' feel like a Congressional Medal of Honor and an 'A-' feel like a slap in the face if the student did not do his or her very best. I can make kids sit through 40 minutes of study hall in absolute silence. I can make parents tremble in fear when I call home.

"You know what I make? I make kids wonder. I make them question. I make them criticize. I make them apologize and mean it! I make them write. I make them read, read, read. I make them spell, 'definitely beautiful,' 'definitely beautiful,' and 'definitely beautiful' over and over and over again, until they will never misspell either one of those words again.

"I make them understand that if you have brains, then follow your heart . . . and if anyone ever tries to judge you by what you make, you pay them no attention. You want to know what I make? I make a difference! What about you?" (author unknown)

This is an important story to share because among noneducators, there is much ignorance about the daily experiences of teachers. Why do you think someone decides to become a teacher? Do you think they do it to eventually become rich? Do you believe most teachers choose to be with children or adolescents because they really despise kids and want to make life miserable for them?

Do you know any public school teachers who want to see children fail in the learning process? Do you know any teachers who prefer that their students do poorly in school? Are there any teachers in your community who would rather their students *didn't* do well on standardized tests? How many really poor teachers are there in the public school that you attended, or that your children attend? What percentage of your teachers were terrible versus exceptional?

WALK A MILE IN MY SHOES

These are meaningful questions. Let's face it, if you're not a teacher, you really don't know what the life of a teacher is like. It's likely that you know a teacher and may even be related to one; but that doesn't make you a teacher and doesn't help you to really know what the life of a teacher is like. Until you've been responsible for the learning of 20 or more students for six to seven hours a day at any grade level *for at least five continuous days*, you know nothing about teaching!

Are the breaks afforded to teachers during June, July, and August really worth putting up with everyone else's kids for 6 hours a day for 180 days of the year? If you're not a teacher, you won't be able to answer that question; so please ask one when you get the chance. The average number of social interactions in a week for a classroom teacher is between 10,000 and 15,000. For that intensity of social interaction each week, perhaps providing a few weeks away from students is imperative for teachers to return with renewed energy and excitement in September each year.

"But," you're saying, "teachers make a lot of money compared to other professionals! Their salaries keep going up and up and all they do is strike and ask for more money." If teachers are lucky, they're asking for more money and getting it. But the facts prove otherwise. Beginning teacher salaries run from $20,000 to $10,000 *less* than those who enter professions such as engineering, mathematics/statistics, computer science, and accounting.[5] As an additional piece of information about beginning teacher salaries, the National Education Association (NEA) has reported that almost one fourth of public-college graduates who become teachers will owe too much in student loans to repay on their first-year salaries.[6]

Before you start complaining about salaries of U.S. teachers, you might be interested in knowing that salaries here rank 12th among 34 other industrialized nations, and near the bottom of all those countries when compared with other nations' gross domestic product per capita.[7] A dental hygienist makes about $67,000 a year. Everyone deserves an opportunity to make a decent living; but a dental hygienist, whose training includes only two years of college, making more than the average teacher with a master's degree is an unfathomable inequity.

An interesting fact that may be a surprise to you is that teacher salaries rose a mere 0.8 percent (less than one percent) in the ten years between 1996 and 2006, according to the Economic Policy Institute. According to the institute, college-educated workers in the private sector had an increase of 12 percent over the same time period.[8] (All this was before the economic fallout of 2008–2009.)

How much has your salary risen over the past ten years? Many teachers cannot afford to buy homes in the communities where they teach.

If one estimated how an average teacher's salary compares to an hourly wage, it would be approximately $30 an hour, which sounds quite reasonable to some.[9] That figure is based only on the work completed at school—which much of a teacher's work isn't. An author of an NEA study from 2001 noted that teachers work an average of 10 additional hours per week outside of the 7:30–3:00 schedule. If you've ever had a conversation with a teacher, you clearly understand the "Sunday evening stress" that goes along with preparing for another week of teaching; but one must also consider the other four evenings that teachers work at home—Monday through Thursday.

THE CHALLENGES OF THE PROFESSION

None of these conveniently collected statistics measures the genuine challenges of teaching each day. Imagine a daily job where the people you work with make a concerted attempt to derail the scheduled events and thus prevent you from reaching your daily work objectives. Students who act disruptive, lazy, tired, emotional, out of touch, hungry, or angry, and many who are completely unmotivated by the activities of the day, bring a reality to teaching that noneducators can't possibly comprehend.

Students' displays of reluctance and apathy can be daunting when middle and high school teachers see as many as 100 to 150 students a day, any one of whom may demonstrate complete disdain as teachers deliver the "sales pitch" that is scheduled to benefit them. Teaching is challenging even when most students are cooperative, because there are so many differences in children's and adolescents' academic skills and cognitive abilities. Students who are all in the same grade level have many learning differences that one who doesn't teach can't even imagine.

Charles Murray, author of *Real Education*, describes the reality of students' abilities and the effects on teaching efforts:

> If you define *grade level* as the tasks that someone of average ability can be taught to do, then the proportion of students who are not at grade level will be approximately 50 percent. If you define *grade level* as the tasks that someone in the top two-thirds of the distribution of academic ability can be taught to do, then the proportion of students who are not at grade level will be approximately 33 percent.[10]

Reaching all students in presenting daily lessons at grade level is the primary test of effective teaching, and every teacher struggles with this task because, of course, of the reality suggested by Murray and confirmed by every teacher in the United States. Students are grouped by age when they enter school—not by academic ability. Teachers can never afford to assume that all their students are at the same place cognitively—students weren't when you were in school, and they're not now!

Some believe that teachers are only responsible for teaching kids the basic three "Rs"—reading, 'riting, and 'rithmetic. Most teachers are primarily interested in doing *only* that and would love to experience a group of students whose only concerns each day were how to improve their mathematic skills, write better essays, critically analyze advanced literature, and seek a cure for cancer. Unfortunately, those who have never taught know nothing of the continual teaching of socialization skills, respect for adults, common U.S. values, and general social behaviors needed to maneuver through adolescent and adult life.

One of the ultimate challenges that teachers experience each day is motivating children and adolescents whose backgrounds are so varied that finding the right combination of activities that actually excites students is often impossible. One other highly challenging role for teachers is being exciting enough to compete with all of the technological games and tools that students have access to daily. Kids have iPods, Gameboys, Nintendo, Wii, constant access to the Internet, and all of the other electronic devices and games that are marketed and sold every year to children and adolescents—now available at their fingertips on their phones.

Who would even attempt to compete with all of these distractions in the hope of being more exciting? And it's not enough to be an "expert" in one's discipline to be an influential or effective teacher. As Gaea Leinhardt from the Graduate School of Education at the University of Pittsburgh describes it, "It's the juggling, the interruption, the compromise with your own sense of control, that make it more complex than being an engineer who knew a lot of math and now wants to come back and stand in front of a class and teach arithmetic. It's much more complex than that."[11]

Many adults are under the mistaken belief that all children and adolescents act with total respect for their classmates and teachers while going through their school day, with complete control of their emotions and social behaviors. An inaccurate picture exists in many people's minds that every adolescent and child enjoys being at school and relishes the opportunities to plunge headlong into the books as if this were his or her last chance to become the next president of the United States, the next Oprah Winfrey, or the next Steve Jobs by virtue of unfailing effort, energy, and excitement for learning. If this were the case, teachers wouldn't have any trouble just teaching reading, writing, and arithmetic.

If teaching were that simple, and all students were cloned from the most cooperative, well-read classmates we ever knew, then anyone with adequate knowledge in any subject area could be a successful teacher. But every educator knows better. David Blair, a professor in the Department of Psychology at Carnegie Mellon University, explains the complexities of teaching: "A good teacher has to be sensitive, to try to figure out where the child is with respect to what they know, and not just whether they know it or not, but what they do know about this concept that's probably right, and what do they know about it that's probably wrong, and how can I build on what they know that's right, and how can I show them the parts that are wrong."[12]

When all of those barriers are successfully crossed and teachers might believe for a few minutes that they are making a difference in the lives of their students, teachers are faced with the constant challenge of two overbearing factors that affect students' learning: a student's attitude and effort. Teachers can believe that they have control over these two critical aspects of learning; but as hard as they try, children and adolescents are just that—children and adolescents.

No amount of cajoling, dancing between the rows of desks, showing YouTube videos, or using fantastical technology can affect the minds of youth who just don't care about learning on any particular day. Any parent of a 15-year-old can probably attest to this fact. On a daily basis, teaching is a more challenging job than most people would ever want to attempt.

Additional Challenges: Helping Students with Special Needs

I suspect most of the public is aware that schools are filled with students with special needs. Some students have learning disabilities, Down syndrome, attention deficit hyperactivity disorder, or autism, and many children and adolescents alike have a variety of physical, emotional, and cognitive problems that prevent them from being able to read without significant assistance and accommodations.

The previous list of learning difficulties is merely the tip of the iceberg of what causes learning problems in school. I haven't mentioned students who have emotional disorders, violent tendencies, or any of a list of emotional and social challenges that prevent them from performing at even an average level, much less at an academically advanced level.

The possibility always exists that these students could disrupt other students' learning without the appropriate accommodations to help them learn. Teachers are responsible for meeting all of their students' needs—and I mean social, emotional, cognitive, and physical—on a daily basis. This makes for more than enough clients—all of whose needs teachers must address at the exact same time.

I challenge accountants, doctors, attorneys, and even auto mechanics with the idea that instead of seeing one client at a time for an hour or two, for a total of 5 to 7 clients a day, each professional, like teachers, see 20–30 at a time, for a total of 150 clients a day. Every professional should ask the question, "Just how successful would I be with each of my clients if I saw 150 a day and 25 of them all at once?" Daniel Moulthrop and colleagues said it best: "Teachers' hours should be compared to those of other high-stress jobs—like air-traffic controllers, firefighters, or pilots—that afford employees a good deal of time off in consideration of the high intensity of the hours worked."[13]

Educators might often say that the day-to-day decisions at school are not life altering—that whatever they choose to do in their classrooms isn't going to have the impact of affecting one's physical health. That said, many events that occur in elementary, middle, and high school classrooms do affect students' *mental* health; but the way we talk about and financially reward teachers, you'd think most U.S. citizens didn't actually value education as much as they say they do. Make no mistake, teachers have chosen this professional path; but a mere $30 an hour just doesn't do justice to the difficult realities of daily teaching.

I Quit!

You might be interested in knowing that the dropout rate for teachers is fairly high. Thirty-three percent leave within the first three years. One of every five teachers leaves the profession before the fifth year of teaching.[14] In urban school districts, the attrition rate for teachers is phenomenal: one in three will leave teaching after the third year.[15] Think about an attrition rate of 33 percent in three years, or if 20 percent of the employees where you work quit within five years. This can't be good. If teaching is such an easy job, why are so many leaving the profession? It turns out it isn't because of the poor pay.

It may surprise you to know that one of the primary reasons that many teachers leave the profession is because they are not able to develop an effective learning environment. In the field of education, we call this poor *classroom management*. Another reason that teachers leave is a lack of recognition from the community or even the principal for their commitment to the lives of their students. The more valued teachers feel, the better their attitudes toward their students.[16]

You Call This Respect?

As if the lack of respect and support weren't enough—neither is the money, as at least one of every five teachers reports having a second job outside of education.[17] Add to that the number of teachers who coach. The money made following middle and high school athletes around a gym or field and riding school buses two to three evenings a week to games during an athletic season compares more closely to working at a fast-food restaurant at minimum wage than to the average salary of $30 an hour for a teacher.

As you might guess, it's difficult for teachers to believe that being an educator is honorable and inherently of intense value to U.S. citizens when they are treated the way they are financially, as well as with disdain in the rhetoric by national politicians, reporters, and newscasters. Moulthrop and colleagues note that a Harris Poll from 2003 reported that "73 percent of Americans would say that teaching . . . is a profession with 'very great' or 'considerable prestige'"; yet a majority of teachers made it clear that they did not feel respected at the level they felt they deserved.[18]

So, you may be wondering, why don't Americans treat teachers with respect? Much of the justification for minimizing the work of teachers in the United States derives from a line of reasoning explained in this passage from Moulthrop and colleagues: "Much of the tension around the status of teaching seems to derive from the feeling that teaching isn't actually that challenging, that even people with little or no training could do the work as well as the person in the classroom. It turns out to be much more complicated than that."[19]

Educational researchers have studied effective teaching for many years and continue to conduct studies to determine how teachers can improve student learning at all levels. One significant factor that educational researchers most assuredly agree on is the value to students of having a certified teacher.

THE VALUE OF CERTIFIED TEACHERS

All fifty states require that all educators who teach in their *public* schools be certified. Federal No Child Left Behind (NCLB) legislation passed by Congress in 2001 reinforced state standards for becoming certified in the public schools, which include (1) holding a bachelor's or higher degree in the subject area taught at seventh through twelfth grade; (2) attainment of full teacher certification at each state's level; and (3) demonstrated knowledge in the subjects taught.[20]

The NCLB guidelines did little to affect the primary requirements for becoming certified as a public school educator that have existed for as many as 60 years. It was common during the 1960s for many schools to still have some lifelong professional educators near the end of their careers who had initially been certified without a four-year bachelor's degree. Exceptions to being certified as a teacher in any public school today are based on the inability to retain certified teachers in many urban schools in certain high and middle school content areas such as advanced mathematics and science courses.

Think about the meaning of the word *certified*; what does *certification* mean? It means that a teacher receives an undergraduate degree in an education major, having completed a set of standards generally met through taking a prescribed set of courses. Each college and university develops a program for certification that is approved by each state's education department.

Certification requirements are established by the state education-department members and approved by a state board of education, and they are generally quite common from state to state. Each state department of education sends an independent team of reviewers to each college and university (private or public) in its state that certifies teachers, to inspect and either approve or disapprove their programs of study for teacher certification. Certification coursework includes general-education requirements, content-specialty courses, and as many as 20 to 50 credits in *pedagogical* courses (courses about the science of teaching).

Within the past 10 years, many state-supported colleges and universities, especially those that originally began as teacher-training institutions, have improved their programs by attempting to meet new and rigorous national standards for training teachers set by the National Council for Accreditation of Teacher Education (NCATE). Many college professors and education-school deans believe that the NCATE standards for training teachers are quite challenging to meet, particularly based on the standards for preparing teachers to teach ethnically diverse learners and students with special needs.

What Does the Research Tell Us about Certified Teachers?

You might be asking, "Does it matter whether teachers are certified?" That question has been answered by a number of researchers. For these studies to be accomplished, there must be a number of uncertified teachers in the public schools—which there are, due to shortages of teachers, particularly in urban districts. Linda Darling-Hammond, a respected researcher in the field of education, reported negative correlations between the percentage of a state's new *uncertified* teachers and the level of student performance on six separate state tests administered by the National Assessment of Educational Progress (NAEP). Students in the K–12 schools in her study who were taught by *certified* teachers did much better on the same NAEP tests.[21]

Two other researchers, Ildiko Laczko-Kerr and David Berliner, in a 2003 summary of research on uncertified teachers, presented some significant findings on the value and importance of certification: "Research provides convincing evidence that subject matter knowledge is necessary *but not sufficient* for teaching well. Without methods courses to learn pedagogical content knowledge, novices [new teachers] are *unlikely* to provide quality instruction" (my emphasis).[22]

There are other significant findings reported by Laczko-Kerr and Berliner, including the conclusion that "education coursework is a stronger predictor of teaching effectiveness than are teachers' grade point averages in their majors or their test scores on content knowledge."[23] So the recent demands in some state legislatures to require grade-point averages of preservice teachers to be at 3.0 are obviously rather moot in ensuring that the public schools are staffed with quality teachers.

Later in that article, Laczko-Kerr and Berliner state, "We agree with Wilson, Floden, and Ferrini-Mundy (2002) who concluded that 'the research suggests that there is value added by teacher preparation (p. 194

of their study) especially the clinical experiences and fieldwork provided through student-teaching.'"[24]

Uncertified and Unprepared: "Teach for America" Stand-Ins

Those teachers who receive their certificate through alternative means, rather than being certified the standard way through an education major at a university "tend to have a limited view of curriculum, lack understandings of student ability and motivation; experience difficulty translating content knowledge into meaningful information for students to understand; plan instruction less effectively; and tend not to learn about teaching through their experiences"[25]

Some value the idea of encouraging those who didn't graduate as teacher educators, did not take an education course in college, and did not become certified to enter the field of teaching. The Teach for America (TFA) program is one of those avenues to alternative certification that places untrained, non-education-majoring, and *uncertified* teachers in classrooms across the United States. Generally, the belief is that these "teachers" (quotation marks are used to note that these are not certified teachers) will be smarter and better prepared to teach than certified teachers—a grossly inaccurate assumption. *College education majors come to college with a stronger academic background than students in most other majors.*

TFA "teachers" are only bound by contract for two years. After two years, most (well over 50 percent) leave the profession—perhaps a good thing since they haven't been educated as teachers. The TFA "teachers'" training is a five-week crash course in how to teach. Predicting their failure is easy based on these teaching candidates' volumes of missing knowledge—particularly pedagogical courses, field experiences, child- and adolescent-development coursework, and the lengthy practice-teaching experiences that education majors receive.

TFA staff usually teach in urban areas, which also causes problems because this is where America needs its best certified teachers. The ugly truth about Teach for America is that this organization garners millions of your tax dollars each year—$21 million in 2010 and $50 million in 2011.[26] One might wonder if most of the money goes to the six-figure salaries of TFA leaders/management and the recruiting fees

TFA charges each school district to hire their uncertified, uneducated "teachers"—about $35,000 for each "teacher" per year.[27]

One TFA chief knowledge officer recently bragged about what TFA "teachers" do in a classroom: tape themselves teaching, plan effectively, and organize objectives into units.[28] The practices he mentioned remind me of the experiences university education programs provide to their teacher candidates in their first two years of college—long *before* they are alone in a classroom. TFA "teachers" unfortunately only learn a minimum amount of information about how to teach during their first year on the job—not *before* they enter a classroom, as traditional education majors do.

Often older adults seeking second career opportunities will choose to become teachers. It is certainly not unusual for these adults to become effective educators—when they receive their certificates through traditional teacher education institutions. Without education coursework and official certification, it is unlikely that any teacher will become effective in meeting students' needs.

James Stronge adds to the advantage that certified teachers bring to a classroom:

- Fully prepared and certified teachers have a greater influence on gains in student learning than do uncertified teachers;
- Teachers with certification of some kind tend to have higher achieving students than teachers working without certification; and,
- Students of teachers who hold standard certification in their subjects score from 7 to 10 points higher on 12th grade math tests than students of teachers with probationary, emergency, or no certification.[29]

Grade-Point Averages

You might want to conduct your own personal survey of teachers by asking a few that you know if they believe that their grade-point averages made them effective educators, or if their scores on the required Educational Testing Service (ETS) certification tests required by many states are accurate indicators of their success in teaching.

It is no surprise to any teacher that these required licensure tests are a waste of money and time for all involved. ETS doesn't mind, though, that your state education department requires these certification tests.

Many individuals associated with the testing companies are making millions of dollars by requiring these tests, and it's surprising that some of these people who are making the money are simultaneously on state boards of education and on the payroll or boards of directors of the testing companies.[30] This is as controversial as former vice president Dick Cheney being on the board of directors of Halliburton, the company that played a considerable role in attempting to rebuild Iraq (see the book *Blood Money*, by T. Christian Miller).

It is clear that certified teachers, trained by the universities and colleges that are sanctioned and approved by the state education departments, make better educators for our children than those who become teachers without being certified. So the rigorous development of our teachers through traditional certification programs is another feather in the cap of public school systems across the United States.

WHAT IS PEDAGOGY?

Meaningful certification requirements developed by state education departments and NCATE provide a future teaching candidate with a solid mix of basic general-education requirements, content-area knowledge for the subject area of certification, and a set of courses in the area of pedagogy. *Pedagogy* can best be described as the science of teaching—so pedagogy courses would cover areas such as educational psychology, child and adolescent development, the science of assessing students, strategies for managing students appropriately, educational philosophy, curricular theory, and strategies for designing effective instructional experiences.

The list goes on, and anyone who has tried teaching knows that effective teaching is *much more* than just knowing and presenting content knowledge—it's knowing how to deliver content effectively that matters the most. Among the kinds of background knowledge that educators need to be effective (as supported by research) are the following cited by Stronge:

1. considerable amount of coursework in education
2. strong background in one's content knowledge

3. formal pedagogical knowledge (information on how to teach)
4. methods preparation courses
5. recent participation in professional development activities (graduate courses, workshops, or conferences)
6. teacher preparation gained from schools of education[31]

Stronge summarizes the research on the value of pedagogical knowledge:

> Teachers who are not formally prepared to teach know little about how children grow, learn, and develop, or about how to support learning differences. Teachers with little or no coursework in education consistently have difficulties in the areas of classroom management, curriculum development, student motivation, and specific teaching strategies. They are less able to anticipate student knowledge and potential difficulties or to plan and redirect the lesson to meet the individual needs of the students.[32]

The final leg of becoming certified is the student teaching experience, in which a teaching candidate spends a semester with a professional educator in his or her classroom in a public school, teaching alongside that person to learn and experience effective pedagogical practices. No college classroom can emulate the day-to-day challenges that accompany teachers' roles in their own classrooms.

That's what makes the student-teaching experience critical to the appropriate development of effective educators. The student teaching experience is serious business, and those classroom teachers who accept the responsibility for training novice teachers have an immense impact on the pedagogical skills and knowledge gained by student teachers.

Education Majors Are Actually Good Students

Some states have established a minimum overall grade-point average that is required in order to become certified—often at or just beneath 3.0. Do you recall your undergraduate overall graduation grade-point average? Was it above 3.0? Many lawmakers believe that this is an appropriate minimum grade-point average, despite the fact that they themselves might well have been below the 3.0 standard following their four to five years as undergraduates.

So, you might wonder—based on some wild rumors—don't college students with the lowest grade-point averages become teachers? Not so! Gerald Bracey reports that in a national study of undergraduates' grade-point averages after sophomore year in college (before they started taking courses in their majors), those who were majoring in teacher education had an average GPA of 2.88—versus those who were majoring in other fields, whose average GPA was 2.87. Teaching candidates also had a higher grade-point average during the senior year—averaging 3.05, versus 2.95 for graduates in other fields.[33]

Three researchers revealed that almost 60 percent of all female teachers from the 1992 high school class came from the top two-fifths of academic ability. These researchers also report the results of an ETS study of prospective teachers' scores on their Praxis II (teacher certification test), which revealed that those in most secondary teaching programs who passed the examination had higher academic skills than average college graduates.[34]

Other researchers have discovered that those teachers who enter the teaching profession through traditional university-designed programs are "[g]enerally more academically able than the average college student of any major, whereas unlicensed entrants into teaching have significantly lower levels of academic achievement than most college students and those in education programs."[35]

Why don't the *Wall Street Journal*, the *Washington Post*, and the *New York Times* carry the results of these studies? Federal Department of Education representatives, presidents, and even broadcasters all admit that effective teachers have the greatest impact on student academic success; but they never go far enough to announce that *certified* teachers make the most difference in student learning.

Why Don't Private and Charter School Teachers Need to Be Certified?

In the late 1990s, I met with all incoming teaching candidates at my institution for postbaccalaureate certification in elementary education. These were graduate students who had majored in some area other than education for their first college degrees and then decided to return to college to become certified teachers. I recall a conversation with one woman about private school teachers:

> "I'm not sure I want to take all of these courses just to become a certified teacher," she commented.
>
> I replied, "You don't have to be certified to teach everywhere. You can teach in a private or parochial school if you'd rather teach without a certificate."
>
> "I thought all teachers had to be certified," she said.
>
> "Not private or parochial school teachers," I noted. "The state department of education doesn't require private or parochial schools to certify their teachers."
>
> She looked at me rather quizzically for a few seconds and responded, "My kids go to private schools, and their teachers are certified."
>
> "Are you sure?" I asked.

I'm not sure she really knew whether her children's teachers were certified or not. Her response to me sounded more like a question than a statement of fact. What percentage of adults understands certification and its implications? It's a fact that private and parochial schools *do not* require that all their teachers be certified.

The percentage of certified teachers in parochial and private schools varies from school to school. The best way to determine how many of the teachers in a local private or parochial school are certified is to call the school and ask. In the archdioceses of Los Angeles, Philadelphia, and Washington, DC, certification is *not* required to apply for or obtain a teaching position. The Archdiocese of Chicago *requires* certification as a criterion of employment, but the New York City archdiocese only *prefers* certification among its candidates for teaching positions.[36]

As for the mysterious charter schools that are popping up in several states, most state policies regarding charter schools *do not* require that all charter school teachers be certified. Five states with charter laws *do not require any* teachers within charter schools to be certified; 13 states require all teachers to be certified in their charter schools; 14 states require a percentage of teachers to be certified in charters—such as 50 percent or 75 percent of the teachers, depending on the state.[37] Ten states have no charter school laws at all; and as you'll discover when you read chapter 8, it's wise that those states don't have charter schools.

How Do Urban Schools Handle Certification Issues?

Staffing urban classrooms is a constant dilemma. New York City public schools hire as many as 7,000 to 8,000 new teachers per year; Philadelphia hires approximately 1,000 new teachers a year. Chicago and Los Angeles also hire more than 2,000 new teachers per year. Trying to replace the teaching core each summer is a daunting task for urban school districts. New York City public schools recently began advertising for teachers internationally, seeking candidates from around the globe to fill its many vacancies.

The solution that many state education departments have applied to address this shortage of urban teachers is to offer temporary certification to almost anyone with a college degree. Temporary teaching certificates are generally effective for two years, during which time these teachers are required to complete the state requirements for certification at local universities.

The Teach for America program has permission from some governing body to put their uncertified "teachers" into urban classrooms—but, as mentioned earlier, this is not a wise move due to the uneducated status of TFA members. Of course, most of them only stay for two years—so they never become certified. After the previous discussion of the value of certification, one can understand the concern that urban parents might have over the hiring of an uncertified teacher.

Finding certified teachers in urban districts is challenging due to the difference in pay between urban and suburban teachers. In one suburban Philadelphia neighborhood, the per-pupil expenditure is at almost $22,000. That is, the money available in that district from federal, state, and local tax revenues, if equally distributed to each student, would equal $22,000. Compare that figure to what students receive a mere seven miles away in Philadelphia: approximately $12,000 per student. That $10,000 difference has an amazing impact on the number of teachers hired, and thus on class size, resources, number of special-education teachers, number of teachers' aides, supplies, and the technology available to both teachers and students.

That monetary difference also impacts teacher salaries. During the early years of the 20th century, teachers who chose to work in urban centers made considerably more money than teachers in the suburbs.

That trend was reversed as businesses and wealthy families moved out of the cities during the 1960s and 1970s (see chapter 10). The result was—and remains—a lower tax base to support urban schools, which has lowered salaries for teachers who choose these jobs. Despite that disadvantage, urban public school teachers still make more money than suburban, urban, or rural private and parochial school teachers.

WHAT IS AN EFFECTIVE TEACHER?

> One of those studies found that the higher the quality of the teachers
> as perceived by students, the lower the dropout rate.[38]

What really makes an effective educator? You know the answer by listening to your children talk about their teachers. But how do you know the teachers who are entering the public schools versus the privates are really the best of the bunch? Quality teaching begins with obtaining a certificate to teach. That's important due to the required courses that form the foundation of an effective educator.

As mentioned earlier, those courses are suggested both by research and by the accreditation organizations for effective teacher-certification programs (e.g., NCATE and state departments of education). NCATE reported in 2009 that 632 colleges were accredited by them, and another 100 were seeking accreditation.[39] Beyond the required courses is a set of teacher traits that actually have a significant effect on teacher performance—all influenced by the education that teachers receive.

Required Effective-Teacher Background Characteristics

Many people have a picture in their heads of how a perfect teacher acts and how that teacher responded to their needs when they were in school (and now responds to their children's needs). But we don't have to rely merely on opinions to know which teacher candidates become better educators. The research base provides years of data to support adults' instincts and knowledge about effective teachers. Stronge writes, "The growing body of research concerned with teacher effectiveness has reinforced the notion that specific characteristics and behaviors matter in teaching, in terms of student achievement as well as other desirable outcomes."[40]

Stronge studied, collected, and summarized the data on teacher effectiveness. His findings reveal a match between what we all know in our hearts that effective teachers do and what researchers have been finding for years. Stronge's list includes the following components:

- the teacher as a person
- classroom management and organizational abilities
- organizing for instruction
- delivering instruction, and
- monitoring student progress and potential[41]

More detailed traits within the "teacher as a person" category include demonstrating care for students; listening to, understanding, and knowing students; demonstrating fairness and mutual respect; showing personal enthusiasm and motivation for learning; and dedication toward the teaching profession. These traits can be taught and are supported by many studies.

These five general categories of effective-teaching traits are all associated with learning effective pedagogy at the college level. Courses mentioned before, such as educational psychology, instructional theory, philosophy of education, and child and adolescent development, are all essential to the successful development of educators.

Do Effective Teachers Produce Higher Student Test Scores?

The philosophy adopted by some and accompanying NCLB policies leaves many educators feeling that perhaps those research-proved teacher characteristics don't matter. Instead, some legislators and businesspeople have subscribed to the impractical idea that one can judge effective teaching based on a teacher's ability to raise student test-score performance.

If one is to accept that premise, then how effective is a suburban or rural educator who helped 8 percent of her students raise their reading test scores from the 94th percentile to the 96th percentile in one year's time? The students' test scores certainly are impressive, but their scores only rose by two percentage points.

If you were to compare that class's rise in scores to that of an urban teacher who takes a third of her 25 students' reading test scores from the 23rd percentile to the 40th percentile, who would you perceive as the most effective educator? You'll have to judge; but you might be able to ascertain that conclusions about effective teaching are not reliably based on the level of students' test scores, or their growth when compared to other students' growth during an academic year.

It might be wise to compare this scenario to coaching. Coaches frequently have incredibly talented athletes, some with years of experience playing their sports before they played for these coaches. In those fortunate years, winning games come easily, but those wins don't necessarily indicate coaching prowess.

In the seasons in which high school athletes come with limited experience and skills, winning means that coaches need to be much better teachers of the game in order for athletes' abilities to improve. Many coaches will tell you that winning games with those less-experienced athletes is much more rewarding than wins with the best athletes. However, those teams with poorer athletes don't win as many games as the teams with great athletes, despite a greater improvement in their skill levels.

Maybe that helps explain why many talented educators take teaching positions in urban school districts, where the student populations are often less academically capable than their suburban counterparts. Many urban educators will tell you that the meaning of success is measured and defined quite differently in urban teaching environments as compared with suburban schools.

But make no mistake, urban teachers are succeeding with a majority of their students, and students' test scores may not reveal that significant success. This comment from Moulthrop and colleagues, however, provides support for the value of effective teaching in urban environments:

> A study in Boston shows student learning gains in both reading and math to be, on average, far superior when they work with an effective teacher than when they work with an ineffective teacher. These types of gains are mirrored in a Tennessee study that shows that effective teachers can help

the lowest performing students make gains of as much as 53 percentile points on standardized tests in a single year.

Over three years, students with effective teachers show as much as an 83 percent gain. These studies also found that effective teaching countered the often predictive effects of low socioeconomic status.[42]

Another researcher reports that minority students who are exposed to "high quality teachers" for three consecutive years make outstanding academic progress.[43]

Some might conclude that private and parochial school teachers are better teachers based on their students' higher test scores. Many questions must be asked to ascertain the accuracy of this assumption. Private and parochial school students don't take state tests, so the tests these students take differ from those taken by public school students in both number and type. Perhaps the most significant factor among private schools is that acceptance is frequently based on meeting certain criteria: previous good grades, cooperative spirit, relatively high scores on entrance examinations, no previous behavior infractions, and absolutely no special learning needs—particularly reading deficits.

Not every child is entitled to attend most private schools—only specifically selected students are accepted. Filtering out students who might skew test results, such as by lowering the school's average SAT scores, is a common strategy among private schools.

Think about that impact on a school's test scores. Accept only the best, and the results are obviously higher test scores. How can anyone make the assumption that private school teachers are better educators than public school teachers when there are such strict controls on the students who attend the private schools?

Salary Makes a Positive Difference in Teacher Quality

Where would the best teachers go to teach? Think about where the best accountants go to work as you ponder the answer to this question. Where do the best CEOs choose to work; where do the best attorneys take jobs? What if you were one of the most acclaimed novelists—for which publishing house would you choose to write? Where do the brightest and most successful doctors choose to work? The answer to these questions in many cases is that the best of each profession go where the money is greatest. Many American businesses like to push for a competitive environment, so that those who are the best are entitled to the most money.

Moulthrop and colleagues describe a typical business model for bringing success to a failing business:

> [If it were a failing school, the company would] find the very best educators available. "Surround yourself with the best people," . . . successful businessmen say again and again. To that end, [the business owner] would recruit the best college candidates, would try to poach great teachers from other schools, offering salaries to encourage the brightest teachers to join. . . .
>
> Treating his potential staff members as highly valuable professionals— who likely have dozens of choices for careers, and myriad firms vying for their services—would ensure that he'd get the best candidates available.[44]

Why would landing the best-paid teaching jobs be any different from practices in the business world? Of course, the best educators would take the teaching jobs that pay the most money. Ever notice how the New York Yankees frequently have the best record in professional baseball? The Yankees organization has won more World Series championships than any other team. Do you know how they do it? They spend the most money to get the best players. Do you recognize a recurring pattern across professions? Why would it be different in higher-paying public schools?

The most money in teaching is in the public schools in almost every community. It is rare, if not almost unheard of, for private or parochial school teachers in any school or community to make as much money as public school teachers—even in the urban centers of the United States.

If education is anything like the corporate world, then you realize that the best educators are teaching in the public schools because that's where the best education money resides. That may sound like a gross generalization, but it's actually not. There are many private school educators, of course, who continue to teach in those private schools for better reasons than the amount of money they make.

The most recent data on teacher salaries for private versus public school teachers reveal the following: Starting average salaries for private school teachers are approximately $10,000 lower than starting salaries for public school teachers. Public school teachers across the United States at the highest steps of the salary schedule earn approximately $15,000 to $20,000 more than private school teachers with similar years of experience. In 2007, the American Federation of Teachers reported that teachers' average salaries were just above $50,000. The top 10 percent of public school teachers earned an average of from $68,000 to $76,000.[45]

Those averages are obviously boosted by the fact that teachers earn considerably more in northern states, where the cost of living is higher than in southern regions. Please remember that the average includes teachers at the top of the scale, the bottom, and everywhere in between those two points. Please *don't misconstrue* these data to make it appear that every teacher in the United States is making almost $80,000 a year. Also keep in mind that teachers make more money, just like MBAs, if they hold advanced degrees.

If you're worried that you are paying teachers too much, this story that recently circulated among teachers may give you a more accurate perspective about the realities of teacher pay.

I'm fed up with teachers and their hefty salary guides. What we need is a little perspective. If I had it my way, I'd pay these teachers myself—I'd pay them babysitting wages. That's right—instead of paying these outrageous taxes, I'd give them $3.00 an hour out of my own pocket. And, I'm only going to pay them for 5 hours, not coffee breaks. That would be $15.00 a day—each parent should pay $15.00 a day for these teachers to baby-sit his or her child.

Even if they have more than one child, it's still a lot cheaper than private day care. Now, how many children do they teach everyday—maybe twenty? That's $15.00 x 20 = $300 a day. But remember, they only work 180 days a year! I'm not going to pay them for vacations! $300 x 180 = $54,000. (Wait just a minute, I think my calculator needs batteries.)

I know now you teachers will say, "What about those who have ten years of experience and a master's degree?" Well, maybe (to be fair) they could get the minimum wage; and, instead of just babysitting, they could read the kids a story. We can round that off to about $5.00 an hour, times five hours, times twenty children. That's $500 a day times 180 days. That's $90,000 a year! Wait a minute, let's get a little perspective here. Baby sitting wages are too good for these teachers. Did anyone see that original salary guide around here? (author unknown)

After reading this scenario, there must be a realization that the salaries of public educators are embarrassingly underfunded, particularly based on what is asked of them daily. New teachers in the era of computers can add to their responsibilities, establishing an eBoard on the school's website to keep parents informed of all assignments (to be updated on a daily basis); responding to e-mails within 24 hours of receiving them from parents; and keeping the electronic grading site updated so that parents can see their children's grades 24/7 in all the classes they take. I quote the comments of Dave Eggers:

> I'm cautiously optimistic that the day will come when teachers are treated with the respect given to doctors and architects and judges and paid commensurately. I do think that it will happen, though it will take decades to change the perceptions of the profession, and to make people see the fairly simple and irrefutable correlation between teacher quality and teacher salaries, between teacher retention and teacher salaries, . . . and the prospects of our youth and the future of the country and teacher salaries.[46]

THE POSITIVE IMPACT OF UNIONIZED TEACHERS

Historic framed stamps are frequently available at the post office for purchase. One of those historic stamps reads in all capital letters, "HONORING THE TEACHERS OF AMERICA" and, in smaller print, "NATIONAL EDUCATION ASSOCIATION." The cost of the original stamp was three cents; so as you surely imagine, it's old: it was issued in 1957.

That was perhaps the *last* year that anyone honored the teachers of America. Sputnik went into space that same year; but that stamp most likely was issued before this, because teachers took a great deal of heat following Sputnik's success. It was allegedly public school teachers' faults that the United States didn't put a satellite into space before the Soviets. Teachers have been bashed regularly since, but the teacher unions even more so.

Former president George W. Bush was heard saying in his first term, "We must end the teachers' unions stranglehold if we are going to have successful schools."[47] His comment demonstrates an ignorance of teachers, how learning occurs, and the role that teacher unions have played in improving the lives of students. Bush's first education secretary, Rod Paige, was equally ignorant when he verbally compared the largest teaching union in America, the NEA, to a terrorist organization.

So what is it that is so bad about teacher unions? Maybe it's that pay issue again. How can anyone deserve the average teacher salary of $50,000 for putting up with children and adolescents for seven hours a day for 180 days a year? And the teacher unions keep asking for more money—imagine that, as you contemplate your own salary and the raises and bonuses you've received over the past 8–10 years.

Unions of every kind are responsible for making people's lives better in protecting workers from unfair management practices and providing workers with needed benefits and safeguards, such as health-insurance coverage; protection from poor working conditions such as asbestos; pay for overtime hours, retirement benefits; paid holidays; vacation days; and due process before being fired for unsubstantiated reasons.

The advantages secured as a result of a group representing the needs of those who share a profession are many—whether it be teacher unions, truck-driving unions, or actor unions, they all exist because employees can't always trust management to protect their needs. Employees who work in management benefit as well from the difficult gains achieved by the collective bargaining of unions—perhaps management personnel don't recognize their gains enough to respect the unions in their own businesses.

Teacher unions are responsible for a number of reasonable protections for those who have entered the profession. Diane Ravitch notes that unions protected women teachers during the early 20th century by permitting them to keep their jobs even if they decided to marry or get pregnant. Before the union protections, they were automatically fired for those two circumstances. Teacher unions helped equalize pay for female teachers so that they eventually were paid as much as men who taught.[48] Unions protect teachers when they choose to teach the required curricula even though parents in the community might want them fired for teaching it.

It is perplexing that teacher unions receive so much bad press. How are teacher unions responsible for poor teaching? This question has never been answered; yet educators continue to be crucified by pundits who decry the NEA and the American Federation of Teachers (AFT). Unionized police officers don't add to an increase in crime; unionized fire fighters have no impact on an increase in fires in a city; and unionized news broadcasters don't cause the ratings for the evening news to drop.

When working conditions are healthy and a trusting atmosphere exists between management and employees, the laborers have more reasons to work productively. Children and adolescents become the beneficiaries of treating educators like professionals, and unions help to ensure the creation of mutually beneficial environments for students and teachers.

RESULTS FROM UNIONIZED STATES

If you enjoy comparing test scores among students from differing states, you may be interested in knowing that *teachers in states where educators are unionized actually have students whose test scores are better than those of students from states whose teachers are not unionized.*[49]

Bobby Ann Starnes reported in 2004 on a study from Arizona State University that "twelve studies reported evidence of higher student achievement in strong union schools." Many states (22 to be exact—mostly southern states) have the "right-to-work" laws that in essence prevent any unionization of schools and businesses. Starns notes that states with teacher unions "receive higher education rankings than right-to-work states."

Starnes noted, "Class size, availability of materials, condition of school buildings, and other factors also illustrate clear differences between right-to-work schools and union schools."[50] There are reasons that unions are necessary in the arena of the teaching profession. Protecting the rights of teachers is imperative to their success—and, according to the statistics, also to children's successes.

"YOU'RE FIRED": THE REAL MEANING OF TENURE

The meaning of *tenure* is often misconstrued and misunderstood. Obtaining tenure does not entitle teachers to a lifetime of employment without any possibility of being released or fired from a teaching position. Tenure only entitles a teacher to a hearing, that is, *due process*, before being released or fired. Tenure laws are designed to protect teachers' free-speech rights and minimize possible political pressures that may affect their performance.

Tenure is obtained in most states by completing two or three years of successful teaching. "Successful teaching" is determined by observations and evaluations of one's teaching; it is usually determined by being formally observed at least three times a year. Principals in each building are responsible for providing feedback and, if necessary, releasing a teacher before he or she receives tenure.

If a teacher does not receive tenure after those two or three years of the trial period, the principal needs no reason to explain why the teacher is *nonrenewed* (i.e., the teacher will not be rehired). Since the teacher has not received tenure, no formal hearing is required, nor does any specific reason need to be provided for the dismissal of the teacher.

Teachers can be nonrenewed for any number of reasons: a decline in students that has led to a need for fewer teachers; the return of a tenured, experienced teacher who was on temporary medical leave; or, for instance, the elimination of a program or position due to lack of funds. Other, not so obvious, reasons for being nonrenewed might include a teacher's personality conflict with a student who has an influential parent; the perception by any given number of parents that a high school teacher is not "giving" students enough As; or the perception by a number of parents, or an administrator, that a teacher's students' test scores are too low.

Tenure exists because teachers are exposed to children's wild imaginations. Imagine going to work each day, doing your job effectively, then being accused of sexual harassment by a co-worker who has the emotional maturity of someone seven years old. Seven-year-olds aren't emotionally or socially mature; so a mere hug to help a child who is in tears over a broken pencil could turn into a sexual-harassment case—incidents such as this occur regularly.

Imagine spending the day with 15-year-olds—who, according to adolescent developmental research, are highly emotionally charged. The adolescent brain is designed to send messages to the emotional center of the brain—the amygdala—rather than the reasoning center of the brain in the prefrontal cortex—the frontal lobe of one's brain. What does this do for a teacher who reprimands a student for inappropriate behavior? The irritated student may then start a rumor about the teacher via text messages that threatens the teacher's job. And what if the parents of that student are just as emotionally immature? A parental phone call is made to the superintendent's office without any prior notification to the teacher that anything is wrong.

Imagine that there are 1,500 fourteen- to eighteen-year olds in the building with you each day—a typical high school population. Every day, teachers have to be extremely careful with their words and actions, and their responses to numerous emotional events. After the day ends, teachers are responsible for saying the "right" things to the parents who may be enraged about inaccurate descriptions from their children about things that have occurred.

Teachers must be protected from the arbitrariness of being fired as a result of such circumstances. For these reasons, plus many other unpredictable circumstances, tenure, that is, an equitable opportunity to defend oneself in a public hearing before being fired, is a necessity in the teaching profession.

If you think that tenure is *unnecessary*, you may want to recall how many U.S. citizens were treated during the McCarthy era in the 1950s—thrown into jail on suspicion of being communists. You may recall the eight U.S. federal attorneys who were fired during the second George W. Bush administration in 2007 for unknown reasons. Protections from such egregious acts are necessary for public servants in our communities.

Unions are *not* responsible for firing teachers—unions exist to protect the right to a fair hearing when teachers are subjected to unreasonable parents' demands, students' false allegations, or school board members' anger about their children's grades. Knowing this should prevent pundits from blaming unions for the hiring of or lack of dismissal of poor teachers.

Certainly, there are many valid reasons why tenured teachers are sometimes released, which we've all heard of—for instance, inappropriate relationships with students; severe alterations of curricula that negatively impact students; excessive absences; or mistreatment of students. None of these behaviors is acceptable, and they certainly warrant firing teachers. Interestingly, private and parochial school teachers are not entitled to these basic protections afforded to public school teachers. Tenure is another primary reason that the best teachers seek and attain professional teaching positions in public schools.

EVALUATING TEACHERS—IT'S NO MYSTERY

Many pundits believe that the education profession has no clear practices or objective means for evaluating teachers. You may have even mistakenly believed that teachers can never be fired and are never evaluated. Evaluations occur frequently during a teacher's first three years in a classroom. Principals are responsible for hiring, evaluating, and firing teachers. If principals don't fire poor teachers, the job is left to upper-level administrators or the school board.

Principals all over the United States use research-based evaluation instruments to determine the needs of teachers. When I use the phrase *research-based* I refer to the fact that an entire body of research on effective pedagogy exists, a body of work that informs and is used to design evaluation instruments. Effective teaching involves a number of specific, measurable practices that are evaluated by principals, including

- lesson planning that is developmentally appropriate for that grade level;
- use of materials that help students understand the concepts and principles taught;
- use of appropriate *instructional* (actual teaching) strategies that help students understand content (such as hands-on learning, discussions, or group work when appropriate);
- appropriate management of student behavior, including effective use of punishment;
- presentation of lessons that encourage creative and critical thinking and problem solving;
- use of assessment strategies that aid in determining what students need assistance on and inform teachers how to help students improve;

- monitoring of students' level of growth and its communication to parents;
- acting professionally in communication with parents and colleagues.

These are a few of the descriptors that are used throughout the United States to determine whether teachers are effectively doing their jobs. These factors are not hidden codes used only if approved by teacher unions. These are research-based factors that affect whether students learn. These effective practices are not debatable; nor should they be influenced by parents, pundits, or politicians. Teachers either demonstrate these professional traits or they do not.

The teaching profession does not need any advice from Bill Gates (college dropout—current billionaire), Michelle Rhee (business/education lobbyist), Arne Duncan (U.S. secretary of education), or Louis Gerstner (former CEO of IBM) about how to evaluate effective teaching. Effective evaluation of teachers is driven by research that has been delivered by the educational researchers who inform the teaching profession.

Teacher evaluation has been this way for at least 40 years, and it continues to be improved via new research findings on how the brain works and the researched effectiveness of innovative teaching strategies. There is nothing "soft" about the process of determining if teachers are effective or not.

Value-Added Models of Evaluation and Merit Pay

Educators are always suspicious of other professions seeking to exploit the education field. One particular group of public-education naysayers is economists. A few economists aren't conducting research in their field, but instead attempting to find a way to "measure" every event that occurs in a classroom.

Some economists propose that teachers be evaluated based on a complex system of data collected from students' test scores, to determine how much growth has occurred during the year—this is referred to as the *value-added model* (VAM). Many unanswered questions exist when attempts are made to connect test scores to one's teaching performance. The greatest barrier to judging a teacher based on students' test scores is being able to completely isolate all of the other variables that affect a child's test score—variables such as students'

- background experiences;
- preschool opportunities;
- previous academic successes;
- parental support;
- attitude and effort.

Other uncontrollable variables for teachers associated with student test scores include

- whether there is a correlation between the test items and the content they teach (*validity*);
- whether teachers know what will be tested so they can appropriately prepare students for the concepts/principles that are tested;
- whether students will give their best effort on high-stakes tests that affect teacher evaluation;
- whether students have access to learning materials, supplies, and books necessary for academic success;
- whether students have resource support services within a classroom.

Researchers have discovered in studying these VAM evaluations that when teachers are subjected to value-added evaluations from year to year, the scores change considerably each year. Michael Simpson, an educational researcher, notes, "*Every respected, independent testing expert in the country agrees that VAM is not a valid or reliable measure for making high-stakes decisions about teacher effectiveness. It is junk science*" (my emphasis).[51]

Simpson adds that the federal Department of Education's "Institute of Education Sciences concluded in a 36-page analysis of VAM research data that 'more than 90 percent of the variation in student gain scores is due to the variation in student-level factors *that are not under the control of the teacher*'" (my emphasis).[52]

To use such arbitrary measures to determine whether a teacher is effective is patently absurd. Even if all the variables were positive for students who were tested, teachers and parents alike realize that preparing students for a single test would dilute the overall education that children and adolescents deserve: opportunities for creative thinking, problem solving, building interpersonal skills, learning cooperation strategies, and designing their own learning experiences that match some of their interests. Multiple-choice tests don't measure these critical cognitive traits—the ones you use every day to be successful in your adult life.

Often noneducator pundits call for merit pay so that poor teachers don't receive a decent salary. The challenge to the merit-pay advocates is determining just who is entitled to merit pay. Can the best teachers be easily identified? Was your list of "best teachers" the same as your neighbor's list of "best teachers"? Was the best teacher the one who raised test scores, or the one from whom students learned more that wasn't measured on a single test?

Is the best teacher the one who raises students' average reading scores 20 percentage points, from the 40th percentile to the 60th percentile, or the teacher whose students' scores went from the 95th to the 96th percentile? Was the best teacher the one who taught more content, or the one who raised students' confidence levels and helped them improve their creative-writing skills? How will the school board determine the best teachers who deserve the most money? Will the students have a voice in deciding, or should only parents choose?

Imagine what happens to your child in school when a teacher is evaluated merely on students' test scores. Your child scores consistently at the top of the scale on the tests, so the teacher ignores her because there are other students who need more assistance, who don't usually do as well. Some teachers are told by principals to ignore the needs of some struggling students because they don't have a chance of passing the state tests. Al Ramirez, a University of Colorado professor, notes,

Policymakers who would impose merit-pay systems should be careful about what they choose to reward because employees will respond to established incentives. The question soon becomes, What will *not* get done? Teaching is a complex profession, and teachers do a lot in the interest of students that really isn't measurable. Yet, many of these hard-to-measure practices, such as counseling students about academic or personal concerns, are crucial to students' lives and of value to parents.[53]

What type of evaluation instrument can be used to measure the everyday social and emotional assistance that teachers provide to our children? Ramirez adds, "Merit pay misses the boat entirely—because good teaching is not about money. Most educators chose the profession out of a sense of calling; they understand they will never get rich."[54] Ramirez raises the following question: Which school districts, in a time of financial crisis, will be willing to increase taxes to pay teachers even more for merit pay? Will your district provide merit pay every year to every effective teacher? Can you afford that kind of increase in your local taxes?

It's clear that merit pay cannot be based on student test scores, because teachers don't have enough control over those variables that affect students' test scores. The state of Tennessee experimented with merit pay from 2006 to 2009. The particular district involved offered to pay teachers between $5,000 and $15,000 more a year based on whether their students' achievement rose by a specific amount during the year.[55]

Independent researchers found that "[on] average, students taught by the teachers taking part in the program *did not* make larger academic gains than those taught by teachers in the normal wage group. The sole exception was in grade 5 in the second and third years of the study. But the effect did not appear to persist."[56] *The final verdict: paying teachers more money for improved student performance just doesn't work.*

The faulty thinking that accompanies merit pay is that someone has to encourage teachers to work harder, and more money is the way to make this happen. Most teachers who don't want to work hard quit. The evidence is in the percentage of teachers who leave the profession by droves each year. Merit pay for teachers in any form is demeaning to the profession, to the responsibilities that every teacher accepts unconditionally to provide appropriate overall care for all children.

Shouldn't Experience and a Master's Degree Matter?

As with accountants, professional football players, CEOs, and politicians, having experience as an educator makes a difference. Novice teachers make many mistakes, and they learn from them. Bill Gates and an economist from Stanford University, Eric Hanushek, have both been telling stories about how experienced teachers shouldn't earn more money because they don't positively affect students' test scores. Unfortunately, these two aren't measuring effective teaching when they speak of test scores. That is a significant distinction: *effective teaching should not be confused with or associated with higher student test scores.*

Several economists have disputed Hanushek's techniques, and revealed different interpretations of test-score data associated with teacher experience and master's degrees. One researcher analyzing over 900 Texas school districts *"found that the single most important measurable predictor of student achievement gains was teacher expertise, measured by teacher performance on a state certification exam, along with teacher experience and master's degrees."*[57]

That's unequivocal support for the exact opposite of the message Gates and Hanushek have been selling. Six other studies by five different educational researchers between 1986 and 2002 revealed the advantages of certified teachers to students' academic growth.[58]

Despite the value of having a master's degree to students' test-score improvement, connecting high test scores with effective teaching is another example of faulty thinking, and a demonstration of ignorance of the essential components of professional teaching. Teaching to the test is simplemindedness—something people could probably train a monkey to do—but teaching for learning requires professionally educated and certified teachers.

It is unlikely that Gates and Hanushek will ever comprehend the distinction between effective teaching and higher test scores, primarily because they haven't engaged in the sophisticated processes of teaching. Their lack of awareness of classroom reality yields an inability to ask the "right" questions in their research. Instead of asking questions about effective teaching and how it affects learning, their faulty thinking leads to collecting *student test score* data rather than *learning* data.

Once teachers have a few years of experience, they often seek a master's degree—in the same way that some of those who graduate from college with psychology, business, or nursing degrees decide to pursue master's degrees. When professionals receive master's degrees they are honored for their newfound knowledge with more money.

Making more money as a result of receiving a master's degree and having more experience in the business is not in opposition to what professional cultures do. Would a mere college graduate with a four-year degree be a great attorney; or does that extra three years of schooling matter? Do engineers really need another year of college past the four-year degree, or can they be experts in the business without the additional year of schooling?

I'll bet that you learned more as you grew into your job or profession. If you have a master's degree, I suspect that added to your skills in your profession. Master's degrees are honored in all professions, because education beyond a bachelor's degree is essential to a professional's growth—and teaching is no exception.

Teachers who pursue graduate degrees use their background classroom experiences as real teachers to advance their knowledge of the profession through new perspectives. A greater understanding of their philosophies and their practices develops as a result of pursuing graduate studies. Another valid reason to pay more for an education master's degree is to honor teachers' pursuit of studying, and learning more about, the continual research that the profession yields. Educators with master's degrees make better teachers because of the many progressive ways they find to improve the learning of all their students, whether test scores rise or not. Using student test scores to determine if master's degrees matter minimizes teachers' responsibilities to help every student grow in all the domains—social, emotional, and physical, as well as academic.

5

INACCURACIES AND ABSURDITIES DELIVERED BY THE PRESS, PUNDITS, AND POLITICIANS

Sometimes I think all reporters must have had terrible experiences in school and are working through their early traumas in print or just using their jobs for payback. Media tend to accentuate the negative generally, but they overdo it for schools."[1]

A seventh-grade girl sings her first solo in the choir; a Down syndrome senior gets to play a couple of a minutes in a varsity basketball game and *both* teams make sure he gets to score a basket; a fourth-grader's home burns to the ground and the next afternoon the PTA has clothes, school supplies, and more; a first-grader comes to school hungry every day and every day he gets a good breakfast and lunch.

Miracles happen every day in public schools. Those who are inside the schools see it constantly. And yet, many on the outside describe our schools as failing or declining and speak longingly of the "good old days."[2]

The Flat Earth Society (FES) is a genuine organization that promotes their theories that the Earth is not actually round. You can Google the organization, and find reasons listed for believing that humans are living on a flat surface. FES believers surely find ways to justify their basic premises. Not one of their reasons for believing the Earth is flat makes sense or is supported by any valid evidence. If you're reading this, it is highly unlikely that you will believe the nonsense promoted by FES.

There's another more notable society that exists. This group doesn't have one single name, a specific leader, or a stated mission. This group exists for the purpose of obliterating America's public school system. Their members are among us: in the press; as members of officially named organizations that sound like supporters of effective educational practices; as politicians; as nationally recognized businesspersons; and even as clergy proclaiming their own inaccurate truths. An accurate title might be the "Destroy the Public Schools Society" (DPSS), based on their inaccurate claims.

The school destroyers' evidence against the public schools is as faulty as the evidence proffered by the FES. The trouble is, the many believers of the DPSS are highly organized, vocal, and well funded. Their purposes for eliminating support for the public schools are varied, but some of them are primarily interested in one goal: diverting taxpayers' money from the public schools and, for some, transferring it into their own pockets. The DPSS spokespersons are the chief detractors.

As you listen to or watch talk shows, newscasts, NPR broadcasts, even comedy shows, you'll hear pundits speaking negatively about public schools. All of their comments are laced with alleged truths; and, when these people speak, not one of them can find a positive note to deliver about the schools.

If you were to say something positive about our schools, it is doubtful that anyone would believe you. You may even have a difficult time believing many of the facts presented in this book because of the constant brainwashing Americans are subjected to by so many high-profile speakers.

I try to convince my students at the university of the effectiveness of our public schools. Many of them will shortly become our public school educators. They react with such surprise when I share my reasoning as to why we should be proud of what we've accomplished due to our strong public schooling system.

Bashing public schools has become a national pastime—a chance for everyone to deliver a joke with a group of friends or acquaintances about how teachers are responsible for the "achievement gap"; opening laughs for a comedian about "terrible" urban schools; must-say lines, such as "We've got to raise the bar," for any politician searching for votes; and the rallying cry and mantra, "More money for schools doesn't raise achievement," for Wall Street advocates who'd rather see their tax dollars spent on war chests that prop up a company's sales and drive up stock-market prices. Perhaps many Wall Street bankers don't understand the value of public schools because they never attended one.

Who are *you* listening to this week to tell you the truth about the progress and value of public education in the United States? What are the chances of your hearing an accurate statistic about public schools on the airways? Who do you know that verbally supports public schools and has the credibility needed to gain your trust?

MISTAKEN COMMENTS ABOUT PUBLIC EDUCATION

Just who is the voice of American public schools—public school teachers, administrators, or school board members? Educational researchers, the parents who choose to send their children to public schools, or perhaps the students themselves? Not usually. Should it be pundits who own the airways—Lou Dobbs (formerly with CNN), Bill Maher (HBO comedian), Katie Couric (formerly of *CBS Nightly News*), or John Stossel (*20/20*)?

Maybe Armstrong Williams is capable of speaking with accuracy on public education in America. You may recall that Armstrong is a conservative talk-show host, who was reportedly paid $240,000 by the Bush administration (your tax dollars) to promote the No Child Left Behind legislation.[3] Let's not forget to consider the limited perspective Davis Guggenheim presented in the one-sided documentary *Waiting for "Superman"* in 2010.

On the list of public school detractors from the business world has recently been the former CEO for IBM—Louis Gerstner, Jr.—a person, like all of those mentioned above, who knows little to nothing about children, teaching, and the education profession. But his voice is not as commonly heard as that of the infamous mere high school graduate (he dropped out of college), noneducator Bill Gates. Gates has pledged some of his money to conduct education research. In Gates's effort to study teaching, he is likely to discover that the critical information he seeks will replicate findings from valid educational studies conducted over the past five decades. A better use of his money would be to pay his staff to examine the progressive research that has already been and is currently being conducted.

Several politicians have bought into Gates's view of education—even the Obama administration has given an ear to Gates's hype. Gates's big money (called *Gates gold* for further reference) has a way of creating strange bedfellows. It's revealed in chapter 6 how Gates gold has negatively influenced educational policy in several states.

Not to be outdone, other business moguls who are trying to eliminate education reality and insert their view of education include the Walton Foundation (think Walmart), which provided $82 million for charter schools, $26 million for school-choice programs, and $116 million to promote school vouchers in several states through TV advertising.[4] Vouchers, when approved by your state representatives and governor, are state tax dollars given to parents to send their children to private schools that they want to attend, instead of that money being spent on your local public schools.

Should former politicians or policy makers, those political appointees to educational posts like Bill Bennett, E. D. Hirsch, or Diane Ravitch, speak for our public schools? Should former federal secretaries of education speak for our public schools? William Bell (Reagan Administration), Rod Paige (first George W. Bush administration), or Lamar Alexander (George H. W. Bush appointee, and now a senator from Tennessee)?

What about Obama's secretary of education, Arne Duncan? Should Duncan, who has a bachelor's degree in sociology and has never actually been a public school educator, speak for the profession? Should Duncan even be a secretary of education? Every public school teacher is anxiously awaiting a president to appoint a former or current public school teacher to lead policy and decision making for America's public schools. Educators deserve at least that, and so does the general public—those 89 percent of parents whose children attend public schools.

Just as Wall Street bankers expect the secretary of commerce to be a former Wall Street executive, and the farmers hope that the secretary of agriculture understands the complexity of the farming industry, so should public school professionals expect an *educator* to be the secretary of education. The education profession is not searching for pseudoeducators such as Michelle Rhee, Paul Vallas, or Arne Duncan to represent them, but instead a person who has taught children or adolescents in a public school as a certified teacher. None of these three has certified-teacher credentials.

If you were to think a genuine public school teacher might have a problem handling the political hot seat, you'd be wrong. Try handling 110 different adolescent personalities a day, getting them to cooperate enough to learn something every day, and then speaking to four sets of parents after school twice a month to resolve grade concerns. No political climate can match the daily stressful challenges of being a public school teacher.

Several reasons exist for the need to hire a public school teacher as the secretary of education, but perhaps the primary reason is that this person should be the foremost representative and spokesperson for America's public schools. A noneducator is simply not capable of comprehending the daily challenges, problems, and successes that occur in classrooms each day. Noneducators lack the philosophical base, pedagogical knowledge, research background, and face time with students to comprehend the profession in ways that would make them adequate representatives of the profession. Without this essential knowledge, they are incapable of creating policies, speaking honestly to legislators, or telling the president what children and adolescents really need at school.

No matter who speaks on the public airways or who posts comments online, those persons who make broad, sweeping public statements of alleged fact about schools and teachers should at least be knowledgeable about the real challenges professional educators face daily. The secretary should be capable of obtaining frequent, accurate research from trusted educational sources. Unfortunately, that isn't the case and hasn't been for a long time in the United States.

WHY POLITICIANS MAKE TERRIBLE EDUCATION SPOKESPERSONS

Politicians are generally uninformed about education matters. People want to believe that politicians mean well when they speak, but that's foolish optimism. Honestly, do Americans need another "education governor" or "education president"?

Imagine politicians running for an office—any office, from school-board member to governor to president. They want to find an issue that resonates positively with every voter within the sound of their voices—whether a Democrat, Republican, or independent. So they choose a winner: they talk about education! Politicians start by saying that nothing is more important than a good education for children. They add that they are in favor of improving education in the geographical area that they represent. Who could disagree?

Politicians become more detailed with their messages as the campaign rolls on, noting publicly that students need higher test scores, teachers need to be better trained, and public schools should do a much better job than they currently are. Everyone cheers, regardless of political persuasion, further encouraging the politicians.

A week before election day, the politician rolls out a few statistics heard from Jay Leno or Lou Dobbs the night before, repeating some absurdity such as "The U.S. is behind every other industrialized nation in reading and mathematics," and, of course, promising to fix the problem. Candidates on both sides of the fence are spreading the same message: "Our schools are broken, and I want to, and can, fix them." No matter who wins, we elect someone who almost always knows nothing about the day-to-day operations of the local third-grade classroom or high school chemistry class.

In traditional fashion, as they take office, they appoint one of their political friends to be an education secretary and the rumor mill continues, without factual basis, with his or her comments. Then, when the budget looks dire, the newly elected politician cuts education spending despite the promises, because, "Well . . . our roads, federal and state prisons, and the latest war are more pressing issues!"

Politicians become the mouthpieces regarding public education in the regions that they represent (county, state, or country); but, unlike in their days as students, they fail to do their homework with education, letting the pundits do it for them. Each time politicians speak they provide even more inaccurate information. As teachers en masse (i.e., the National Education Association [NEA]) begin to disagree with their grand plans for "fixing" the problem, politicians start to develop a negative perspective of education unions and teachers in general.

Educators' messages, if accepted by others, will mean that politicians will need to seek more revenue, but that doesn't fit the politicians' plans of merely acting the part of education advocates. They didn't actually mean that they could or would do something about education problems. Now politicians become defensive because otherwise they'll need to actually engage in resolving issues that weren't originally part of their leadership plans. Education issues are perhaps perceived by politicians as an easy aspect of their campaigns. It is not likely that politicians expect education to be a controversial issue that warrants reasoned debates or significant time and resources.

As with George W. Bush's first secretary of education, Rod Paige, instead of the truth being sought, a comment such as "The NEA is a terrorist organization" is blurted by a politician in front of the cameras. As it did in 2004 with Bush II, relationships with educators can only go downhill from this point. The tragedy in all of this inaccurate rhetoric is that the general public never actually hears the truth about their schools from politicians.

Americans have to go elsewhere for accurate information about the public schools. So whom do Americans turn to in the absence of accurate information? The media—and what a mistake that has been.

THE LIES "THEY" TELL YOU

Who's Complaining, and What Qualifications Do They Have?

Every month someone who is well connected in the media makes a disparaging comment about public schools in the United States. Here are some examples of the lack of "R-E-S-P-E-C-T" that educators and the public schools have received over the past few years.

The following comment is from news anchor Dobbs on his own show with CNN News in 2006: "Bush is not addressing the issue that the public schools failed to educate an entire generation of Americans."[5] Don't you wonder of which generation Dobbs was speaking? Are you worried it might be your generation, your partner's, or your children's?

Do you wonder what that "lost" generation is currently doing? Do you suppose they are all unemployed due to their inadequate education? Are they hardened criminals, or did that generation actually contribute positively to the gross national product? The most pressing question some might have about that generation is, "Are they happy?"

Perhaps you heard this comment by an author, Harry Spence (author of *Tough Choices or Tough Times*), about the American public school system: "It's one of the weakest in the advanced industrial world."[6] Spence made this pronouncement on National Public Radio in 2007. Some may be confused by that characterization—*weakest*—but considering the many successes Americans have created as an "industrialized" nation, perhaps Spence will change his mind.

U.S. citizens are fairly advanced when it comes to creating and developing industrialized products—a valid sign that the U.S. public education system is successful. U.S. citizens invented and developed the iPad, Google, pooperscoopers, Snuggies, smart bombs, and drones, and the United States placed a man on the moon first. Can't Americans chalk successful "Yankee ingenuity" up to an effective public education system?

In 2010, someone from the United States invented the drills that saved several trapped Chilean miners. The United States sends medical aid to countries around the globe. Americans send heavy machinery invented, designed, and mass produced in the United States, airplanes to rescue people, and entire armies to undeveloped places no other country will go. It takes many people to accomplish these amazing feats of technological, military, and medical invention—most of them public-school graduates. Spence's analysis of our public schools is clearly a sweeping inaccuracy.

Here's another zinger: "The public schools are abysmal in Memphis."[7] This comment is from an author, Michael Lewis, who wrote the book *The Blind Side*, which became a movie in 2009. Lewis describes in his book the journey of professional football player Michael Oher, as he escapes urban Memphis during his high school years via a wealthy family living nearby.

Lewis's background is not that of a school evaluator, administrator, or teacher; nor is he a former student in, or the parent of a child in, the Memphis School District. Lewis attended a private college-preparatory high school in New Orleans before attending Princeton University. He became a bond salesman before embarking on a writing career.[8] None of his accomplishments would qualify him to be any kind of an "expert" on public schools anywhere; but he can surely make general comments that reflect the similar ignorance of many about public schools.

A former vice-presidential candidate proclaimed, "Education in America has been in some sense in some of our states just accepted to be a little bit lax."[9] Sarah Palin shared these thoughts during the 2008 vice-presidential debate. Palin's background knowledge on the subject of several topics has been questioned by a number of people. In her defense, though, her words are less incendiary than most we've heard over the past five decades. Perhaps she didn't want to dismiss the many public school graduates of her home state of Alaska.

Cornel West, a high-profile professor of religion and the director of the program on African-American Studies at Princeton University, had this to say about the public schools one evening on Maher's HBO political program: "We have a disgraceful school system." One could certainly appreciate Professor West's qualifications as an expert on religion and African American issues, but not as an educational researcher.

What is it that qualifies Dr. West as a spokesperson for public education in the United States? What is it that would make him describe our system as "disgraceful"? One example to share with West is the success of many African American students following the *Brown v. Board of Education* Supreme Court decision of 1954. That landmark decision led to the eventual desegregation of public schools and created a meteoric rise in graduation rates and higher test scores on national examinations among African American students (see chapter 10). West may have even been one of the beneficiaries of the 1954 decision!

Recently, a group of people with the significant-sounding label of the National Council on Teacher Quality (NCTQ) proclaimed that "states have 'broken, outdated, and inflexible' policies in place that protect ineffective teachers and ultimately harm student learning."[10] In my 20 years as an educational researcher and college professor, I have never seen our educational programs at our university or any on the East Coast subjected to the simple and limited standards for teacher education quality mentioned on NCTQ's website.

Colleges of education voluntarily choose to be evaluated by and meet the standards of the National Council for Accreditation of Teacher Education (NCATE). Every college and university that wants to provide professional teacher certification for their graduates must also meet state education-department standards. The national NCATE standards and every state's education-department standards change regularly based on current research provided by educational researchers.

Very few, if any, of the staff at NCTQ have doctorate degrees, which is the primary standard used by the education profession for those collecting and disseminating accurate research data. It's a pity that NCTQ hasn't established high standards similar to what they expect of others for their own data collecting and reporting staff.

Some NCTQ board members have been or are associated with charter school organizations, including Edison and the Thomas B. Fordham Institute, which lobbies for more charter schools. NCTQ is funded by several groups, including ExxonMobil and the Bill and Melinda Gates Foundation. Accepting donations from these sources doesn't sound very "nonpartisan." In 2005, NCTQ even received some money from federal tax dollars, despite the disclaimer on their website noting that the company does not receive any *direct* monies from the federal government.[11]

Several of the staff members at NCTQ are former uncertified Teach for America "teachers." NCTQ's agenda may be providing opportunities for more unqualified and uncertified teachers to enter public school classrooms. That seems antithetical to their stated mission of improving teacher quality.

Davis Guggenheim, a man who appreciates making money as much as the rest of us, created a new project to get rich. He was the producer of *An Inconvenient Truth*, Al Gore's explanation of the danger of climate change—a documentary that actually contained some significant facts related to the problem. Guggenheim's 2010 venture, *Waiting for "Superman,"* was intended to be an emotional appeal to fix the public schools. Unfortunately, the film is a combination of cheerleading for charter schools and for merit pay. It is also a serious attack on teacher unions. According to one critic, *Waiting for "Superman"* "makes reformer Michelle Rhee [former Washington, DC, CEO of schools] look like Princess Leia, and union leader Randi Weingarten look like Darth Vader."[12]

The book that accompanies the "Superman" documentary contains this line: "And despite decades of well-intended reforms and huge sums of money spent on the problem, our public schools haven't improved markedly since the 1970s."[13] Naturally, no data accompany that remark—no evidence that there is any truth to these words. Yet the phrase was picked up by a CNN broadcaster and has been repeated regularly since the documentary was released.

The reality is that high school graduation rates have increased considerably since 1970, when the graduation rate was at 75 percent, compared to a rate of 86 percent in 1990;[14] plus, more students are applying to and attending college now than ever before. The National Center for Education Statistics reported in 2009 that, in the decade from 1999 to 2009, the number of bachelor's degrees awarded by U.S. colleges and universities increased by 33 percent.[15] How could anyone suggest that our public schools haven't improved for the past four decades with so much data proving the opposite?

Wouldn't someone wanting to produce a film about public education have some experience with it, for example by having been a student in public schools, by having earned teaching credentials, or by having collected volumes of data on schools? Guggenheim fails those tests miserably, and he received his high school education from Sidwell Friends School in Washington, DC—not exactly a public entity. Recent presidents have sent their children to Sidwell Friends—Presidents Carter, Clinton, and Obama—which gives an idea of the clientele who usually attend that school. How would Guggenheim know about what most public schools are like if he's never experienced anything other than a Friends school in Washington, DC, as a student; never interviewed teachers in public schools; and failed to cite recent research? Bias without experience or research can be the worst ignorance, especially when the story is available to a national audience.

Shortly after the documentary was released, Guggenheim stated during an interview on CNN's *American Morning*, "Overall we're failing millions of kids," and later added, "because schools have been a problem for so long." When asked by a CNN broadcaster how the public could help with the problems he articulated in the movie, Guggenheim unashamedly responded, "Start by going to see the film."[16] It sounds like "the inconvenient truth" of producing "Superman" is greed—not reasoned debate or truth telling about the value of public school teachers or schools in the United States.

The Education Ignorance of Bill Gates

How does it sound for John Glenn, a former astronaut and U.S. senator, to advise IBM on how to improve sales? How about if Joe Torre, famous baseball manager, lashes out against farmers, explaining how they need to do a better job harvesting their corn crop? And, what if Matt Damon, famous actor, suddenly develops a strategy for preventing Wall Street bankers from making too much money, a strategy that is later considered by Congress for a new federal law?

These three scenarios seem absurd to me, and probably to you as well. In the world of business, amateurs aren't entitled to "hold court" or propose new laws that negatively affect the value of a business for which they are not members. What if an adult college dropout who had made millions of dollars in a business having nothing to do with education told the public how to repair a profession in which he had never engaged? Within the past few years, Bill Gates, with no college degree, no education training, no experience as a professional educator, and no research credentials has become somewhat of a public school "spokesperson" and called a "reformer" by pundits.

Here are a couple of Gates's 2005 comments: "America's high schools are obsolete . . . and broken, flawed, and underfunded"; and "Even when they're working exactly as designed, [they] cannot teach our kids what they need to know today."[17] It might have been somewhat understandable if he had made these comments in an editorial; but instead he unleashed his ignorance at a 2005 conference of governors and chief education officers from all fifty states. Of course, the greatest fear is that the governors may have believed Gates.

Why would Gates be invited to speak as an education expert, having dropped out of college? No one in America can even become a teacher without at least a four-year college degree and a teaching certificate— and now, Gates knows more than they do about education? How are Gates's education opinions any more believable than those of the man called "Joe the Plumber" from the 2008 presidential election?

Mr. Gates announced in late 2010 that he didn't like the idea of an educator with a master's degree making more money than one with a bachelor's degree.[18] He doesn't think that more seniority as a teacher should lead to more money. But what does he know about the *business* world and seniority?

Does Gates believe a person with an MBA deserves more money than one fresh out of college? Does he believe that a 20-year veteran of IBM deserves more money than one with 5 years of experience? Should Gerstner and Gates receive more money than those with fewer years of experience in their businesses? Perhaps; but as reported earlier, educational researchers have found that a master's degree actually improves teaching.

One often hears about how wonderful the public education system is in Finland. Finnish students' test scores on several international comparisons have always been quite high. There are several reasons that Finland does so well, reasons explained in chapter 3. One reason that researchers would suggest that Finland does well is because since 1979, *all teachers are required to earn at least a master's degree in education in a content area to accompany their education bachelor's degree.*[19] It's reasonable to suggest that those advanced degrees are having an impact on teacher quality and, thus, student learning.

Gates doesn't know enough about effective teaching for policy makers or the general public to value his comments. Gates also hasn't accessed much of the research on effective teaching—which he seems to believe needs to be conducted for the first time. The greatest injustice to teachers is hearing a person who has never taught tell them that class size doesn't matter in helping students achieve more—another education inaccuracy from Gates's mouth. Gates is right about one thing—education does matter—and his lack of it as a researcher in education makes his public pronouncements null and void to education professionals, as they should be to policy makers.

How would businesspersons feel if Gates spent millions to uncover a better accounting system? Would auto companies welcome Gates's plan for finding a better way to build safe vehicles? Would Walmart accept a study from Gates to encourage lowering their prices on every item? And would the U.S Congress accept Gates's ideas for trimming the number of representatives and senators to half of the current number? Most would be saying, "Mind your own business—not ours," which is exactly how professional educators feel about his onslaught of ignorance on the education profession.

Recently, Gates embarked on a new venture of hiring several educators without much research experience to initiate a study on effective-teaching traits. He and his wife spent $45 million for a two-year study of effective teaching, called "The Measures of Effective Teaching" project.[20] Gates intended on studying the work of 3,700 teachers across the United States.

The humor in all of this for teachers and principals is that educational researchers have studied effective teaching since at least the 1950s. Numerous volumes of research on effective teaching exist, which Gates could acquire and read in less than three months, if he only realized that the data had already been collected. If he were a researcher in the field, Gates would know this.

Instead, Gates chose to hand out $45 million to six school districts to uncover dated research while replicating previous studies. In March of 2011, Gates revealed his complete ignorance of educational research and understanding of teacher education training when he bragged in a *Wall Street Journal* article that he had found an innovative way of helping teachers improve their practice.[21]

His paid researchers videotaped educators in the act of teaching, then showed the video to them later, at which point they critiqued themselves. Since the 1970s, numerous research articles and professional conference presentations have been presented on the value of videotaping feedback for teachers. Most educators are hoping that Bill and Melinda Gates become bored with their search for education answers and instead choose another hobby.

WEEKLY REPORTERS TAKE THEIR SHOTS AT PUBLIC SCHOOLS: *NEWSWEEK* AND *TIME* REPEAT MORE OF THE SAME IGNORANCE

Researchers and practitioners in the field of education know that weekly magazines are written to inform the general public on significant news events. It seems that whenever there is a paucity of news to report, *Newsweek* and *Time* find journalists to issue *their* latest perspectives on public education.

During the spring of 2010, two journalists, Evan Thomas and Pat Wingert, took their shot at education issues—and what a negative shot it was for public schools.[22] The cover of *Newsweek* for March 15, 2010, was black with chalklike white written over and over again with the words "We must fire bad teachers." The words "The Key to Saving American Education" were written in the middle of the page.

I explained in chapter 4 that educational researchers have clearly noted time and time again the significant effects of quality teachers on student learning. Thomas and Wingert took liberties with several facts to spin a story that might make one believe that the public schools are the only schools with poor teachers.

Lines such as "Much of the ability to teach is innate" and "Although many teachers are caring and selfless, teaching in the public schools has not always attracted the best and the brightest"[23] *couldn't be more inaccurate*. Instead of citing recent research that proves the opposite about public school teachers' academic backgrounds, these authors chose instead to roll out these epithets without citing any evidence to support their claims.

RESEARCH-BASED FACTS ABOUT PUBLIC EDUCATION

Course Content Required to Become a Teacher

In addressing the "teaching is innate" comment, it is important to recognize that the reason for the existence of colleges of education in universities across the United States relates to the highly in-depth research base on effective teaching, with classes covering topics such as

- appropriate philosophical perspectives and their impact on student learning;
- educational psychology and the importance of applying it in classrooms;
- components of successful lesson planning;
- choosing appropriate curricula;
- classroom-management strategies;
- assessment strategies, both formative and summative, for determining what students know and helping them progress;
- instructional processes that are effective for the lessons being presented;
- *developmentally appropriate* practices (i.e., practices suitable for a particular age group);

- cultural responsiveness;
- questioning strategies that match lesson objectives;
- professionalism.[24]

Infants aren't born knowing all this information. Going to school for 13 years of one's life doesn't make one a professional educator. Does reading a magazine magically make someone a journalist? Every teacher who becomes certified knows about these principles. It is highly improbable that a teacher candidate progressing through a teacher education program at a university would not be exposed to these ideas. Colleges' and universities' teacher education programs are all approved by state and national accreditation boards that insist the universities' programs contain the essential elements noted above.

Teacher candidates' evaluations and grades during their student-teaching semesters are all based on the tenets of effective pedagogy listed above. The fact that preservice teachers are being taught these principles and graded on them explains why the ability to teach is not and never has been primarily "innate."

Teachers Are Highly Successful Academically

Evidence also exists to refute Thomas and Wingert's assertion that "teaching in public schools has not always attracted the best and the brightest." Gerald Bracey reported in 2004 *that college students majoring in teacher education had higher grade-point averages than students in all other majors.*[25] Other researchers have noted that for students enrolled in education programs, "58% of all female teachers from the high school class of 1992 came from the top two quintiles of the ability distribution of high school graduates."[26]

These same researchers also reported an Educational Testing Service study of prospective teachers' scores on their Praxis tests (teacher-certification tests), noting that those who passed in "most secondary education fields had higher ability than the average college graduate."[27] Other researchers have discovered that teachers who are trained in traditional university-designed programs are "generally more academically able than the average college student of any major, whereas unlicensed entrants into teaching have significantly lower levels of academic achievement than most college students and those in education programs."[28]

Several pundits have gone on TV and reported to the press that universities are doing a poor job of educating teacher candidates. Once again, no facts are ever presented in their comments—they're generally parroting a false comment they heard from an inaccurate source.

Accurate Facts about Tenure

Another partial inaccuracy reported by Thomas and Wingert is this comment: "In most states, after two or three years, teachers are given lifetime tenure. It is almost impossible to fire them."[29] Every teacher can be fired any day of the week for behaviors that are unfitting of a professional educator. Every year hundreds of tenured teachers are relieved of their duties due to poor teaching, by principals who evaluate them.

The idea that tenure protects teachers from firing is grossly inaccurate. Tenure only ensures a teacher of a hearing before being officially fired. The concept of tenure is also addressed in chapter 4; but for immediate clarification here is an explanation by the Missouri State Teachers Association concerning the reasons for firing a tenured teacher:

- If the teacher has a physical or mental condition that renders him or her unfit to instruct or associate with children.
- For immoral conduct.
- For incompetence, inefficiency or insubordination in the line of duty.
- For willful or persistent violation of Missouri's school laws or the local school district's published policies or regulations.
- For excessive or unreasonable absences.
- For conviction of a felony or a crime of moral turpitude.[30]

Thomas and Wingert go on to blame teachers' unions for schools keeping poor teachers, rather than the true culprit—the failure of principals to fire poor teachers. Principals are responsible for determining who belongs in the classroom and who doesn't. Effective principals, just like the effective bosses where you work, are responsible for getting rid of those who don't perform well.

The mail-carrier union doesn't fire poor mail carriers; the American Federation of Television and Radio Artists union is not responsible for firing poor TV broadcasters; and the Air Line Pilots Association isn't in the business of firing their members who fly planes. The boss fires employees, so any attacks on the teachers' unions as the cause of poor teaching or the reason for poor teachers not being fired seem absurd.

One of the primary problems with the *Newsweek* article is that the authors cite statistics from organizations that have no interest in collecting accurate data or supporting what actually works in public schools—groups such as NCTQ, Teach for America, and the Education Trust. Not one of these organizations is concerned with supporting the data that are collected by genuine educational researchers. Most of the members of these organizations have never been teachers, have never been researchers, and probably would rather not see more taxes used to support public schools.

Thomas and Wingert fail to report any data from studies conducted by the thousands of researchers from the American Educational Research Association—studies reported in the peer-reviewed journals *Educational Researcher, Review of Educational Research, Educational Evaluation and Policy Analysis*, and the *Journal of Educational and Behavioral Statistics*. Every education journalist and even politicians could report studies from these trusted resources.

Anyone involved in education policy and decision making could access articles from the journal *Phi Delta Kappan*, or the accurate data that Bracey revealed for years (e.g., *Setting the Record Straight*; the annual "Bracey Report on the Condition of Public Education"). Another trusted source is the Association for Supervision and Curriculum Development's monthly journal, *Educational Leadership*, which has been published since 1943 and includes numerous studies.

The authors who contribute to *Educational Leadership* describe effective classrooms in which teachers use research-based curricular and instructional practices, classroom management techniques, and cultural responsiveness, as well as many other research-proved strategies. How could so many journalists miss the resources available in the Educational Resources Informational Center (ERIC) database—available for the past 25 years?

REPORTERS' LIMITED BACKGROUNDS

Thomas and Wingert each received private school educations—Wingert admitting that she attended Queen of the Rosary School in Chicago, and the biography of Thomas reveals his schooling experiences at Andover Academy. These two may have never actually been in a public school, which would create another serious layer of ignorance of how most public schools work in America. Even if they didn't attend public schools as students, reporters can visit and collect data from schools or access information from the thousands of educational research studies that have been and continue to be conducted.

Another frequent *Newsweek* contributor to education opinions is Jonathan Alter. Alter has become a cheerleader for Bill Gates, singing his praises as the great "reformer" of schooling. If you're curious about whether Alter knows anything about public schools, then you may be interested in knowing that he graduated from the very private, prestigious, expensive Andover Academy High School in Massachusetts, like Thomas did.

Private schooling experiences don't provide one with an understanding of the genuine issues that affect our typical public schools in America. Educational researchers are required to reveal their bias when they conduct studies—why can't journalists be required to do the same, so that when the public reads *their* accounts of facts, everyone knows that the authors' views will be severely impacted by their limited experiences?

Different Story—Same Ignorance

Time magazine journalists tried to upstage *Newsweek*'s attempt to destroy public schools' reputation with their September 20, 2010, issue. By the fourth sentence of her article on the public school–bashing documentary *Waiting for "Superman,"* journalist Amanda Ripley had initiated her attack, stating, "So for a movie about America's malfunctioning education system . . . ."[31] That descriptor—*malfunctioning*—used to label America's entire education system is an interesting way to portray the schools that 89 percent of U.S. children attend.

An investigation into Ripley's credentials to ascertain her research background in educational realms partially explained her inappropriate use of *malfunctioning* to describe public schools. Her resume isn't what might be expected for someone hired to write about public school issues: she holds a B.A. degree in government. We should expect more from a giant media corporation such as *Time*.

Ripley's attempts at providing accurate information are so interlaced with her opinions that genuine teachers would easily recognize Ripley's ignorance about the profession. When she writes, "First, thanks partly to the blunt instruments of No Child Left Behind, we can now track how well individual students are doing from year to year—and figure out which schools are working and which are not," she demonstrates her lack of knowledge of what occurs each day in a classroom.[32]

For well over 25 years, numerous educational researchers have detailed the absurdity of using the traditional "blunt instruments" (e.g., any externally created state test, SATs, Iowa Tests of Basic Skills, California Achievement Tests) to determine students' knowledge or lack thereof.[33] All classroom teachers know and reveal knowledge of their students' skills and abilities long before the state tests are given in March or April of each year.

Teachers explain what kids can do when they grade and return assignments, have conferences with parents, and complete report cards. Students' growth is *not* a secret to teachers until an expensive state test is given once a year in April. Teachers can predict every one of their students' general standardized-test scores long before they receive the results four months later.

How can teachers calculate students' grades, provide feedback for growth, and determine what to teach the next week without constant formative assessment? OK, that wasn't fair—use of the word *formative*. Noneducators aren't familiar with formative assessments—the day-to-day analyses teachers use to determine what to do the next day.

Journalists fail to use *formative* because they are not trained educators—not teachers—and they are not educational researchers. Is it too much to ask that journalists might speak to teachers to discover how they help students *before* they write the final drafts of their articles? Is anyone curious about who's editing these articles at the magazine headquarters?

Teachers are taught to recognize when students don't comprehend ideas, when students need additional help on a concept or misunderstand a principle that is taught, and when students aren't working to their level of ability. Formative assessment is learned in a teacher education program at the university. You won't find the word *formative* in *Time* or *Newsweek* because journalists aren't talking to enough public school teachers.

Public Education: Continually Helping Kids with "Wretched" Home Lives

Here's another absurd quote from Ripley's article: "We now know that that it is possible to teach every kid, even poor kids with wretched home lives, to read, write, and do math and science at respectable levels."[34] Once again, every teacher from the dawn of the profession has been teaching "poor kids from wretched home lives . . . to read, write, and do math and science at respectable levels."

Ripley's great-great-grandparents may have been something like those "poor" kids—perhaps immigrant students whose parents worked two jobs each and had no time to interact with their children, and whose lives were defined by challenging circumstances. Even if her ancestors weren't "poor kids," there have always been and will always be poor kids in our schools. It's unlikely those *poor kids* will be in the schools where those authors went to school, though—like Andover Academy.

Ripley continues with her erroneous reporting on the next page, with a genuine whopper: "Teenagers are now less likely to graduate from high school than their parents were."[35] All Ripley needed to do to prevent that inaccuracy was track the graduation rates in this country since 1900, when it was about 3 percent, to today's rate of 89 percent.

The public should notice what teachers have been doing for years—helping families move from the lower class socioeconomically into the working class, the middle class, or perhaps the upper class. *Public* education is based on a philosophy of equal opportunity for every child, so that every American can benefit—just as Thomas Jefferson envisioned centuries ago. Public education is responsible for the ability of Ripley and millions of other descendants of immigrants from the 1800s and 1900s to eventually attend college.

The public school system's assistance in helping lower-socioeconomic-class students graduate from high school and enter college continues today, as evidenced by the number of poor Caucasian, Hispanic, and African American students who never would have attended college even 10 years ago! Certainly in the past two decades, Mexican and other Hispanic immigrants from several countries have flooded America's public schools.

According to a recent study from the Pew Hispanic Center, 16 percent of Hispanic high school graduates earn four-year college degrees.[36] A rise in the number of students attending college is certainly considerable when compared to 20 years ago, and public school education is the primary contributor to those improved numbers—especially for lower-income families. A 2009 survey completed by over 250,000 college freshmen, released by the *Chronicle of Higher Education*, revealed that 73 percent were White, 11 percent were African American, 9 percent were Asian American, and almost 10 percent were Mexican Americans and other Latino students.[37] Most Latino immigrant families are not sending their children to private K–12 schools; thus, these statistics reveal more success for our public schools.

In reviewing the *Time* article, we see that Ripley, like every other private school graduate, adds her own ignorance about hiring and firing teachers in charter schools as compared to public schools, with the following comment: "At these schools [charters], principals can hire their own staff. If teachers consistently fail to help their students learn in ways that can be measured, they are asked to find another job."[38] Again, Ripley echoes the words of previous authors with no evidence to support her biases against public schools. In most public school districts, principals *do* hire their staff and *are* responsible for their firing. Conversations with principals would reveal how frequently teachers are released from contracts.

Another Set of Troubling Inaccuracies

Time's companion article in the September 20 edition, "How to Recruit Better Teachers," was equally disturbing to public school educators due to reporter John Cloud's limited and biased perspectives. Cloud reveals his ignorance of the research on teachers' successful educational backgrounds with the comment, "We hire lots of our lowest performers to teach, and then scream when our kids don't excel."[39]

Cloud, however, couldn't be a better cheerleader for Teach for America, an organization that likely furthers low student performance by placing uncertified teachers in many urban classrooms across America. Cloud generally whines about teachers' salaries, and reveals ignorance about how teachers are evaluated.

With a little research, Cloud could have revealed a study that was commissioned by the U.S. Department of Education in 1983, whose intention was to prove that college students who entered the teaching profession *were not* good students. Bracey notes what happened to that research: "*When the report found teachers to be about as smart as anyone else in college, the report was buried.*"[40]

Bracey discovered the report through a conversation he had with David Imig, the president and CEO of the American Association of Colleges for Teacher Education (AACTE). This organization is recognized nationally for conducting and disseminating research on effective design and implementation of teacher education degree programs across the United States.

The AACTE has promoted effective university teacher education programs since its inception in 1948. The AACTE does not have a political agenda—it exists to provide research in support of effective college teacher education design. Education professionals recognize the value and research the AACTE provides. Why can't journalists and politicians refer to this trusted source, instead of spinning their versions of negative press about public schools?

Both the *Newsweek* article by Thomas and Wingert and the equally appalling writing by Ripley and Cloud in *Time* reveal a definitive lack of research on the authors' parts. Educational researchers are responsible for turning over every stone to reveal genuine facts. That educational researchers realize this information is available and find it becomes a valid reason to choose resources other than *Newsweek* or *Time* for accurate information about public education.

Every public school teacher who read the Ripley article must have laughed out loud after reading the "poor kids" line, realizing the sensationalism used by reporters to get the general public to read these fictional accounts of the state of public education. Based on the inaccuracies of these two articles and the severely limited research conducted by the journalists who wrote them, perhaps *Newsweek* and *Time* should be placed in the newsstands next to *People* magazine and *The National Enquirer*.

It's no secret that when people want accurate information on how to invest money, they don't rely on a politician for information; questions about how to repair one's car don't go to *Newsweek* or *Time* reporters; economic experts aren't reliable for questions on infant formula; and Bill Gates is the last person Americans can trust for the best research on how to teach children or adolescents! Americans need education-journal articles written by educational researchers and classroom teachers to inform them on educational matters.

The best sources for information about what is really happening with the public schools in your community are the education professionals who work there. Until all Americans begin to seek accurate sources of information about their schools, the public schools will be under attack by those with political agendas and plans for profiting from your children. I hope you won't buy their snake oil, or fear walking off the edge of the earth.

WHEN GOVERNMENT AND BIG BUSINESS GET COZY

More Lies and an Expensive Agenda

An educated people were, and still are, considered a danger, not to democracy, but to the wealthy who profit from other people's labor.[1]

Funny thing: Japanese officials don't want to say anything bad about their schools; our officials don't want to say anything good about ours.[2]

As head of the Federal Communications Commission, Reed Hundt went to former Secretary [of Education] Bennett and asked him to support legislation that would bring Internet infrastructure to both public and private schools. According to Hundt, "He told me he would not help, because he did not want public schools to obtain new funding, new capability, new tools for success. He wanted them, he said, to fail so that they could be replaced with vouchers, charter schools, religious schools, and other forms of private education.[3]

It's difficult to imagine that a former secretary of education, Bill Bennett, would forsake America's public school system, which currently educates 89 percent of U.S. children. His words bring into question which government officials actually support the premise of public education for all. America's public education system is responsible for creating a reality of the dreams that so many Americans have had: in the past, in the present, and for the future. Who would destroy such a powerful avenue for Americans to improve the quality of their lives?

Former education secretary Bennett is not the first government leader to attempt to derail such a successful system. Previous officials with intent to diminish public schools include former presidents Ronald Reagan and George H. W. Bush. Former president George W. Bush also did his share to tarnish our public school system's reputation, and successfully gained allies from big business to help with the process.

Public education is under attack by numerous culprits; but as K–12 education enters another year of strangulation by No Child Left Behind (NCLB) policies, educators and parents are piecing together the relationship between unreasonable government policies, big business, and reckless educational practices. The curtain is slowly being pulled back, and even noneducators are beginning to see who's delivering the rhetoric and creating policies that actually destroy public schools, rather than helping them. The driving philosophies behind recent poor educational-policy decisions are not research based—they're market based—an unforgivable solution for the children and adolescents who are affected by it all.

THAT PESKY REPORT THAT STARTED
THE RUMORS: *A NATION AT RISK*

This trend of being a pseudo education spokesperson, an expert or adviser for public schools with no knowledge of what children are like or how schools operate from a professional's perspective, certainly has a long history. It is interesting that these attacks were unleashed with vigor during the Reagan presidency, as told by educational researchers David Berliner and Bruce Biddle:

> In 1983 the Reagan White House began to make sweeping claims attacking the conduct and achievements of America's public schools—claims that were contradicted by evidence we knew about. . . . Related hostile and untrue claims were soon to be repeated by many leaders of the Reagan and Bush administrations. The claims were also embraced in many documents issued by industrialists and business leaders and were endlessly repeated and embroidered on by the press. And, as time passed

even leading members of the education community . . . began to state these lies as facts.[4]

The specific document with many inaccuracies that effectively damned public schooling was *A Nation at Risk* (ANAR), a report written by a team of primarily *noneducators* led by Reagan administration officials.[5] Two of the several committee members were principals, and two were high school classroom teachers; but every other member was from a university, a school board, or the private sector.

Reagan didn't originally want ANAR written, and was mostly interested in some rationale for completely eliminating the federal Department of Education. When the report was released to the public, the press jumped on it due to its controversial nature.

The opening salvo was probably the most damning:

> We report to the American people that while we can take justifiable pride in what our schools and colleges have historically accomplished and contributed to the United States and the well-being of its people, the educational foundations of our society are presently being eroded by a rising tide of mediocrity that threatens our very future as a Nation and a people. What was unimaginable a generation ago has begun to occur—others are matching and surpassing our educational attainments.
>
> If an unfriendly foreign power had attempted to impose on America the mediocre educational performance that exists today, we might well have viewed it as an act of war. As it stands, we have allowed this to happen to ourselves. We have even squandered the gains in student achievement made in the wake of the Sputnik challenge. Moreover, we have dismantled essential support systems which helped make those gains possible. We have, in effect, been committing an act of unthinking, unilateral educational disarmament.[6]

Reagan administration officials began to see that ANAR might help in his reelection bid for 1984. Democrats were focusing on domestic issues and how the country needed to resolve those through electing a new president. Reagan aides saw ANAR as a way to gain favor with women voters, who they predicted would favor a more domestic agenda, and thought many women might interpret the ANAR report as an effort by the Reagan administration to address domestic issues.[7] It was a ploy that may have helped, but support for public education was never one of Reagan's goals.

If the authors of this report had initiated any genuine search for the truth about U.S. education at the time, they might have written a much different report. On the other hand, why write an accurate report if the news would be positive? How could President Reagan have claimed that the successes of public schools were due to his actions after being in office for only two years prior to the report's publication?

Berliner and Biddle—highly respected educational researchers—describe the problems with ANAR:

> It made many claims about the "failures" of American education, how those "failures" were confirmed by "evidence," and how this would inevitably damage the nation. (Unfortunately, none of the supposedly supportive "evidence" actually appeared in *A Nation at Risk*, nor did this work provide citations to tell Americans where that "evidence" might be found.)[8]

The findings were rather insignificant; but publishing ANAR created a renewal of the national pastime of bashing public schools, public school teachers, and the value of teacher education. Reagan probably never intended for this general distaste for schools to occur, since he graduated from a public high school in Illinois.

BUSINESS INTERVENTION IN PUBLIC EDUCATION

> Precious little of the press coverage explores in depth the implications for a democratic society of the for-profit businesses running public schools. In addition, right-wing think tanks such as the Heritage Foundation, Hoover Institution, American Enterprise Institute, Cato Institute, Hudson Institute, Manhattan Institute, and the Scaife Foundation, not to mention business organizations such as the Business Roundtable, have succeeded in steering public policy and national debate by placing spokespersons in mass media and government to assure a business-oriented perspective when it comes to making decisions about the future of public priorities such as schooling, health care, social security, and the environment.[9]

Perhaps the most appalling result of ANAR was the unwelcome intervention of the private sector in educational issues. In particular, a group of businesspersons calling themselves the Business Roundtable (BRT) established the Business Coalition for Education Reform shortly after 1989. This group has pushed for the development of standards for learning and more tests for students, and for schools to do a better job preparing students for the *workforce*. Kathy Emery and Susan Ohanian, however, describe the BRT's real agenda:

> Corporate fat cats are determined to deform the schoolhouse, to poke a huge hole in the very notion of what it means to live in a democracy. In the name of preparing workers for the global economy, we get hyperacademics: kindergarten twisted from a children's garden into a high-skill zone, with blizzards of worksheets and threats of failure; we get third graders vomiting on the tests that will determine whether they move on to fourth grade; we get high schoolers weak in bibliographic reference skills and trigonometry denied a diploma.[10]

More Business Influence: From Content to Performance Standards

Gerald Bracey, a genuine educational researcher, in speaking about the influence of business in education, relayed this comment that emphasizes the inappropriate role that business has played in how we educate children: "Teachers are pilloried and innocent children are intellectually abused for failing to learn under the drill-for-skill, test-em-often methods advocated by the Bush ["W"] administration, by both political parties, and by the biggest lobbying group in Washington, the U.S. Chamber of Commerce."[11]

What group could be farther removed from comprehending education issues than the Chamber of Commerce? None of their members are professional educators; yet these businesspersons are heavily lobbying Washington and your state legislators to alter reasonable educational policies that ensure effective teaching and learning.

Content Standards Appear

Bracey is referring to the renewed involvement of the business community in influencing legislators to accept new paradigms about teaching and learning that run contrary to what teachers and educational researchers know children and adolescents need. Business intervention started in the late 1980s, and by the early 1990s businesspersons had developed an interest in developing and influencing standards that schools should teach. Two types of standards exist: *content* and *performance*.

When the state education department chooses a set of items that children should know by the time they finish first grade, they are establishing *content standards*. Content standards sound reasonably safe, *but only when every student is working at grade level*. Many people might think that everyone with whom they attended school was on grade level in every subject; but it's wrong to assume that. Just because students sit in the same classroom and have birthdays within a year of one another doesn't mean that they are all at the same level in reading, mathematics, social studies, science, art, music, or physical education. All 100 people in a high school graduating class aren't valedictorians; nor do they all make the all-state soccer team or receive music scholarships to college.

The challenge that teachers have in attempting to get every child to understand the content standards established for each grade level in every subject is the overwhelming fact that every child is different. Their brains are just as different as their bodies. The business community jumped on the idea of establishing content standards for every child at every grade level in every subject. The problem was that no one in the business community pushing that agenda had ever taught children or adolescents. And yet, the content standards came, and now every state department of education has long lists of what every child should know in every subject at every grade level.

The development of content standards didn't help students learn more or learn faster, as was the thought process from the business community supporting the standards plan. The standards were rolled out, educators saw them, and many attempted to teach them all. The problem was, the BRT didn't produce children who grew faster. Remember the Chia Pet advertisement: "Just add water and watch it grow!" Children aren't Chia Pets. Teachers knew the result of higher *unrealistic* content standards would be student and teacher frustration, with many failures. The teachers were right, as professionals are apt to be in their own fields.

One reason that businesspeople like content standards is that they want to be sure that when students graduate from high school, they are prepared to do the work that new technology has created for America's working class. Businesspersons want "work-ready" soldiers prepared to take orders and fill their quotas for the day.

The willingness of state education departments to adopt the business communities' content standards started a trend that has ruined not only high school education, but particularly the joy of learning in kindergarten and the primary grades. *New standards meant that kindergartners were expected to learn most things that kids had previously learned in first grade.* Growing didn't matter anymore; knowing a lot of facts did!

Emphasis placed on kids learning at their own pace is called *developmentally appropriate practice* (DAP) by child development experts. DAP is particularly critical to choosing content that children can understand within their age and developmental range. Kindergarteners should be painting, drawing, and playing outside quite a bit during each day, to run off steam and promote cognitive development through large and small motor activities. Nap time each afternoon has vanished in full-day kindergartens. The result is a room filled with tired, restless children with greater academic expectations pushed down their throats and an inability to understand or take in more information.

Parents can thank the *standardistos*, as Ohanian calls them, for orchestrating this unreasonable set of expectations for learning and foisting them on children at every grade level. For years during the 1990s and early 2000s, educational researchers lamented the pushing down of curriculum from upper to lower grades, which places more stress and unreasonable demands on children and adolescents at every grade level.

Educational researchers have a term they use to describe giving students more difficult concepts to learn before they are ready—*hothousing* the curriculum. The BRT's agenda caused these unreasonable demands to be placed on children, all across the United States. The standardistos have created a nightmarish world of *conveyor-belt education*—no learning, but a continually moving curriculum that is an inch deep and a mile wide.

There's no time for painting, drawing, recess, music, or physical education; but content standards make for a fun read for those who are curious about what they can't remember from their past years in school. Now teachers have to waste time on professional development days to align their curriculum with each others' at higher grade levels, to ensure that students don't miss anything—educators call it *curriculum mapping*. What a waste of time *mapping* is for them, when they could be determining how to help those students who will never be on grade level.

We Have Content Standards—Now We Need Tests to Measure Them

Perhaps due to the influence of the BRT, several states in the late 1980s initiated a paper-and-pencil standardized test that kindergarteners were required to pass to advance to first grade. Have you ever seen a kindergartener try to hold a pencil, and then try to darken a circle with it—all within a limited amount of time? It's akin to cruel and unusual punishment.

Testing kindergartners could almost be considered abuse—the kind that used to be sanctioned when children were permitted to work in factories from the age of seven or eight. Federal legislators stopped those abuses when they passed child-labor laws. Seventy-five years later, both U.S. houses of Congress reversed their wisdom by ignorantly approving NCLB legislation. (See chapter 9 for details on NCLB.)

Among several southern states that initiated kindergarten tests in the late 1980s, the failure rates for developmental reasons were rather disturbing: the average percentage of kindergarteners that failed was at 10 percent.[12] The effects of early failure on elementary-age students is appalling—about 40–50 percent of those students who repeat a grade eventually drop out of school. The Florida Center for Children and Youth reported in 1990 that the additional cost of educating retained kindergarteners through third-graders in Florida for that one year was *over $143 million.*

Spending more money in taxes for education probably isn't what the BRT had in mind when they pushed for more standards and tests. The testing initiative defines the problem with noneducators determining what schools should look like and how educators should do their jobs—it not only defies logic and hurts students; it also costs the public more.

Every state in the union had adopted mandated tests for students by 1990. The costs of all of the standardized tests administered by each school district are phenomenal. The taxpayers in each state bear the burden, as a result of businesspersons and politicians exerting their influence over the education field. If businesspersons knew how testing mandates affect what they are paying for local public education, and what little value tests are to teachers, they'd probably vote to eliminate them.

Unfortunately, the public didn't question these costs or the absurdity of testing students once a year on material that had little significance to their overall growth. As the tests became more acceptable, testing-company business leaders reaped the rewards of testing costs and added another plan that created a high-pressure situation for children and teachers.

The business world had a strong ally in government by this time—George W. Bush. The perfect storm began to develop over land in the Northern Hemisphere, right between the North Atlantic and North Pacific oceans. Big business, educational management organizations, rich people who didn't want to pay to support public schools, and business appointees to education-related government positions came together. These culprits created No Child Left Behind, thus designing a neglectful federal policy that continues to ruin public schooling for every child.

Now That We Have Tests, Let's Establish Performance Standards

Performance standards make schooling even more disgusting for children than content standards. *Performance standards* are established levels of success on tests or assignments. An example of a performance standard for physical education might be, "Every child must jump over the hurdle to pass third-grade physical education." Performance standards always sound foolish when we connect them to physical feats; but the business community and local politicians love to use the term *standard* when they stand at a podium in front of people. If only they understood what it means.

Performance standards are used to establish a minimum level of accepted success on tests. After the BRT had their wishes come true through content-standard adoption, they next sought performance standards for every child in America. NCLB language matched the needs of big businesspersons who didn't want to support public education. NCLB punishes students and teachers who don't meet a minimum score on reading and mathematics tests by closing the school and having it taken over by a private company.

These private companies run charter schools and are called *educational management organizations* (EMOs). EMOs are perhaps best represented by Edison Learning Incorporated, a company that gained control of numerous urban schools in the late 1990s and early 2000s. Other EMOs include companies such as the Knowledge Is Power Program (KIPP) or Achieve, who step in and try to change students' test scores by switching teachers, principals, and content, and usually providing less money to run the schools. (See chapter 8 on EMOs and charter schools.)

It would have been easy for anyone to predict that not all children and adolescents would succeed in "jumping the hurdle in third grade" or, in this case, receiving high enough scores on reading and mathematics tests to be *proficient* (the label NCLB utilized). As children continued to fail to meet performance standards, more charter schools suddenly opened in urban districts. As EMOs took over schools as charters, more testing materials were sold to ensure that students received the appropriate preparation for another round of tests.

Charter schools took over public schools, and big business reached its hand into public tax dollars through the charters. As more students failed to reach the performance standards, vouchers were proposed and sometimes approved to further alienate public schools and blame their teachers for the problems (see chapter 8). Public education has been hijacked by a few unsavory businesspersons, and NCLB is the bullet train pulling big business along for the best ride of its life at taxpayers' expense.

The political climate around 2002 that encouraged highly inappropriate measures for evaluating children and the bashing of public schools is best described by Emery's and Ohanian's creative lyrics to a song with which you might be familiar, "If You're Happy and You Know It":

> If you cannot find Osama, test the kids.
> If the market hurt your Mama, test the kids.
> If the CEOs are liars
> Putting schools on funeral pyres,
> Screaming, "Vouchers we desire!"
> Test the kids.
> If you have no health insurance, test the kids
> Your retirement's a game of chance? Test the kids.
> If the GPA ain't growin'

And corporate greed ain't slowin'
And White House con is flowin'
Test the kids.
If your schools they are a crumbling, test the kids.
And the Congress it is a bumbling, test the kids.
CEOs want competition.
And public school demolition.
They're on a hunting expedition.
Test the kids.[13]

True to form, NCLB opened the door to one stark, unhealthy reality—measuring children each year would be the only way for the federal government to justify financially supporting children's and adolescents' learning. The floodgates opened, and business filled the gaps through every available policy created through NCLB.

Diane Ravitch, who had a miraculous awakening in her own thinking about the negative impact of business influence on education policy, notes in her 2010 book:

Each of the venture philanthropies (Gates, Walton, the Broad Foundation) began with different emphases, but over time they converged in support of reform strategies that mirrored their own experience in acquiring huge fortunes, such as competition, choice, deregulation, incentives, and other market-based approaches. These were not familiar concepts in the world of education, where high value is placed on collaboration.[14]

Policies that destroy the relationship between teachers and the communities in which they work deny parents opportunities to participate in their children's lives. NCLB policies have ripped schools away from professionals and placed them in the hands of corporate leaders lacking a philosophy of teaching, learning, and caring for children. The corporate fat cats are knee deep into education now, and their assault continues through the airways.

IGNORANT THOUGHTS FROM BUSINESSPERSONS

The *Wall Street Journal* runs articles regularly on education issues, and one has to wonder if this didn't become a part of their repertoire until after *A Nation at Risk*. In 2008, shortly after the election of President

Barack Obama, another icon of Wall Street, Louis Gerstner, Jr.—former CEO of IBM—decided to unleash his version of what we should do with public schools in America—namely, *abolish all local school districts except for about 70 of them.*[15]

Louis must have been very upset that a Democrat won the presidential election to offer such a drastic proposal. Does Gerstner want the local public school that your children or your grandchildren attend to be abolished? It's difficult to imagine how his background experiences can be used to promote education policy for professional educators or researchers who spend their days helping America's kids grow. An example from his economic life is that he received an offer of $21 million to take the CEO job at IBM approximately 10 years ago.[16] Gerstner is so far removed from the reality of everyday life for an average U.S. citizen that his solutions to educational issues are, at best, foolish ramblings.

Arne Duncan, secretary of education in the Obama administration, announced on a CNN education special in 2011 that the United States had 2 million high-skilled jobs that went unfilled and had to be shipped overseas because America didn't have enough graduates in mathematics and science to fill the positions.[17] It's improbable that those jobs were ever available to U.S. graduates because Gerstner and other business leaders often ship their companies' jobs overseas, where they likely aren't required to pay a minimum wage, pay for health insurance, or support public education. Perhaps Duncan should speak to Gerstner and the BRT about what they can do to decrease unemployment in the United States.

More Intruders—With No Educational Know-How, but Plenty of Cash

Another high-profile spender that influences local politicians and federal representatives is the Eli and Edythe Broad Foundation, which spends millions each year to support training noneducators (businesspersons, attorneys, and other noneducators) to become school principals and higher-level administrators in charter schools. These alleged "professional educators" pose as experts on teaching and advocate for longer school days and years while trying to dismantle the tax base in urban centers that supports schooling for all students. These billionaires masquerade as education experts, touting generally unresearched solutions to public school policy while promoting certain candidates for public office who will support their views and financial interests—meaning an opportunity to avoid paying more taxes.[18]

Rita Beamish, who works for the Center for Public Integrity, reported in May of 2011 on the amount of money some entrepreneurs were pouring into their pet education projects in attempts to influence federal and state education policy—and not generally in a positive way. These are the "donations" for the following "Moneymen," as Beamish calls them, over recent years:

- Michael and Susan Dell—$400 million for charter schools, school leadership programs, and access to advanced placement classes;
- Eli and Edythe Broad—$440 million on leadership training, charter schools, and teacher effectiveness;
- Walton Family—$538 million for charter schools and voucher programs;
- Bill and Melinda Gates—$3 billion on smaller high schools, charter schools, and researching merit pay for teachers.[19]

Often this money supports political candidates who share the billionaires' beliefs about how schools should operate. Unfortunately, their theories are poorly planned, lack a research base, and never work in real schools, so that they do more to damage public education than help. Beamish makes it clear in her reporting of the analyses on these foundations' efforts that they have failed to have a positive impact on education in America. That won't, however, prevent them from spending money to influence public school policy and reduce their tax responsibility.

It was revealed in 2011 that the billionaire Koch Brothers provided several thousand dollars to Wisconsin governor Scott Walker's campaign coffers. The reason the information was so revealing was that Walker attempted to dismantle the collective-bargaining rights of teachers, firefighters, and other public employees as soon as he took office. The proposed legislation was seen as a vicious attack on the value of public employees.

You might wonder, as education writer Ravitch did, about corporate interest in public affairs, particularly the monetary influence of the Walmart Corporation:

> Why should it be surprising that a global corporation that has thrived without a unionized workforce would oppose public sector unions? Nor should it be surprising that the Walton Family Foundation has an ideological commitment to the principle of consumer choice and to an unfettered market, which by its nature has no loyalties and disregards Main Street, traditional values, long-established communities, and neighborhood schools.[20]

Ravitch's comments echo the concerns that much of the business community isn't interested in supporting local public schools. They *are* interested in dismantling them or making a buck from children and adolescents who are required to go to school.

The Free Ride for Big Business

What does business have to gain from bashing public schools? A short history lesson might explain it all. During the 1940s–1960s, urban centers—for example, New York, Chicago, Detroit, and Philadelphia— were booming business locations. Corporations had their executive offices there as well as their factories. Those corporations were responsible for paying their share of property, income, and payroll taxes, like you currently are—taxes that supported the public schools in their cities and states. Any teacher who wanted to make almost a decent living moved into the city to teach, where the most money could be made.

During the late 1960s and early 1970s, big business decided to leave the cities. They took the tax base, the jobs, and the upper-, upper-middle-, and middle-class families out. All they left were the buildings, many of which are still standing in urban centers—eyesores to all. What started shortly after the mass exodus of big business from the cities was a game by states to try to lure big businesses back into some locations in the state—usually into the suburbs, where bedroom communities used to exist; these were soon to become "business and bedroom communities."

The game was this: state legislatures bidding for big businesses felt compelled to offer incentives for businesses to return and build in their states, thus bringing in the promise of more jobs for their citizens. State legislators decided to give up a valuable source of income to get businesses back—tax revenues from income, real-estate, personal-property, and local taxes. The promise was this: if you build your drug company, auto-manufacturing plant, or Wall Street–trading company in our state, we'll waive your responsibility for paying a number of taxes for 10 years.

One gubernatorial candidate from Michigan promised in 2010 that any corporation that moved into the state and decided to take over a previously owned abandoned building would pay "no sales tax, corporate income tax, real property tax, personal property tax, or any other state or local tax for up to 12 years."[21] Imagine, if that occurred in several states (as it has), how much revenue a state would be giving up for its children who attend public schools? Someone has to pick up the tax burden left by big business not paying its share—that would be you, private citizens receiving an increase in local taxes to support local schools.

It appears, as you've guessed by now, that businesses don't want to be subjected to the same taxes that individual citizens pay. These *less than altruistic* entrepreneurs are interested in dismantling the public schools so they can stick more money into their pockets. It's not likely that their actions will translate into greater pay for a majority of the employees. Who benefits from businesses not paying taxes? The CEOs such as Gerstner, formerly of IBM, who wants to dismantle the public schools your children attend.

These types of tax incentives exist in at least half the states. In some states it's real-estate- or sales-tax breaks; others offer businesses the opportunity to opt out of state income taxes for a few years. Big businesses are searching for another loophole or genuine gift from any state they can find.

These actions translate into business leaders inserting their opinions about what our schools should look like and how to continually reduce their operating budgets. Businesses attempt to lower their tax burden by advocating negative educational practices that affect children and teachers, such as

- increasing class sizes;
- eliminating teacher unions that might encourage paying teachers a decent salary;

- encouraging the use of vouchers to provide state money to families to send their children to private schools, so the public schools receive less revenue;
- increasing the number of tests that children take so that companies such as McGraw-Hill reap millions in reward;
- requiring graduation tests so that more students drop out of school, thus lowering the state and local education budgets and tax responsibilities;
- requiring "data gathering" so as to promote business products created to analyze data (IBM has a product that could help your local school—just ask!);
- discouraging teachers as effective evaluators of student growth, so that test companies' products are justified as the "only" option for determining student growth;
- proposing the elimination of paying teachers for receiving additional degrees and training (one of Bill Gates's new ideas [remember, that guy *without* a college degree]);
- implementing merit pay, so that teachers aren't paid for their experience and the many immeasurable successes with students; instead, only a few receive more money, so that it won't cost the business community so much in taxes.

A simple Google search regarding the relationship between the Bush family and the McGraws of the McGraw-Hill Testing Company reveals a cozy and long-term friendship. It shouldn't be any surprise that the NCLB legislation passed in 2002, during the first George W. Bush administration, required more testing among younger children in every state.

Taxpayers are responsible for funding the out-of-control costs for these unnecessary tests (see chapter 9). McGraw-Hill and other companies, such as Kaplan, Sylvan Learning, TestU, and Princeton Review, are cashing in on selling your local schools the tests themselves, guidebooks to state exams, textbooks allegedly aligned to the state tests, and online programs that train kids to do well on test items. As is often the line when someone has you under his or her control, the politicians, test companies, and test-prep-material companies have a phrase for taxpayers—often unwilling consumers of their products: *Who's your daddy?*

Teachers no longer rush to sign a lucrative contract in U.S cities—because the tax base is long gone, as are the reasonable salaries that left with big business. The taxes that could support education in urban areas have vanished; and no one seems interested in equalizing state funding formulas so that all children in your state would receive equal funding for their education (see chapter 10).

Educational research articles are not published by businesspersons such as Gerstner or Bill Gates in the journals that define valid education research. No journalist from *Newsweek* or *Time* has ever conducted genuine educational research, and no U.S. secretary of education has ever been a researcher in the field. Americans should not take these people seriously when they write about proposals for how to fix public schools. They're not experts—they don't even know enough to be called amateurs, and they fail to cite accurate information when they do write.

The painful and dangerous reality is that the businesspersons, the philanthropists, and the candidates they support through campaign donations are altering the way America educates children. Their inaccurate ideas, faulty beliefs, and influence on state and federal policies are harming children and adolescents in previously never-imagined ways. Ravitch notes a major flaw in giving so much authority over education policy to businesses in her book *The Death and Life of the Great American School System: How Testing and Choice Are Undermining Education*:

> There is something fundamentally antidemocratic about relinquishing control of the public education policy agenda to private foundations run by society's wealthiest people; when the wealthiest of these foundations are joined in common purpose, they represent an unusually powerful force that is beyond the reach of democratic institutions.[22]

Jefferson's primary reason for initiating a system of education for all U.S. citizens was to promote and encourage engagement by all in the democratic process. Gates, Broad, the Koch Brothers, and the Waltons are poised to take public education away from local communities.

REALITY . . . PLEASE! WHAT THE RESEARCH REALLY TELLS US

The Sandia Report—Hidden from View

Those who like mysteries and the idea of an official cover-up will appreciate this story of how George H. W. Bush administration officials purposely hid essential findings that supported U.S. public education. Bush, president from 1989 to 1993, decided initially to take a more honest approach than Reagan on education issues by commissioning a group of independent researchers to study how public education was doing in the United States at the time.

The research was conducted in 1990 by officials working at Sandia National Laboratories, a branch of the Department of Energy and the Atomic Energy Commission, and the resulting report was released under the title *Perspectives on Education in America*. Bush had commissioned the report because he was the self-proclaimed "education president."

The study revealed many positive findings about America's public schools based on numerous measures, as described by educational researcher and writer William Smith:

> The Sandia researchers examined dropout statistics, test scores, international comparisons, educational funding, and numerous other measures. When possible, they compared data over time. As Mary McClellan (1994) reported, the Sandia researchers stated, "To our surprise, on nearly every measure, we found steady or slightly improving trends."[23]

The most significant finding was that the public schools in America were actually doing fine, as noted by the authors in the line, "There is no system-wide crisis."[24]

The intrigue began when the deputy secretary of education at the time, David Kearns, a former CEO of IBM, was quoted as saying to the Sandia researchers, "You bury this or I'll bury you." Reporters for *Education Week*, a weekly newsletter for educators, revealed a comment that surfaced from the release of the document to Bush administration officials: "Sandia researchers were told that the report would never see the light of day, and that they had better be quiet."[25]

Bush-administration officials suppressed the report with the excuse that it would undergo peer review. Bush officials obviously had enough authority and power to prevent the Sandia Report from being released until it appeared in its entirety in the well-respected *Journal of Educational Research* in 1993. By then, of course, President Clinton had taken office.

The Sandia Report was an opportunity for a federal representative and government leader to finally support the gains, successes, and positive aspects of America's public schools. Instead, a report was buried—some believe to prevent taxpayers from supporting their local public schools.

Other Little-Known, Significant Findings about Our Public Schools

It seems that some people think the Scholastic Aptitude Test (SAT) administered to college-bound students might provide valid information on the effectiveness of America's public schools. This is faulty thinking because most adolescents and/or adults don't go to college. If one were searching for an indicator of U.S. education success, SAT data wouldn't be a wise choice. The SAT only measures learning for those students interested in going to college—and only to colleges on the East Coast or West Coast, since college-bound students in the Midwest take the ACT test.

Suppose, though, that someone believed the SAT was an indicator of the strength or weaknesses of U.S. public education on the East and West coasts. The test is not designed to permit everyone to do well, as are most standardized tests, because it is a norm-referenced test. Those types of tests are specifically designed so that if too many students begin to perform well, then questions must be made more difficult to ensure that only a select few do well and most everyone else falls in the middle range of ability.

The first group of students who took the tests were from the states of New York and Massachusetts, and the tests were normed just before 1940 from these particular students—who were White and male and had attended private college-preparatory high schools. *Norm-referenced* refers to the fact that the tests are initially given to a select set of students who share certain traits, and future scores for the test are ranked and established based on how well this initial population of students scored.

The first SAT would be influenced by the fact that the test was *normed* or scored based on the abilities of a few privileged individuals. Imagine how different that population was from the current high school test takers. Even in 1996, the SAT test takers included over a million students, of whom 58 percent were female, 71 percent were White, 25 percent came from homes with yearly incomes of less than $30,000, and 83 percent attended public schools. The average mathematics SAT score went to its lowest point in 1982 (492), then rose from year to year to a high of 520 in 2005. The average verbal SAT score also went down to its lowest level in 1983 (only five points lower), but then rose to its high in 2004 and 2005.[26]

It's amazing that SAT scores could remain nearly constant when one considers how diverse the population of college students is now compared to 75 years ago—a sure sign of the successes of public education over the past several decades. The Department of Labor announced in 2007 that among 18- to 24-year-olds nationally, 40 percent were enrolled in two- or four-year colleges. That's progress that makes a difference in the lives of American citizens, thanks to public schools.

Tests of public school students have increased from year to year at the state level; but one test, the National Assessment of Educational Progress (NAEP), is a national reading and mathematics test that has been given to certain public school students since 1971. Bracey reported that scores in both reading and mathematics have increased steadily or stayed the same for nearly 35 years.[27] Instead of seeing this as a negative change, Americans should embrace the relatively small changes as a fairly positive finding.

The immigration rate of the 1980s and 1990s exceeded that of every other decade in American history other than the period between 1905 and 1915. The influx of this many immigrant families creates innumerable challenges for public school teachers. Yet those NAEP scores still remained stable, despite the influx of hundreds of thousands of English-language learners.

The NAEP and SAT scores are not very accurate measures of genuine learning in classrooms across the United States; yet if critics are seeking any version of truth, why aren't they willing to admit the relative success of public education in the United States based on these data? As is evident in comments mentioned above by many high-profile pundits, the facts about public schools are rarely known, understood, or studied carefully enough to reveal the truth.

The number and frequency of inaccurate comments constitute a definite liability to public schools and the families that depend on their neighborhood schools to promote success for children. In addition, more serious implications exist as a result of these inaccurate public appraisals of America's public schools.

WHY THE TRUTH MATTERS

Public education is a defining and unique American symbol of democracy. Without the opportunity for every U.S. citizen to receive a free and appropriate education, the issues we start wars over, the international causes we support with rhetoric, and the monetary costs we endure to support many countries' development of democracy are feckless ventures. When Americans support the development of democratic governments elsewhere, they're putting their own soldiers'/citizens' lives at risk so that others can experience the American way of life.

Studies of other countries' attempts to replicate our system fail because the United States has adopted an educational system that prides itself on inclusion: everyone is entitled to the benefits of being educated fully until the age of 18, not merely the upper class, not merely Caucasians, and not merely those with "adequate" physical and mental health. When our country goes to war, we're fighting for democracy that supports our public education system.

Any attempts by businesspersons, politicians, movie producers, or the wealthy to dismantle the U.S. public school system via privatization, less funding, or inaccurate verbal attacks weaken the very core of what it means to be a U.S. citizen. The current trend of bashing public schools and dishonoring their teachers has the following negative effects:

- It discourages support from key government officials—presidents, Congresspersons, governors, and state legislators.

- It relieves legislators at both the state and federal levels from providing the necessary taxes and funding to provide adequate support to promote every child's growth.[28]
- It discourages teachers from continuing in the profession.
- It encourages local communities to reduce education budgets.

Continuous attacks on our public schools lead to a less-educated electorate, and results of that outcome are easy to predict:

- a smaller proportion of the total population prepared for productive lives;
- a rise in the prison population;
- a rise in the number of adults and children on monetary public assistance;
- a rise in the unemployment rate;
- a rise in the number needing federal assistance for medical insurance, retirement, and Medicaid.

WHO CAN WE TRUST TO TELL US THE TRUTH?

William E. Smith notes accurately in his 2009 book, *Restoring Honor to Public Schools*,

> No group of professionals is more underrepresented in decision making about their own area of expertise than educators. The exclusion extends not only to teachers, but to administrators and educational scholars as well. As a result, the people who are shaping public school policy in America have little or no knowledge about educational research or practice.[29]

Teaching is a profession. Being a *professional* means that a teacher is college educated in the science of how to meet students' cognitive, social, emotional, and physical needs. Teachers aren't like people in other public-supported careers, such as police officers, firefighters, or mail carriers—the training and learning required to be a professional educator is supported by researchers, and has been for decades.

Random adults searching for a career cannot just become teachers with two weeks of training. The Teach for America program is an example of a failed attempt to take non–education majors from universities and make them teachers, with a minimum of training—maybe five weeks at best (see chapter 4). Anyone who has had the opportunity of taking a three-month-long teaching assignment knows the responsibilities of doing teaching right and how difficult it is—every day!

Occasionally I read an article in a newsmagazine in which the authors use the word *reformer* to describe someone who frequently speaks about education issues: people like Bill Gates, Davis Guggenheim, or Michelle Rhee. When education issues arise in the press, Rhee is frequently interviewed by national news organizations, despite her limited background knowledge of the research on teaching, learning, child development, and teacher education. Now Rhee, who has never been certified as a teacher, has no education degree, and taught for a mere three years, has a new agenda that is another quick fix to improve U.S. schools.

After being fired from her position as head of DC schools in the fall of 2010 by the new mayor of Washington, DC, Rhee decided to start her own organization to fix public schools. Among their goals: "taking on special interests, such as teachers' unions, . . . dismantling teacher tenure and seniority-based incentives, . . . [and] using standardized tests to evaluate teachers."[30] None of these goals is supported by research to improve teaching or learning. I foolishly thought that Rhee would develop a clearer understanding of the meaning of tenure after she was fired immediately from the DC schools without the hearing or due process to which tenure entitles teachers; but, alas, her new organization proposes eliminating tenure.

Rhee's views of the realities of teaching, the challenges that poverty creates for children, and the limitations placed on teachers for ensuring academic success for every child are at best parochial. Her comments indicate the views of someone who is highly naive about the real life of teachers. She's not an education reformer—she'd be better described as a high-profile "actress" who's been thrust into the spotlight by the media and is likely receiving "donations" from Gates, the Walton family, and the Broad Foundation to attack public schools as she continues her speaking tour. Professional educators and educational researchers see the description *reformer* as a false label for Gates, Rhee, and Guggenheim.

PROFESSIONAL EDUCATORS AND EDUCATIONAL RESEARCHERS: REAL REFORMERS

To be considered a reformer in the education profession, one has to be a researcher with the credentials and background knowledge to influence the lives of children and adolescents. Many reformers exist in education, researchers who have made an impact on teaching and learning: John Dewey, Robert Slavin, Gloria Ladson-Billings, Linda Darling-Hammond, James Beane, Nancie Atwell, Donald Graves, Lucy Calkins, Howard Gardner, and David Perkins, to name a few.

Rhee and Gates aren't making the kinds of contributions the trusted researchers mentioned above have to our profession—they're more *false prophets* than *reformers*. Their views of teaching and learning demonstrate a lack of extensive teacher training and ignorance of the educational-knowledge research base.

Along with Gates and Rhee, others who also lack a comprehensive understanding of the teaching profession are most journalists, TV-news anchors, politicians, presidents, business leaders, CEOs, movie producers, U.S. secretaries of education, ministers, and everyone else who has *never* taught children or adolescents. So which resources should journalists, education-department personnel, news broadcasters, and politicians actually read?

The list of recognized educational researchers and experts who have no political agenda is small among those in the public eye; but those of us in education know whom we can trust to deliver accurate information on this critical issue—genuine truth about our public schools. They don't support the status quo—they research and reveal the truth about what matters in the classroom. The list is not extensive, but among the heroes of public school teachers and educational researchers are

- David Berliner, a renowned educational researcher from the University of Arizona, and coauthor of *The Manufactured Crisis: Myths, Fraud, and the Attack on America's Public Schools*; and *Collateral Damage: The Effects of High Stakes Testing on America's Schools*;
- Alfie Kohn, an education realist and writer, and author of numerous books, including *The Homework Myth: Why Our Kids Get Too*

Much of a Bad Thing; and *The Case against Standardized Testing: Raising the Scores, Ruining the Schools*;

- Richard Allington, an internationally respected reading researcher and author of *Big Brother and the National Reading Curriculum: How Ideology Trumped Evidence*;
- William E. Smith, a public school educator, former college professor, and author of *Restoring Honor to Public Schools*;
- Susan Ohanian, who helped us challenge the idea of standards when she wrote *One Size Fits Few: The Folly of Educational Standards*, and who cowrote *Why Is Corporate America Bashing Our Public Schools?*
- Linda Darling-Hammond, a renowned educational researcher, former president of the American Educational Research Association, executive director of the National Commission on Teaching and America's Future, author of dozens of publications about education, and author of *The Flat World and Education: How America's Commitment to Equity Will Determine Our Future.*
- The late Gerald W. Bracey, an educational researcher and fact-checker who wrote several books that provide absolute, accurate data on public schools: *The War against America's Public Schools*; *Setting the Record Straight*; and his last book, *Education Hell: Rhetoric vs. Reality.*

ADVANTAGES OF ATTENDING PUBLIC SCHOOLS

Almost every adult has an opinion about whether private or public schools are better for a child's K–12 education. The debate about private versus public is a rather moot point in most of the nation because there are so few private schools compared to all the public schools. Remember that 89 percent of U.S. students attend public schools.

The reasons provided for believing that private schools are better than local public schools are rarely based on accurate data or information. If accurate data were used, the public schools would overwhelmingly be the best choice due to several significant factors that noneducators fail to recognize or comprehend. Charter schools are so unique that a separate chapter exists for the details on their organization and questionable value to state taxpayers and the children who attend them.

Stories always exist about children switching from a private school to a public, and the opposite situation, in which someone found it necessary to leave the local public schools and attend a private one instead. On the East Coast, private and parochial schools are much more numerous than in the middle of the United States. Suburbs near major metropolitan areas generally offer many alternatives to local public schools. Approximately 40 percent of the school-age children within my public school district boundaries attend some sort of private or parochial school—an unusually high percentage compared to most suburban and urban areas of the United States.

Many charter schools also exist in urban areas. Charters are relatively new on the educational landscape, and they are a combination of public tax dollars and private funds and are regulated by state laws that govern their operation. Unlike under public school law, each state's laws for charter schools are quite different, and this has an impact on their effectiveness (see Chapter 8).

In almost all American towns, rural areas, and suburbs, the local public school is the only option. Public schools are in every corner of the United States: a total of approximately 99,000 schools with almost 50 million students, according to the latest data from the National Center for Education Statistics (NCES). Some public schools in remote areas of the western states are one-room schoolhouses, with one teacher providing an education for a few students at varying grade levels. Most public schools obviously have much larger populations.

PUBLIC SCHOOLS REQUIRE CERTIFIED TEACHERS

The greatest difference between public and private schools is what matters the most: certified teachers. Every state has certification procedures and guidelines, and every public school teacher must be certified. Certified teachers are not required in private or parochial schools, and not all teachers are required to be certified in charter schools (check your state charter school guidelines for details). As detailed in chapter 4, certification is the critical trait of effective teachers that cannot be ignored if one is searching for teaching excellence.

Some political pundits, businesspersons, and recently even some governors have suggested that certification is *unnecessary*; but they are completely unaware of the research on certified teachers' significance to students' successful learning. There is no debate among educational researchers about the powerful influence on children and adolescents of certified teachers.

The combination of receiving a college education and an emphasis on many educational courses can never be overlooked or ignored in the teaching profession. Teachers' content-area knowledge is certainly needed for them to be able to respond intelligently to students' questions; however, expert content knowledge is never enough to be a successful educator.

What Certified Teachers Learn before Obtaining a Job

Certified teachers have learned about the following, as is critical to their success in helping students grow academically:

- the developmental processes of children and adolescents—cognitive, social, physical, and emotional needs—that must be considered before learning can occur;
- educational psychology, taught in courses that emphasize how students' brains work and how teachers can use this information to positively affect learning;
- evaluation and measurement, taught in courses that provide teachers with strategies for determining what students know and how to use the information to improve learning;
- research on the primary reasons that teachers are unsuccessful—classroom-management strategies that help teachers create healthy learning environments;
- the many teaching strategies, and their effectiveness with students—this field is also called the science of teaching (pedagogy) and is critical to teachers' success;
- experiences in actual classrooms, which college education majors gain through field experiences, with teachers and university supervisors providing guidance for how to improve—this includes a student-teaching experience, in which the college senior is paired with a professional classroom teacher and practices teaching, with constant feedback each day of the semester.

Anything less than these college experiences for teachers in training denies children and adolescents access to a well-trained professional educator.

Examples of Uncertified Educators

For those who have attended college, perhaps the greatest evidence of the meaning and value of trained, certified teachers lies in the *ineffective* teaching quite common at universities. Universities value advanced degrees, and college professors are hired based on the primary criterion of having received an advanced degree in their content area. But knowledge is *not* enough to be a successful educator. Anyone who has attended college recalls the miserable teaching that could emanate from professors in any discipline. College professors may be experts in geology, history of the Western Hemisphere, women's studies, advanced algebra, or economics, to name a few disciplines; but, they may simultaneously be possibly the worst teachers one has ever experienced. College professors with terminal degrees in a content area don't magically become effective professional educators due merely to their expert knowledge in their fields.

If public school educators at every grade level were hired based only on being an expert in a field of study, high school graduation rates would probably match those of universities—about 63 percent.[1] Instead, average graduation rates for public schools are closer to 90 percent. This percentage is based on the *status dropout rate* determined by the percentage of 16- through 24-year-olds who are not enrolled in high school and who lack a high school credential. A high school credential includes a high school diploma or equivalent credential such as a General Educational Development certificate.[2]

Certified teachers are trained to and know *how* to teach, not merely *what* to teach. Uncertified teachers are permitted in and are sometimes a majority in private, parochial, and charter schools. Most parochial schools do not require teachers to be certified (see chapter 4). Private schools also do not require certified teachers; and, as noted, charter-school laws differ from state to state. Some states only require half of the teachers to be certified at charter schools, other states require 75 percent certification, and a few states require that all charter teachers be certified.

PROVIDING SUPPORT FOR STUDENTS WITH SPECIAL NEEDS

Students who are gifted, autistic, have a learning disability, or face social and emotional challenges; or who have physical disabilities, Asperger's syndrome, Down syndrome, fetal alcohol syndrome, mental retardation, or other low-IQ challenges are permitted by law to attend and receive appropriate educational services in public schools. In essence, every child in America is entitled to a free and appropriate education regardless of any learning challenge.

Federal Public Law 94-142 was first passed in 1975, mandating these services for students with special needs at public schools, and it has been reauthorized several times since. That's a pretty tall order for schools in your neighborhood, yet these services are offered daily in the public schools.

Public schools make accommodations for students with severe different-learning needs, as well as for those with specific needs for help in reading or mathematics. Reading specialists are available at most public schools across the United States, working with children through their schooling careers from kindergarten through twelfth grade. Students may have one of several learning disabilities, from dyslexia to dysnomia to dyscalculia, and the public schools in every neighborhood have teachers trained to assist these children.

Perhaps you know of a child who is academically gifted. In some states, *giftedness* is determined by a specific intelligence quotient (IQ) test score of 130 or above, and your local public school is there to provide for these students' learning needs. Maybe your child has specific physical disabilities, for which your local school district must also provide assistance.

BARRIERS TO ATTENDING PRIVATE SCHOOLS

In private schools, students are not entitled to receive any of the services for students with special needs, and, in fact, these special services seldom exist in private schools. Often private schools require high IQ or achievement-test scores for children to be admitted. A few years ago, a neighbor mentioned that her second-grade daughter, who was attending a private elementary school at the time, would be getting tutoring for mathematics since her math scores on an achievement test were too low for her acceptance into another private all-girls school. Her daughter's acceptance at the new private school was contingent on specific high test scores.

Another local private school noted the following information on its website, regarding who can attend:

> [This school] admits the best-qualified applicants without regard to religious, national, or racial background. When selecting applicants, the Admission Committee considers a number of factors. In addition to admission testing, school achievement, and a classroom visit, the Committee takes into account the student's ability to handle college preparatory work and to show good citizenship.[3]

As if the high academic standards are not enough, the child/adolescent must also "show good citizenship" in order to be admitted.

Public schools can't deny acceptance to children or adolescents with low test scores, a learning disability, a physical disability, autism, a reading difficulty, mental retardation, or "bad" citizenship. Another private school noted this on its website:

> 1st through 5th grade applicants take an independent psychological test which can be administered at one of several different agencies which are familiar with [this school]. Applicants for 6th–12th grade take a standardized admission test, the ISEE (Independent School Entrance Exam) or the SSAT (Secondary School Admission Test).[4]

Some children and adolescents have emotional and social disabilities. Their behaviors can be unpredictable, and they are often in trouble at school and with the law. Private schools can expel these students immediately. Where will they go when they are thrown out of their private schools?

Public school educators know these troubled students will be placed in their classrooms and provided the assistance required to help them grow and improve. These students are difficult to teach, but teachers are trained via certification at the universities to handle these challenges. The testing services, additional teaching aides, and special education teachers are all a part of the state and federal mandates to help these students at public schools. You cannot expect this kind of comprehensive support from the private or parochial schools, and sometimes you cannot even expect it from the charter schools in your state.

One more aspect of attending private and parochial schools is the cost of tuition. For six private and parochial schools within a 20-mile radius of Philadelphia, tuition costs *started* at $18,000 a year for kindergarten and averaged $28,000 for each year of high school. All that money should entitle children to certified teachers, at least; but it doesn't necessarily, depending on school or state policies.

Multiple Choices for Curricular Interests

High school should provide a variety of curricular choices, that is, many opportunities to study topics that interest adolescents. Local public schools offer many opportunities for students at all levels of academic ability.

Some students are interested in auto mechanics more than trigonometry; hair-salon training rather than Shakespeare II; anatomy rather than physics; advanced band/orchestra as opposed to vocal music; or history of the 20th century as opposed to Advanced Placement (AP) history. The choices are many, and the public schools offer the most varied opportunities to match one's interests and abilities with the appropriate academic career track. Students are able to choose between pursuing a career in a hair salon and entering a traditional four-year college.

Public high school guidance counselors provide advice and support to students as they make decisions about their classes or choose possible colleges to apply to in their junior and senior years. Public funding of schools provides the resources for hiring a variety of content-area teachers; obtaining required materials, from art supplies to beakers for chemistry; and providing advanced training for teachers who choose to teach AP courses. Public schools are able to offer so many choices due to the local interests among community members and the influence adults can have on *their* local public schools.

High school students are provided with all levels of courses in different disciplines. This means a chance to take Algebra II instead of trigonometry, or AP English rather than business English, based on academic strengths and interests. Private schools often place every student in the same career-track courses because only one or two possible tracks are offered.

Financial resources matter. Money in public schools emanates from the local community and is used to meet the needs of the residents in that community. In many U.S. communities, adolescents' educational interests and needs are quite diverse, so that schools are forced to offer both trade/career routes—that is, courses such as carpentry or auto repair *and* AP or honors courses for the college-bound student. Approximately 55 percent of U.S. high schools offer AP courses for students, and the federal government recently allocated funding for the development of more AP courses in public schools.[5]

Disadvantages of Small Schools

Many parents choose to send their children to private schools so that their children will have the opportunity to be in smaller classes. Smaller class size does make a difference, as long as students are with certified teachers. Trading larger classes for uncertified teachers can be a costly decision. Smaller high schools may offer greater opportunities for involvement for adolescents. Some urban school districts have attempted to create small learning communities within their large high schools, to help students be recognized and have their needs identified and met in a smaller venue.

Bill Gates jumped on the small-school bandwagon initiative from 2000 to 2008 by contributing $2 billion to several schools across the United States, in an effort to make the high schools smaller.[6] What Gates didn't understand was that schools that are too small don't have the resources needed to offer what many larger public schools offer, such as

- advanced courses in mathematics and science;
- electives;
- advanced placement courses;
- career and technical education.[7]

One could add to this list a whole host of extracurriculars, from band to theater to athletic teams.

Middle and high school extracurricular programs provide adolescents with many opportunities to experiment with and begin to find specific nonacademic activities that match their interests and talents. Extracurriculars include a chance to participate in theater, dance, art, orchestra, band, and other clubs (e.g., technology, chess, cheerleading). Athletic activities often provide the only motivation for some students to attend school, and they exist for both males and females at all grade levels after sixth grade in most public schools.

Private schools in the Philadelphia area generally offer the same variety of athletic teams as the public schools; but they are limited in the opportunities they provide to students in the junior high or middle schools due to a lack of resources for coaches and equipment, and limited space for gyms and athletic fields.

Herein lies the problem with many private and parochial small schools. With fewer financial resources, fewer teachers are hired, and the result of a school's having a small student body is that there are fewer opportunities available for private school students than are offered to public school students in larger schools. U.S. public schools are ultimately designed as comprehensive units, providing opportunities for every child and adolescent in the local community. Private, parochial, and charter schools do not have the same responsibility to local community members, and generally that restricts the effectiveness of those private entities.

THE BEST TEACHERS OBTAIN POSITIONS IN PUBLIC SCHOOLS

The other most obvious difference between private and public schools is teacher talent. Private and parochial schools have a bad reputation for paying teachers poorly. America's best teachers take jobs in public schools, where the pay is often 50–60 percent greater than salaries at private and parochial schools. The list of private school teachers who are certified seeking positions in the local public schools is long, since they seek to earn better salaries.

Related to the private school/public school pay discrepancy is the issue of pay differences between urban public school teachers and their counterparts in suburban public schools. Recently, education pundits and some politicians have publicly announced that better teacher talent might be drawn to urban schools if they were paid more money. If one believes money matters in attracting better teacher talent, then it follows that the best teachers are in public schools.

IF YOU THINK EDUCATION IS EXPENSIVE . . .

A visit to Washington, DC, affords one the opportunity to see the Internal Revenue Service (IRS) building. The following words are etched on the side of the building: "Taxes are what we pay for civilized society." The exact level of *civilization* Americans desire is certainly controversial from time to time.

The public might be reminded about the significance of those words on the IRS building when they hear about another group protesting against paying taxes. The fact is, federal and state taxes have been reduced considerably over the past few years. *USA Today* reported in the spring of 2011 that *U.S. citizens were paying the smallest share of income taxes since 1958.*[8] More specifically, the total of local, state, and federal taxes dropped to 23.6 percent of income. The tax rate was 27 percent from the 1970s until the 1990s.

Another way of comprehending one's tax rate is that someone with an income of $100,000 pays $23,600 in taxes in 2011, versus $28,700 in 2000 and $27,300 in 1990. Being *civilized* has gotten cheaper, despite the high costs consumers pay for every other product they purchase. We should see people standing in the streets applauding the government for reducing the tax burden, rather than protesting against paying more.

Beyond the guilt that tax protestors should demonstrate is the question begging to be asked: How could our tax burden be the lowest it's been since 1958? What does one gain as a result of paying taxes? Many advantages, from running water and flushing toilets to roads that come directly to driveways, among dozens of other perks that those from some other nations don't receive. Near the top of the list of advantages to paying taxes is access to a free, quality education for the citizens of each community.

A frequently seen bumper sticker is this one prompted by educators: "If you think education is expensive—try *ignorance*." In trying to imagine what *ignorance* would be like, one might picture images of the country of Haiti following the earthquake of 2010. A year following the quake, little had changed in the infrastructure of leveled buildings, and many residents were fighting off an outbreak of cholera spread due to living in tent cities in close proximity to one another, having poor quality water to drink, and poor sanitation conditions.

In the Haitian situation, ignorance prevents the community from meeting physical needs so long after the quake; ignorance prevents Haitian leaders from protecting residents from outbreaks of disease; ignorance prevents the pooling of financial resources to build sewer systems, water-treatment plants, and basic homes for the many displaced residents; and ignorance plays a part in not knowing how to start again.

One reporter noted, "Half of Haiti's children are not in school, nor were they before the 2010 earthquake. Most Haitians are not educated. Many can't read about how to add chlorine to their water or why they should not wash dishes, clothing and drink from open streams, which serve many as latrines and sewers."[9]

The events during and after Hurricane Katrina in New Orleans were pitiful, but not anywhere near as bad as the ignorance that exists in Haiti, and its effects on lives there. Public education made a difference in New Orleans because education lifts the lives of every resident in the United States through the advances that occur in our communities as a result of everyone being educated. Education may be costly—but not as costly as ignorance!

ARE YOU PAYING ENOUGH IN TAXES?

Taxes at the state and local level are the primary means of supporting local schools. In many states, personal-property taxes—the taxes levied on the assessment or value of one's home and attached property—are used to support one's community schools. Personal-property tax is more stable than sales or income taxes because it does not fluctuate as much when communities have recessions. When the community spends local tax dollars to improve or build schools, parks, and other structures, property values generally rise.

If you're like many Americans, the last accurate appraisal/assessment on your property may be 10–20 years old. Imagine that the house you've been making mortgage payments on is actually worth what you paid for it 20 years ago instead of the actual value of the home, which is what you'll sell it for when you're ready. It's difficult to imagine that most people won't receive at least 25 to 75 percent more for their houses when they sell them, compared to what they originally paid, if they've kept their houses for 10–20 years.

Despite those probable huge profit margins and the actual value of many homes today, local residents are not lining up outside the local courthouse to demand a more accurate tax assessment. Many residents continue to pay a fraction of the level of taxes that they should be paying to support their local schools, fire and police departments, and recreational services. Maybe residents shouldn't complain so much about that local property-tax assessment.

So, what happens to the personal-property tax dollars that are used for educational purposes? The majority of every tax dollar for education goes for staff salaries—superintendents, assistant superintendents, curriculum coordinators (perhaps 5–10 per district, depending on the number of schools), building principals, assistant principals, and teachers. This figure is about 80 to 85 percent of the total district expenditures.

This relatively high percentage often scares taxpayers, especially businesspersons, because the private sector's personnel budget is about half of this. Some reflection on the reason for the high percentage of money spent for salaries would be that schools aren't using raw materials to create a product, aren't shipping the product, and aren't advertising their product as businesses do. The *products* are children, and meeting their needs requires human resources—teachers, administrators, special-education personnel, and teacher aides.

The remaining 15 to 20 percent of the budget is highly regulated by state and federal laws. That money is spent on meeting building codes, testing requirements (see chapter 9), breakfast and lunch in many districts, and special-education services. Special-education services may involve additional transportation costs for students with special needs, teacher aides, technology to meet some students' special learning needs, and perhaps medical services for some students.

The percentages of local and state government monies provided to a school district are about equal to one another, at around 45 percent each, totaling 90 percent of the incoming funds. The remaining 10 percent comes from the federal government.[10] Federal funds are not always a predictable source of income, because they are based on Congress and the president agreeing to fund programs such as Title I for lower-socioeconomic-class students and allocating money for special-education programs and services as required by the Individuals with Disabilities Education Act.

Since 2002, the No Child Left Behind (NCLB) legislation has created much greater costs for U.S. public schools due to the testing requirements. Many state education budgets have increased considerably due to the frequent *underfunding* from the federal government as far as covering the required testing costs. Since the testing is required as a part of NCLB, states must tax more to cover the costs. Many critics have complained of the unfunded component of NCLB.

Some pundits and media broadcasters complain that Americans pay more for education every year, yet get nothing in return. This is based on believing that paying more should lead to higher student test scores. Once again, it is critical that taxpayers understand that *money being spent is for educating children and adolescents—not for raising their test scores*. Higher test scores is not an indication of investment gains or a definitive sign of educated children and adolescents.

Children are not stock options affected by the market pressures in China and Japan each week. They are not raw materials on a conveyor belt, waiting for a hammer and some glue to be added to magically create equally and perfectly sized widgets—or higher test scores. The raw materials that enter the halls of public schools are all from different lots and somehow of irregular shape, size, and tensile strength. Some can be easily manipulated and changed according to an adult's timetable; but most revert to their original shape and form when they leave the building each day, despite pressure from teachers.

Understanding the nature of children and adolescents and how that affects their learning is critical to preventing the faulty thinking that paying more taxes will magically increase test scores. Public educators want children to grow—but they can't provide a written guarantee on the side of the box (child) promising an increase in their reading scores—*or your money back*. Tying test scores to taxes is more than mere ignorance—it's dangerous to kids, because it leads to high-stakes testing situations that deny children the kinds of learning opportunities that actually lead to growth (see chapter 9).

The cost of educating children and adolescents will not go down any-time soon in the United States, for several reasons:

- More children and adolescents attend public school in the United States than ever before.
- More students are staying in school longer than previously, when dropout rates were higher. If more students stay in school longer, it will naturally be more expensive.
- Special-education laws have been expanded, requiring more re-sources to meet the needs of students with special needs.
- The costs associated with paying for services rise almost every year, so the services used to keep schools running (including electricity, heat, gas for buses, school lunches, books, and salaries) rise, as must the revenues to cover the costs.

How difficult is it to comprehend this scenario? The United States has more children in school than ever before. Therefore, more buildings are needed to house them; more buses to get them to and from school; more teachers to provide a quality education; more administrators to cover the new buildings; more books to educate them; more lunches to feed them; more nonteaching personnel to handle other school needs; and more extracurricular activities.

It shouldn't be a surprise that the cost of education is higher today than it was 30 years ago. The shocking aspect is the lack of tax revenue coming over the past 10 years. The Congressional Budget Office re-ported in 2006 "that one-third of recent federal income tax reductions have gone to the top 1 percent of income earners."[11] That is a whopping loss in income for state and federal governments. Who's going to pick up the slack?

You are—if you're not in that top 1 percent! Altering the tax code to relieve multimillionaires leaves the tax burden to lower-class families. Corporations are getting their tax breaks, too, as Everhart notes:

At the federal level, there has been a dramatic decline in the amount of the federal tax burden being paid by corporations, from 26% in 1950 to 10% in 2000. Data from other states reveal a similar trend. In 1970, corporations generated 45% of the state property tax revenue; some 30 years later, that percentage had declined to 16%. Indeed, in the state of

Oregon, through creative accounting schemes, some 70% of corporations pay the minimum corporate tax—a paltry $10.[12]

The first thing learned in macroeconomics at college is, "There's no such thing as a free lunch." Economists, Wall Street executives, big businesses, and politicians should apply that basic economic principle in understanding the necessity to fund public education in America. Education doesn't come for free, and the same is true for every other federal program that leads to Americans being *civilized*.

ADVANTAGES OF ATTENDING SCHOOL WITH DIVERSE POPULATIONS OF STUDENTS

Many Americans value the ethnic diversity that is found in many public schools. At my youngest daughter's local public school, three of her friends are all 100 percent of their ethnic heritage: one Colombian American, one South Korean American, and one Indian American. And her best friend is 50 percent mixed European American and 50 percent Persian American.

What can children learn from diverse friends? They learn about different ways of seeing the world, rather than merely seeing it from a western European view (a *Eurocentric* view). Children might hear stories from their friends' ethnically diverse parents about their recent struggles as immigrants. Students may experience a new way of handling conflict that differs from the American approach, which is often described as violent or aggressive. Children can listen to a folk story from another part of the world that has a different moral from the American stories they know.

Having ethnically diverse friends provides opportunities to listen to diverse languages and perhaps discover a need to learn a different language. The possibilities for new ways of seeing the world through the eyes of friends' ethnically diverse families are limitless. These advantages for personal growth can't be met through traditional schooling experiences in all-White schools where everyone has similar socioeconomic backgrounds. Many parents search for the same diversity in the student populations of the public schools that their children attend.

Teachers in any community have an opportunity to enlighten their students with their diverse backgrounds and experiences. Teachers often share stories about their travels and their diverse family backgrounds with students. Educators share a common goal for all of their students: that they will all leave the community for the outside world someday so as to develop a different view of *their* world.

In ethnically diverse schools, children receive some of that education—completely unplanned, yet so powerful an influence on their personal growth. These opportunities rarely exist in the small private schools across America. Understanding ourselves as U.S. citizens is much easier when we can share in the experiences of those who bring a diverse background to our communities and our schools. Those experiences are part of the *hidden curriculum*—that stuff that we really want our children to learn but that isn't in any of their textbooks.

Local Control: School Boards

Most people may not know the requirements to be eligible to be a school board member in their communities. It's not likely that most citizens have ever considered the question. Every parent in communities across the United States should know the criteria because school board decisions impact children's and adolescents' lives.

The only two criteria for being eligible for school board membership are residing within the school-district boundaries and having reached voting age. No other credentials are required. One doesn't need a college degree, one isn't required to have children attending the local public schools, one doesn't need a degree in education, and one can be absolutely clueless on education issues. School board members don't need to read the paper, watch the news, or read books. They merely need to live in the community where the schools are located, have enough interest to run for the position, and get elected.

School board elections vary from state to state, based on state law. School board members in almost all states are elected by the public. In a few other school districts, board members are appointed by the county commissioner; and in some urban communities, the mayor has control of the local schools and appoints a school board. If any community member can run for the school board, then the board has a possibility of representing a majority view of the community members.

How School Boards Reflect the Local Community

A majority of the school board members in the Dover Area School District of rural southeast Pennsylvania voted in 2004 to require high-school biology teachers in the district to read a statement regarding *intelligent design*, a label intended as a substitute for creationism, alongside the teaching of evolution in their classes. Board members who supported the intelligent-design addition to the curriculum believed in the value of teaching an alternative view of how humans inhabited Earth, and their perspectives must have reflected many fellow citizens' views.

Since the statement didn't reflect the Pennsylvania state-required content for biology, some teachers refused to read it. Several district parents of high school students filed suit in federal court *against* the idea of reading the intelligent-design comments. In the subsequent fall, 2005, school board elections, every one of the board members who had voted in favor of inserting intelligent design into the biology curriculum was ousted.

School board members are intended to represent the views of their communities. The makeup of school boards is unique in every district. The school boards where I taught in Iowa and Wisconsin, in rural areas, were composed of several farmers, some with college degrees. Where I attended school in the suburbs of Chicago, school board members are now almost all college educated, and their professions range from attorneys to businesspersons to stay-at-home parents.

In a community where I lived in semisuburban northern Virginia, just west of Washington, DC, the school board members were selected by the county board of commissioners, and included federal employees as well as farmers at the time. And in my current community in suburban Philadelphia, almost all of the school board members are attorneys, doctors, professors, or other professionals—all certainly college educated, many with advanced degrees.

It's clear that school board members generally reflect the local community in most cases—hopefully a majority of the local community demographics. Exceptions may exist in urban centers, where school boards *may not reflect* the majority of the community. The reason for the difference is that urban school policies are often controlled by local mayors, so the board members are likely to be chosen by the mayor and represent his or her preferences for school policy.

Hopefully, school board decisions aren't as controversial as the situation that occurred in Dover over intelligent design; yet it does represent how the makeup of school boards can be altered when a majority of community members don't agree with board decisions. The Dover situation clarifies how local perspectives can influence what gets taught (curricula) and how subjects are taught (instruction).

Certainly, curricular decisions ultimately reside with the school board; however, superintendents are the leaders of school districts, and their views are most often represented and supported by school boards. Board members take advice from the superintendent, primarily due to superintendents' educational training, experience, research background, and certification as educational administrators or supervisors.

When superintendents make decisions that are in conflict with the views of a majority of school board members, superintendents may be, and often are, fired. They are also fired when their ideas or actions don't reflect a community's values. Superintendents are sometimes fired when bond referenda are passed or not passed, when students' test scores are not high enough for some, or when they violate local laws, such as being arrested for driving under the influence of alcohol or drugs.

These checks and balances that exist in the public school domain are critical to the schools belonging to the local community. Decisions about what curricula are chosen, how much information children should learn, which athletics the district provides, how much money to spend on the band uniforms, whether new schools will be built, whether teachers will receive any raises or better insurance coverage, and whether to adopt new textbooks should belong to local community members. That's an advantage of public schools that is nonexistent in private schools.

When State and Federal Laws Steal Local Control

Local control of schools ensures that the community's will drives how children are educated, rather than leaving the decisions to a few with the loudest voices or the most money. Perhaps one of the tragedies of local public education since 1990 is the overbearing decision making by state and federal governments and the impact of recent state and federal legislation.

State governments began taking control over local school-district policy during the late 1980s and early 1990s, when each state adopted a mandated test for students in certain grade levels. The negative influence of testing on teacher practice and genuine student learning are almost impossible to describe (see chapters 9 and 10).

A new era of federal policy control of public schools was ushered in when the NCLB legislation was passed in Washington in 2002. Approved by an unprecedented majority of legislators and President Bush, the testing mandates and accompanying accountability for student test scores of NCLB have managed to wrestle considerable decision making from local school boards on curricular issues. Local school budgets are also highly affected, with test preparation, testing materials, test dates, and curricular materials to match tests predominating.

The successful future of local school decision making may be determined by the willingness and ability of local communities to stop the testing mandates and return schooling policies to local teachers, administrators, and parents. These teachers and school administrators most frequently also represent local citizens as graduates of their public schools and want the community to reflect their values for what it means to be well educated.

Seeing how NCLB has severely affected public school policy clarifies why the Founding Fathers left the responsibility for education to the states rather than permitting the federal government to intrude. That's the beauty of public schools—the manner in which they preserve and honor local community values and are governed by local residents who represent a variety of perspectives. These principles are upheld via public schools in every community. NCLB is threatening the previous local control of public schools. It's time for local communities to wrestle Washington politicians to regain control of their traditional educational rights and decision making.

8

CHARTER SCHOOLS AND VOUCHERS

Tax Dollars Down the Drain

Based on 19 studies, conducted in 11 states and the District of Columbia, there is no evidence that, on average, charter schools outperform regular public schools. In fact, there is evidence that the average impact of charter schools is negative.[1]

Business leaders like the idea of turning the schools into a marketplace where the consumer is king. But the problem with the marketplace is that it dissolves communities and replaces them with consumers. Going to school is not the same as going shopping. Parents should not be burdened with locating a suitable school for their child. They should be able to take their child to the neighborhood public school as a matter of course and expect that it has well-educated teachers and a sound educational program. . . . The market is not the best way to deliver public services.[2]

The state of Pennsylvania hosted a meeting of interested adults, which I attended, during the spring of 1996 to explain the state's new opportunity for starting schools that weren't entirely public or private schools; but instead called *charter schools*. Approximately 30 people attended the meeting, hosted by a representative from the state's education department. The representative explained how applications could be completed and submitted through local school boards to start charter schools.

After about 30 minutes of the presentation, several of those in attendance began arguing rather loudly about something. The conflict escalated quickly. Soon two of those present threatened one another, as if fisticuffs were going to erupt. How can adults who resolve disputes with their fists be responsible for operating a school?

My introduction to the charter school movement was a sign that the idea of anyone off the street having permission and support from the state legislature and governor to start and maintain the operation of a school was a poorly devised plan. Many educational researchers, if given the opportunity, could have predicted how the entire national charter-school movement reflects the poor judgment of the attendees at that initial meeting in the mid-1990s.

Every education policy approved by any legislative body must positively affect two critical components: the new policy must create an improvement in the act of teaching or cause an improvement in students' learning. If a policy does neither of those, it has no value to the schooling process. Charter schools and vouchers have no positive effect on teaching or learning.

WHAT ARE *VOUCHERS* AND *CHARTER SCHOOLS?*

Vouchers: Public Taxes Used to Send Students to Private Schools

Schooling in the future United States was reserved for the wealthy when this country was settled by Europeans. That reflected the beliefs of the northern Europeans in power here. The fact that only the wealthy were educated meant that only private schools existed, in which parents paid for their children to be educated. Fortunately, the philosophy of education for everyone followed a few decades after the United States became an independent entity.

Education for all has never been a free venture. Taxing individuals and companies began as a way of financing schools and sharing the costs once the public school process gained momentum. Parents who would rather their children go somewhere other than the local public school are permitted to continue sending their children to a private school; but these parents are not exempt from paying their share of the costs for educating other children in the community at the public schools.

A *voucher* is payment to a family from state or federal tax dollars to send children to a private or parochial school instead of a public K–12 school. Vouchers existed long before the introduction of charter schools in a few communities. Some states approved state tax dollars for parents to send their children to private schools as early as the late 1800s.

Some southern states approved vouchers for parents during the 1960s, after the *Brown v. Board of Education* Supreme Court decision had mandated that states provide equal opportunity for African Americans to attend formerly all-White schools. These southern-state vouchers promoted further segregation of schools in the South and were eventually deemed illegal. The federal government has approved the use of federal taxes to support vouchers for children in the Washington, DC, schools for several years, providing $7,500 to families to send their children to private and parochial schools at the expense of American taxpayers.

The idea of providing state tax dollars to families to send their children to private schools continues, with several states having joined the roster of those permitting taxes to be spent on vouchers. The theory is that children might receive a better education at a private school than they would at their local public school. Voucher programs are much more common in urban areas than they are in rural or suburban communities, so most communities are not affected by them, except when federal legislators approve them, as they often have.

Attempts by federal and state legislators to initiate vouchers occurred often during the 1990s and have been promoted frequently since. The successful passage of voucher laws is limited across the states, where they are more often voted down rather than approved by either state legislators or residents.

Some states and local urban communities permit vouchers to be paid to parents in urban areas to attend suburban schools on the outskirts of the city. These types of vouchers exist in St. Louis, Milwaukee, and Boston. Only a certain number of seats are available for students in the receiving schools. Lottery systems are used in these situations to determine who receives the vouchers. Boston reportedly has a waiting list of several thousand students each year seeking seats in suburban schools.[3]

Milwaukee led the way historically with vouchers in the early 1990s and has several thousand students who use vouchers to attend both private and other public schools based on choice. Over $100 million was spent on the program during the 2006–2007 academic year. Most of the costs are covered by Milwaukee-area residents paying additional taxes to support the program.

Vouchers for all U.S. children were first proposed by President George W. Bush in the original version of the No Child Left Behind Act (NCLB) of 2001. Legislators cut that from Bush's proposal, but Ohio representative John Boehner was adamant about leaving that part of the proposed bill alone, as a Catholic high school graduate himself. Bush tried again, and this time limited the proposal to six U.S. cities, but it failed to pass the legislature on this second attempt.

Bush finally proposed vouchers one more time for the DC schools only, and this time it was attached to a bill to keep the federal government running. The bill passed, giving DC residents the opportunity to use a voucher under the name of the DC Opportunity Scholarship Program.[4] The problem was, and still is, the following: How far will $7,500 go in the DC private school arena? Not far, as the typical tuition at private schools in the DC area is at $20,000–$30,000.

Are Vouchers Legal?

Seventy-six percent of voucher money used in Arizona has gone to private and parochial schools. When public monies are used to support private or parochial schools, many question the constitutionality of such expenditures: how can public dollars be used to support specific religious or political points of view when such narrow perspectives are not permitted in public schools supported by public taxes? A few state and even U.S. Supreme Court cases have addressed the issue of separation of church and state for educational reasons.

Vouchers used in Cleveland, Ohio, in the mid-1990s were challenged in the Ohio Supreme Court and supported by the court's decision. That decision was struck down by a federal district court and the Sixth Circuit appeals court, primarily on the issue of public money being used to send children to Catholic schools. The case was reversed in 2002, when the U.S. Supreme Court ruled in a 5-4 decision to permit the use of vouchers despite the religious indoctrination evident at the Cleveland Catholic Schools at public taxpayers' expense.

When Jeb Bush was the Florida governor from 1999 to 2007, he tried, with legislative support, to amend the state's constitution to permit vouchers after the state's courts had struck down voucher laws. In 2006 the Florida Supreme Court reversed the state law, permitting tax-paid vouchers for students to attend private schools. At issue was concern that the law violated the state's constitution requiring free public schools. This clause in most states' constitutions protects children by supporting their right to a free public education.

California residents had an opportunity to either support or oppose the use of tax dollars for private schools in 2000, when Proposition 38 was placed on the ballot. As is the problem with the use of vouchers in any state, *accreditation was not required of the receiving schools* by the state department of education or any other education-accrediting bodies. California residents defeated the proposition by a final percentage vote of 70.6 to 29.4.

When the entire state's residents have an opportunity to either approve or disapprove the use of vouchers, it is highly likely that vouchers will be dismissed on a large scale as they were in California. In a referendum in 2007, for example, 62 percent of Utah residents repealed vouchers previously passed by state government. When state legislators vote on using vouchers, the political party in power is likely to prevail, generally speaking, with conservatives usually in support. The U.S. Supreme Court decision to support vouchers was a testament to political and, perhaps, religious views and their influence on the approval of vouchers—at that time there were five avowed Catholics on the Supreme Court.

Other support for vouchers comes from some wealthy people who put their money where their mouths are: the Walton empire (Walmart), for instance, spent $42 million in political support to pass voucher legislation across the states. When you watch an advertisement in support of vouchers, just think of your local Walmart![5]

VOUCHERS: MORE PROBLEM THAN SOLUTION

One of the greatest concerns with the use of vouchers is the amount of money given to private schools that may not meet the standards of or reflect the views of a majority of U.S. citizens. Parochial schools have been in existence for hundreds of years, and are not so controversial in urban centers across the United States.

Would the U.S. Supreme Court have ruled the same way to support vouchers if the case had involved a private or charter school developed by Muslims, one specifically designed to teach Afrocentrist values, a school where only Spanish was taught, or a school supported by hate groups such as the Ku Klux Klan?

Public schools are committed to providing a nonsectarian perspective because every American is entitled to receive a free and appropriate education. U.S. public school teachers are expected to demonstrate respect for all religions and all political perspectives as long as those perspectives aren't in violation of the laws of the state. Certified teachers learn this in their university education training.

Cream skimming is used to describe a strategy common to both private and charter schools. When private and parochial schools are permitted to choose which students will attend—usually only the top academic students—they are cream skimming. Private and parochial schools may choose to take only those students

- with the best test scores and grades;
- who don't have any learning disabilities or other special needs;
- whose behaviors are always cooperative, as opposed to students with a history of suspensions;
- whose skin color matches that of the board of directors;
- whose parents' political perspectives match the school directors';
- whose religion matches the school's stated mission.

Private and parochial schools do not have a responsibility to cater to the needs of all students. Based on their opportunity to exclude whomever they like, many Americans wonder how their public tax dollars can be used to support the biased perspectives that may be taught in private and parochial schools.

Local control of schools occurs through the design of school board elections. When parents have concerns about their local public school, they can attend school board meetings and voice their concerns, and they can remove the school board members through voting in elections. Public school budgets are affected through referenda, when parents are permitted to either approve or disapprove the annual budget, the building of a new school, or the purchase of new band uniforms. Local control matters, as it should when decisions affect our children.

There are no mandates for local control at private or parochial schools. Teaching, curricular, and instructional decisions are determined primarily by the priests and nuns who run Catholic schools and the directors of private schools, who may "guard the doors" to prevent the "wrong" students from becoming part of the student body. Put simply, private and parochial schools have the option of dismissing students or denying their acceptance based on their perspectives about children who apply for admission.

State guidelines for what to teach (curriculum) and for implementing effective teaching practices; scrutiny of how state funds are used; testing mandates; and requirements for hiring certified teachers are all null and void at private and parochial schools. Private and parochial schools are exempt from all local, state, and federal education policies.

Who's Left in Public Schools after Vouchers Are Distributed?

To suggest that a level playing field exists among public- and private-school students would be absurd. Vouchers provide opportunities for some students to leave local public schools, primarily in urban districts. When these students leave the public schools, the students left are often from immigrant families or from families in such poverty that parents aren't able to take a voucher and use it at private schools because they cannot afford the tuition even at the level of a mere $3,000–$9,000. Tuition at private and parochial schools long ago surpassed those levels on the East Coast. Vouchers for less than $10,000 are useless at most private and parochial schools.

Do Children Receiving Vouchers Grow More Than Those Who Don't?

One of the most overwhelming concerns with vouchers is that families receiving them should be assured that their children will attend a better school, where teachers are better and learning is occurring more frequently than at the local public school. Evidence *does not* support this conclusion, for several reasons.

The most damaging evidence affecting the value of vouchers is the lack of certified teachers at private and parochial schools. You may recall from the description provided in chapter 5 that certified teachers are more highly qualified than uncertified teachers. Many factors that affect the academic success of students are determined by the quality of the knowledge that teachers bring to a classroom. The science of teaching (pedagogy) is garnered through the certification process. Certified teachers are knowledgeable about

- developmental traits of children and adolescents;
- the psychology of learning;
- planning processes;
- classroom-management practices;
- specific strategies for teaching varied content;
- assessment processes and how to implement them effectively;
- reflective practices that help them improve their teaching.

Uncertified teachers learn none of these skills prior to entering a classroom. Leaving the teaching of these strategies for after a teacher enters the field leads to poorer teaching and less learning. Both of these failures are more likely to occur in private and parochial classrooms devoid of certified teachers.

Lower Test Scores in Receiving Schools

According to data presented in several studies, students *do not have* better test scores when they use vouchers. Gerald Bracey discovered the following:

> After two years of the Opportunity Scholarship program, researchers found no differences between kids with vouchers and a matched group in the D.C. public schools. Nor did they find any significant impact for kids who were the top priority to get vouchers, those from schools that NCLB had already labeled as "in need of improvement."[6]

The most recent federal budget approved by both houses of Congress includes more federal tax dollars for this unwarranted, unsuccessful voucher program in the DC schools.[7]

Things were not much better in the Milwaukee voucher program. Five years of data revealed no differences in reading scores among public versus private schools, and a slight difference in mathematics test scores. Researchers studying the Cleveland, Ohio, voucher program "found no academic advantages for voucher users; in fact, users appeared to perform slightly worse in mathematics."[8]

In one state, the following organizations publicized opposition to vouchers in 2011:

- American Civil Liberties Union
- Americans for Religious Liberty
- Americans United for Separation of Church and State
- [state] Association for Supervision and Curriculum Development
- Education Law Center
- League of Women Voters
- NAACP (state chapter)
- Public Citizens for Children and Youth
- [state] School Boards Association
- [state] League of Urban Schools

This list represents a large cross section of diverse viewpoints, all opposed to using state taxes to send children to private and parochial schools. These collective voices are typically ignored by state legislatures and governors as they approve tax dollars for vouchers.

Voucher laws that have been implemented have not played out the way that proponents wanted or dreamed. The voucher battles over using public taxes for private schools continue and present the need for continued educational research to determine their effectiveness. To date, little evidence exists that vouchers are improving teaching or learning—meaning that they are a waste of taxpayers' money and educational resources.

ANOTHER FAILED BUSINESS ENDEAVOR: CHARTER SCHOOLS

The fight to approve vouchers failed in several state legislatures in the early 1990s. As a result of those failures, other business groups attempted to find another way to influence public policy on education funding. One of the strategies for making an end run around failed vouchers was the invention of the *charter school* in the early 1990s. Charter schools are primarily financially supported by public taxes—even when they are hundreds of miles from your home. Most charter schools exist in urban areas.

The principle of creating charter schools is to provide an alternative to the local public school. If that's the case, then the charter school should, in theory, be a better place for children and adolescents who attend it. Approximately 26 states permit charter schools, but those states establish a maximum number of charters that may be developed. Ten states do not permit the development of charter schools.[9] Of those states that have charter laws, the following rationale is generally used to support their implementation:

> (1) increase opportunities for learning and access to quality education for all students, (2) create choice for parents and students within the public school system, (3) provide a system of accountability for results in public education, (4) encourage innovative teaching practices, (5) create new professional opportunities for teachers, (6) encourage community and parent involvement in public education, and (7) leverage improved public education broadly.[10]

Many might be curious about why their state legislature and department of education would offer another group of people with no track record, experience, or training in the education profession an opportunity to reinvent the wheel of education with fewer guidelines and regulations than public schools have always been required to meet. Another concern can be expressed by asking why state legislators wouldn't "encourage innovative teaching practices, . . . create new professional opportunities for teachers, [and] encourage community and parental involvement" in all public schools through enhanced legislation, instead of trying to create whole new entities to reproduce what many successful public schools currently do.

It seems extremely redundant and absurd to spend more money on a new system, particularly if the new system takes tax dollars from the public system and offers no advantage to the students who attend the charter schools. To date, the evidence is clear that charter schools are no panacea for students who struggle in public schools.

States' school-charter laws designate who approves the start-up of the school and oversees the development, progress, and evaluation of charter schools, as explained in this description:

> In California . . . there are three types of authorizers: the governing board of the school districts, county boards of education, or the state board. In Pennsylvania, individuals or groups seeking to establish a charter public school must apply to the local school board of the district in which the school will be located. Generally there are four types of entities allowed to authorize charter schools: the local school board, state universities, community colleges, and the state board of education.[11]

Charter schools are both public and private in the way they are financed. State and federal dollars support the development of new charter schools, along with some private money—thus making charters educational management organizations (EMOs).

Charter school laws' requirements differ from what's expected of public schools in each state. For instance, the percentage of required certified teachers varies in each state based on its charter laws. I mentioned in chapter 4 that 14 states with charter laws require from 50 to 75 percent of charter school teachers to have certificates; 13 states require all charter school teachers to be certified; and 5 states don't require any charter school teachers to be certified.

History of the Charter School Movement:
The Failed Edison Experiment

Many adults who graduated from high school between 1990 and 2000 recall their homeroom periods each morning: 10 minutes of Channel One news with 2 minutes of advertising. It was businessperson Chris Whittle who attempted to make money from adolescents and public schools with his Channel One idea. Each school that was interested signed a three-year contract that entitled the school to a 19-inch-screen television set mounted at the front of each classroom, along with a satellite dish and cables to connect to local cable television.

The payoff for Whittle was in the advertising that consumed 2 minutes of the 10-minute news program required to be shown each morning in every classroom with a TV set. As long as at least 90 percent of the classrooms had TVs, there were no fees charged to the schools for using Channel One.

Whittle succeeded in that venture before he initiated the EMO school movement in the early 1990s. Whittle named his school business the Edison Project, and it became the first EMO. Whittle, through his new company, attempted to garner contracts with schools or state education departments to make a profit from public schools.[12]

He announced that he could run schools for less money than the state or local communities could. The first Edison schools were *for-profit schools*—designed and run for the sole purpose of making money. Not all charter schools are for-profit schools, although many of the Edison Schools are currently charter schools.

Other companies pour money into charter schools to shore up state tax-dollar support for them. Bill and Melinda Gates contributed $466 million to charters over several years. The Walton family (Walmart) put $272 million into charter schools, while the Eli and Edythe Broad Foundation sank $97 million into charters from 1999 to 2010. One other giant among charter school investors is the Michael and Susan Dell Foundation from Texas, which handed $66 million to charters.[13]

If you're curious about the reasons for these hefty investments, a spokesperson for the Walton family noted his theory of competition among schools as a means of raising student test scores. This flawed thinking of businesses' obsession with public schooling is noted in chapter 6. Outsiders' financial support does more than buy cheap toilet paper for schools' restrooms; it has also been used to support the "right" candidates for school board elections in cities where charter schools exist.

Diane Ravitch reported that in 2000, both Walmart heir John Walton and Eli Broad contributed over $100,000 to prevent a certain school-board candidate from being elected in San Francisco, due to the threat that the candidate opposed the inclusion of more charter schools.[14] The philosophy of Edison Learning Inc. (its most recent name) is guided by the promise of saving money. Running schools as a business to primarily save money puts children at risk on many levels.

Business-run schools also affect the neighboring communities in negative ways in an attempt to save money. I've visited Edison schools in which students didn't have enough textbooks to go around. Kenneth Saltman reports that Edison schools "standardize curriculum and control the ownership and distribution of school materials and resources."[15] The only way for Edison schools to be profitable is to cut corners. This is not a sound philosophy when the cost cutting negatively affects students' learning, as it always does.

Edison Schools spread throughout several eastern cities during the early 1990s. During this same time period, more state legislatures across the United States began approving the development of charter schools. By the mid-2000s, states with charter laws had seen considerable increases in the number of charter schools allowed.

Each time a new charter school is approved by a local school board, more state and local tax dollars are siphoned from the local public schools. One report from Ohio revealed that additional funding for charter schools in 2011 rose to millions of dollars above the funding for the state's public schools.[16] Public school students are the losers in this sad scenario.

Where Are the Professionals?

Edison schools are known for changing the administration in the public schools they take over so that they can hire fewer—and often untrained and uncertified—building principals. These schools pay teachers less than public schools and avoid teacher unions, so as to save costs on extracurricular jobs and on additional workloads for teachers who are not protected by a collective-bargaining agreement. Edison usually finds outside contractors to do food-service and custodial work—contractors that are not unionized.

Many of the EMOs use similar tactics to run their charter schools. The concern among many is that the state dollars charter school CEOs receive are not used to support student learning, hire effective teachers, or obtain essential school supplies, but, instead, go to CEO salaries. Educating children and adolescents is not intended to be a money-making proposition. Teachers, administrators, and schools boards are responsible for ensuring that children get what they need to grow.

Making money from educating children doesn't fit the purpose of learning. Saltman notes,

> These companies [e.g., Edison, Knowledge Is Power Program, Achieve, and other charter-school companies] aim to use tax money to run public schools and extract profits for investors from the money that would otherwise go to pay for smaller class sizes, more books and other supplies, and higher teacher salaries. . . . Public school students are being instructed in pledging themselves to the corporation.[17]

Seeking to educate children and adolescents cheaply creates more losses than it does benefits. The reality that charter schools drain dollars from the local public schools cannot be denied when the state legislative bodies refuse to raise taxes to support public education but do increase funding for charter schools.

Additional federal funding for charter schools has also drained dollars from *magnet schools*. Magnet schools are specialty schools, initially opened well over 30 years ago throughout several urban centers for the purpose of providing a focused, themed educational experience for children and adolescents in both elementary and secondary schools. Other, hidden purposes of magnets were to keep higher-socioeconomic-class students in urban settings, prevent White flight to the suburbs, and provide an alternative to some neighborhood schools for ethnically diverse students.[18]

Magnets were supposed to offer a curricular program more advanced than what was offered at local public schools, and students were admitted based on having good academic backgrounds. Most magnet schools were advertised as schools for academically gifted and talented students.

Recent reports, however, have revealed that in St. Paul, Minnesota, ethnically diverse students in general public schools are scoring better on state tests than the students at the city's magnet schools. Advocates for the magnets claim part of the problem is a lack of federal funding for these schools—drained again by taxes going for charters.

Why Haven't You Seen an Edison School in Your Neighborhood?

Edison didn't receive permission to "take over" any suburban or rural schools, but instead was granted permission by governors, state legislators, and mayors from large cities to "manage" some urban schools—schools where students weren't scoring as high on test scores as those students from higher socioeconomic backgrounds living in the suburbs. The reason most citizens of a state are not aware of the money spent for charter schools is that they are seldom aware that charters exist, since they don't see them nor are their children likely to ever attend one.

Saltman reported in 2005,

> Most students at Edison schools are African American or Latino. Edison does not run any schools in communities that could be characterized as economically privileged. Because public schools are funded mostly by local property taxes, wealthier communities can spend more for school buildings, teaching supplies, administration, extracurricular programs, and technology. They can also pay higher salaries and attract the teachers and administrators they want.[19]

Once a charter school or an EMO moves in and sometimes takes over what previously was a public school, the charter is required to follow federal guidelines regarding attendance for anyone who lives in the area. As more charter companies were created, however, some EMOs found a way to improve test scores: accept only the students who could ensure higher test scores than neighborhood struggling students.

A significant difference in student demographics has been appearing in the latest charter schools. Higher percentages of Black, Hispanic, and low-income students were in the local public schools but not attending local charters. The public schools also had many more students with special needs and immigrant students whose primary language was not English. As I mention below, the charters find ways to dismiss students who don't fit the student profile that ensures better cooperation and higher test scores.

THE EDISON TRACK RECORD—NOT A GOOD ONE

The Edison schools have had a stormy time of improving anything in the education world. Many Edison schools have been booted out of the city schools they entered due to low test scores, large teacher-attrition rates, and problems with company leadership.[20] Other difficulties occurred for Edison in 2001/2002, when some of their schools were accused of cheating on state tests. At about the same time, U.S. House of Representatives member Chaka Fattah, from Philadelphia, ordered an investigation of Edison Schools.

Edison was originally scheduled to take over all the Philadelphia public schools, but was only working in 20 Philly schools by 2008. Philadelphia's School Reform Commission voted that same year to dismiss Edison from four schools, noting that students were not performing well enough to satisfy the commission.[21]

Several Edison teachers from Wichita, Kansas, admitted in 2002 to being told "to do whatever it took to make sure students succeeded on standardized tests" by someone with authority at the schools.[22] Wichita began dropping some contracts with Edison shortly after that. Edison teachers in San Francisco reported being asked to use rigid teaching styles via a reading curriculum delivered using a script (no variations permitted). Foreign languages were not taught, nor were bilingual education classes offered for non-English-speaking students in Edison schools in Philadelphia.

Experienced teachers were not common in Edison schools. The average teaching experience was 5 years at Edison schools in 1998, versus a public school national average of 16 years.[23] The fact that states' charter laws do not require all teachers to be certified has probably influenced the dropout rate for Edison teachers. Edison teachers in San Francisco filed a grievance against their superiors for not being paid for working 7 percent longer hours in 1999.

HAVE WE LEARNED OUR LESSON?

I've addressed the Edison "experiment" in order to demonstrate what occurs when people other than trained education professionals are responsible for making schools work. Edison lost its contract with several schools in San Francisco in 2001 for a number of reasons, according to a school board report:

Allegations in the report include [the following:] special education students were "counseled to leave Edison"; "some parents were told that

Edison 'was not the place' for their children"; the company also failed to provide the district with financial records that track spending of public money, particularly expenditures to help low-income students; parents of African American students "were told that Edison might not be 'the right school' for them, . . . [with the parents saying] the school's teachers and staff treated black students differently from students of other ethnicities [sic]"; teachers . . . were [according to their testimony] victims of "extreme coercion" to sign a petition in support of the original charter.[24]

Finally, a report was issued that Edison received close to a million dollars more than it needed to spend during one of the years of the contract. All but one of the San Francisco board members voted to give Edison 90 days to repair the damage. When that wasn't accomplished in a satisfactory manner, Edison lost the contract to run the schools. Edison lost 18 more contracts following the San Francisco incident.

ACCOUNTABILITY, ANYONE? ARE CHARTER SCHOOLS PRODUCING BETTER TEST SCORES THAN PUBLIC SCHOOLS?

Public education is now a highly accountable business, thanks primarily to the language drafted by George W. Bush's education secretaries in the NCLB legislation. Every child's test scores are public knowledge, and the impact of those scores can mean the demise of the school as a public entity. The NCLB language permits public schools with low student scores to be seized by the state department of education and handed over (conveniently) to an EMO who can then dismantle the structure that it has taken years to create.

Anyone can follow the money trail to notice that the political support for charters was built before the NCLB legislation was passed. How many federal legislators did the rich foundations have in their pockets when the bill was passed in 2001? As a result of states' charter laws, providing some flexibility in the running of charter schools, one might expect some pretty exciting activities and resources pumped into the schools. One educational researcher reports, "Without question, there is no evidence of 'revolutionary' breakthroughs by EMOs with respect to curriculum, instructional strategies, or use of technologies."[25]

I suspect the EMOs are too busy trying to save money and put it in their pockets to provide students with the best technology or, better yet, the best teachers and administrators that money can buy. Evidence of prioritizing putting money in the bank versus supporting student learning occurred in Philadelphia with Edison schools in 2003.

The CEO of the Philadelphia Public Schools at the time, Paul Vallas, notified Edison, which was running several schools, that it would have to spend the same amount per pupil that the other city public schools were spending. Edison was being provided as much as $800–$900 more per pupil, but the tax money was evidently not being spent on students as much as placed into the hands of Edison leaders.[26]

Since 2002, student test-score statistics in charter schools have not been better than in the local public schools, and have often been worse. Perhaps legislators weren't able to predict these outcomes. Charter school advocates do much to dismiss students' poor test-score performances, but there's no hiding reality. As early as 2002, a *New York Times* report revealed that public school students in Cleveland, Ohio, had higher test scores than Cleveland's Edison students.

Researchers found in 2004, by examining scores on the National Assessment of Educational Progress, that charter school students had lower test scores than public school students by close to a half year in mathematics and reading in fourth and eighth grades.[27] The same tests revealed that fewer charter school students reached mathematics and reading proficiency levels than public school students. When socioeconomic levels were added to compare test scores, public school students eligible for free or reduced-priced lunches also did better than similar charter school students.

Ohio has a report-card rating system that it uses to grade all its schools. A report released in 2011 revealed that

only 21 percent of charter schools rate "effective" or better; whereas 72 percent of traditional school buildings and 88 percent of traditional school districts rate "effective" or better on the state report card. In fact, 46 percent of public school buildings rate Excellent (A) or Excellent with Distinction (A+), while 45 percent of charter schools rate in Academic Watch (D) or Academic Emergency (F)—success rates that are almost exactly opposite one another.[28]

The charter-school advocates certainly don't want to know about the summary-of-research study conducted in 2006 by researchers from the University of Illinois for the National Center for the Study of Privatization in Education at Teachers College at Columbia University. The researchers, Christopher Lubienski and Sarah Thule Lubienski, summarized their analyses of several studies comparing private, charter, and public schools with the following comment:

> Overall, the results of this study suggest that, despite the many difficulties faced by public schools, they appear to be performing relatively well when compared to demographically similar private and charter schools, without the remedy of major, private-style structural reforms in their governance and management. These findings question the idea of an inherent superiority of the private sector in education. Furthermore, the data here suggest significant reasons to be suspicious of claims of general failure in the public schools, and raise substantial questions regarding a basic premise of the current generation of school reform.[29]

Educational researchers continue to study charters, with many similar results. Researchers for the Center for Research on Education Outcomes in 2011 reported that 37 percent of charter schools performed significantly worse than their counterparts in the local public school systems.[30] Since their inception in the middle 1990s, more than 650 charter schools have closed across the United States.

What if local communities closed that many public schools? Comparing the value of public schools to charters by using the closing data above indicates a critical need for the stability that public schools bring to all communities across the United States. It would be unfathomable to have public schools closing every other year in our communities, like many of the EMOs.

The philosophy of a quality education for all is not embraced or supported by the idea of charter schools or vouchers. Neither provides the quality of schooling that American students receive on a daily basis from their local public schools—even in the worst circumstances. A continuation of further development of, funding for, and political support for charters and vouchers runs completely against the philosophy of education that the foundations of democracy rest upon.

NO CHILD LEFT BEHIND
Damaging Public Education

The schoolmaster, always severe, grew severer and more exacting than ever, for he wanted the school to make a good showing on "Examination" day. His rod and his ferule were seldom idle now—at least among the smaller pupils.[1]

In a way, the reforms that aim to save America are actually putting America in danger. NCLB is sending American education into deeper crisis because it is likely to lead to increasing distrust of educators, disregard of students' individual interests, destruction of local autonomy and capacity of innovation and disrespect for human values.[2]

Only someone ignorant or dishonest would present a ranking of schools' test results as though it told us about the quality of teaching that went on in those schools when, in fact, it primarily tells us about socioeconomic status and available resources.[3]

It is difficult to imagine that Mark Twain, quoted in the first epigraph above, may have been subjected to harsh treatment similar to what many children endure today during the one-day test performance required by the No Child Left Behind (NCLB) law. The only difference between Twain's school anecdote and schools in the 21st century is that most states have banned physical punishment at school. However, the psychological pressures on children as a result of NCLB most likely exceed the damage caused by paddling students.

The second quote above is from Yong Zhao, University Distinguished Professor in the College of Education at Michigan State University, who received his education in China before coming to the states as an adult. His vision of the ill effects of the NCLB legislation reveals an "outsider's" objective view of the "Education Armageddon" created since NCLB went into effect. Sadly, Zhao's description of the effects has become reality.

As a lifelong educator, I have seen America's public school teachers sink deeper into depression every year since NCLB's inception in 2002. NCLB's problems outweigh any solution predicted by those legislators and policy makers who devised this disastrous plan—some unknowingly, others with a clear objective of destroying the reputation of our public schools. Gerald Bracey, a trusted educational researcher, shared his thoughts on the primary purpose of passing NCLB: "Why would an antiregulatory administration [Bush II] impose tons of regulations on public schools? Because the goal of NCLB is the destruction of public schools, not their salvation. NCLB sets the schools up to fail and be privatized."[4]

Most legislators were and are too ignorant on education issues to comprehend the effects of such poor public policy on children, teachers, and the way we educate humans. After almost 10 years of NCLB, every legislator has the responsibility to listen to administrators and teachers to discover its ill effects. Bracey characterized the NCLB policy as "a weapon of mass destruction."[5] The effects of NCLB on teachers and children reveal the damage it's caused.

WHAT LED TO NO CHILD LEFT BEHIND?

No Child Left Behind is federal legislation that was passed during the first year of the George W. Bush presidency. It was almost a unanimous approval vote by the Senate, and it had at least 380 votes of approval in the U.S. House in 2001, before being signed into law by Bush in January of 2002. Passage of NCLB wasn't the first intrusion of federal mandates on states' education responsibilities. The National Defense Education Act (NDEA) of 1958 was one of the first among federal laws that opened the door to the federal government providing money to states for public schooling.

NDEA was created for a sole purpose: so that the United States would beat the Soviets in the "space race," thus placing our missiles in space ahead of the Soviet Union's—a goal prompted by a genuine red scare! NDEA provided $887 million for education that could support national security—particularly training scientists. For students during the early 1960s, new money meant the "new math" that was supposed to make all children and adolescents mathematical geniuses. Perhaps there was hope that some teenagers might then create their own homemade rockets, which the feds would promptly confiscate in an attempt to improve America's chances of winning the space race.

Ten *titles* (separate sections) were part of that education law intended to create more top scientists. One of those was Title I, which *prohibited* federal control over (1) curriculum (what schools teach), (2) administration (which people become the local education leaders), and (3) personnel (teachers). Those were the "old days," when federal legislators knew that education was and needed to be a state issue and, better yet, a concern and domain belonging to local communities.

Legislators in the 1950s knew that education issues and laws did not belong to someone in Washington, DC, looking for the next new "fix" in order to get reelected. NCLB became that fix for President Bush, and every legislator who voted for it. Unfortunately, long after it was supposed to be reauthorized, many legislators are afraid to mention NCLB, realizing just how contentious it is. Federal legislators are not sure if their support for either dismantling NCLB or voting to reauthorize it will get them reelected. If you want to confuse a candidate running for reelection or for the first time, just ask what his or her stand is on NCLB.

President Lyndon Johnson signed into law the Elementary and Secondary Education Act (ESEA) of 1965, an extension of the original NDEA signed by President Dwight Eisenhower. The improved ESEA provided monies to states to help educate children from low socioeconomic circumstances. *Title I* was the program most associated with the 1965 passage of ESEA, and that program has provided millions of dollars over the past four and a half decades to help children learn to read all across the United States. As a result of Title I, federal dollars were being poured into the coffers of primarily urban *and rural* school districts that needed federal monies to make up for a lack of state dollars.

For many years after 1965, federal money for education was primarily restricted to Title I funds. Few questions were asked; but during the years following 1965, large cities in the United States changed considerably. Businesses moved out of the cities, taking not only families with them, but also the tax base that supported city schools.

Title I money was advantageous to urban schools that lost their tax bases when many wealthy and middle-class families, as well as businesses, left the cities. State legislatures weren't responsive to the plight of urban families, many of whom were recent immigrants. Title I became a relied-upon funding source because state legislatures and governors didn't cough up the lost revenue to city schools.

Following the antitax talk of the 1980s Reagan era, and the unsubstantiated report *A Nation at Risk*, written by Reagan advocates, talk of accountability began to loft through the halls of Congress. I imagine the thought process was akin to, "If we're going to provide federal monies to those schools, they have to prove they are doing their jobs."[6] Faulty thinking about how to educate children was rampant among legislators and businesspersons as they began to see a way via new education policies to limit their tax responsibilities.

Big business began flexing its muscles, having profited so well from "Reaganomics." Some businesspersons began writing about education as if they had the answers to everything, such as a couple of CEOs from IBM who wrote a book called *Winning the Brain Race*.[7] Ignorant fallacies about how to educate children and adolescents became daily news when 24/7 news stations popped onto our cable television stations and needed a topic that every broadcaster thought he or she was an expert on—education.

In the late 1980s and early 1990s, presidential wannabes began running on slogans such as "I'll be your education president." The first Bush tried that, but easily lost the title when business appointees to his education department did their best to bury the Sandia Report after its independent authors revealed how successful U.S. public schools actually were (see chapter 6). Talk of content and performance standards began about the same time, as did the institution of state tests for every child—a multimillion-dollar expense from which state taxpayers may never recover.

As each state legislature endorsed state testing, the test companies lined up for their daily feeding—the multibillion-dollar industry began lobbying in the state houses and in DC. The result could have been predicted by every third-grader in America back in the early 1990s, when "teaching for thinking" was popular in public schools: the development of a new law that would require accountability for public schools based on—you guessed it—students' test scores.

Shortly after the passage of NCLB, each state board of education and state legislatures had to receive the approval of the taxpayers to implement the procedures associated with the law. It was a choice for states— no state was required to adopt NCLB regulations. Each state legislature and board of education could have declined to follow NCLB policies. Unfortunately, every state approved NCLB, with the approval in some cases based entirely on the contingency that the money received from federal Title I funding would be lost if the state did not agree to follow NCLB rules.

The fatal flaw in NCLB is that it is not designed to change two essential schooling components: children's abilities to learn better or educators' abilities to teach better. Any policy or law that fails to address these two aspects is meaningless to the success of the schooling process. The extent of the damage to effective teaching caused by NCLB legislation is beyond any measure after 10 years of this absurdity. Several states have announced their refusal to follow NCLB protocol as the expectations for student success reach impossible levels within the next two years.

The Impossible NCLB Requirements

NCLB requires yearly testing, beginning with third-graders and currently extending through eleventh grade, in only two subjects: reading and mathematics. Even students who are taking Advanced Placement classes for college credit during their junior year of high school must take a state test to see if they are *proficient*, along with receiving college credit as they pass their AP examinations. It seems absurd that students need to be assessed on minimum reading and mathematics skills while they are passing Advanced Placement tests for college credit.

Proficient is a word adopted by policy wonks to mean that students have scored high enough on a test to be considered smart enough for that grade level. If you notice that this definition seems rather vague, you're right. For a student's test scores to be viewed as reflecting proficiency, each state education department's test experts (no one knows who these people actually are) sit in a room together and choose a number—any number—to be their cutoff point for labeling a child as proficient on the state's adopted and taxpayer-supported reading and mathematics tests.

When NCLB was first instituted, state education departments set a score that they believed was fair; but it was a shot in the dark because standardized tests had never been *misused* this way. As the years passed following the initiation of NCLB policy, proficiency cutoff scores were lowered in most states, for a valid reason. Each year that NCLB is in effect, more students must become proficient—until 2014, when every child in the United States is required by the law to be on grade level or proficient.

The year 2014 will be like no other, because the promise of every child in America being on grade level cannot be compared to any other miracle that's ever occurred. There'll be serious celebrations in the streets all over America! It's difficult to imagine that pundits will have any more negative comments to make about public education when this occurs—which is an impossibility. Only the U.S. Congress could pass such a lemon.

If someone works for any state's department of education, that person serves at the discretion of the governor. If the governor wants more students to be proficient, then he or she might ask to have the test scores required for proficiency to be lowered so that more students are proficient and the governor looks good—good enough to be reelected! This is the rationale sweeping state departments of education across the nation for arbitrarily setting and altering proficiency scores. When more students are proficient, state department of education members may also keep their jobs.

Making Adequate Yearly Progress

If a certain percentage of students, as stipulated by NCLB, become proficient, the school district makes what's called *adequate yearly prog-*

ress (AYP). The reward that each school district wins for having made AYP is its share of Title I monies from the federal government. If too many students (a percentage determined by NCLB) fail to obtain a proficient score on the state reading and mathematics tests, the school district loses its share of Title I monies; these funds are generally quite considerable for urban schools that have many students from low-socio-economic-status (SES) families.

The percentage of low-SES families determines how much Title I money is available to a district; more poverty equals more Title I money. Every district in the United States receives Title I money, and it is used primarily to help struggling readers.

Where would you predict the most Title I money would go in a state? Which school districts would you predict would have the lowest student test scores? There's no prize money for your correct response in realizing that large, urban school districts need Title I money the most, and are the most likely to have low test scores due to many circumstances beyond the control of educators.

Other NCLB details affect school practices: AYP is also determined by other, student-controlled factors, such as graduation rates and number of expulsions. As long as a district meets the established marks for success on all those matters, it will also continue to receive its Title I money.

If a district's students fail to make AYP for two consecutive years, then students may transfer from that school and attend another school: public or private. Schools that don't make AYP from three to five consecutive years are *taken over* by the state. A takeover usually means that an educational management organization (see chapter 8) such as Edison or Knowledge Is Power Program is offered a contract by the state department of education to run the school. Students are also permitted to apply to attend any private school nearby.

The absurdity of the transfer policy is that private schools are not responsible for meeting any of the requirements of NCLB or any other federal mandates, because they don't receive federal tax dollars. Private schools are not required to accept any students who fail to meet their entrance requirements, including any who can't afford the tuition. In addition, many private schools have limited space and resources, which would prevent them from being able to accept more students even if they were kind enough to do so.

Chicago Public Schools personnel reported in 2004 that they were required to offer 200,000 students a choice to go to different schools due to the number of students who were not proficient on state tests. A serious flaw in the plan was that only 500 spaces were available to the 200,000 students who had the option of going to another school.[8] Do you suppose any legislators considered the challenges presented by their approval votes for NCLB? The word is that most legislators didn't actually read NCLB before they voted for it. Experienced educators should have been asked to review it and make recommendations to their legislators regarding the validity of the plan.

All of the NCLB plans sound fairly reasonable, *but only to noneducators*. Educational-research findings were never considered as reasonable sources to reference, nor were the professors who conduct such research invited to help cowrite NCLB. If research had been considered, students' test scores would not have been the method for determining schools' successes. NCLB policies were developed by legislators and legislative assistants—people who have never been classroom teachers or administrators. It's also obvious to public school educators that most of the designers of NCLB were private school graduates and therefore people with a deep ignorance of the way public schools operate and the clientele that attend public schools.

It may sound simplistic or perhaps appear to lack in-depth analysis to criticize NCLB as poor policy based on the lack of education credentials among the designers. However, NCLB's negative effects on basic, well-known learning and teaching practices are so obvious to classroom teachers and educational researchers that one can only surmise that the authors had no idea of what actually occurs when children learn. Even parents are now beginning to understand NCLB's flawed theoretical ideas, as their children experience impractical teaching/learning situations in efforts to prepare them for a single test.

A Pot of Gold for Test Publishing Companies and Educational Management Organizations

NCLB was also conveniently designed to create a marketplace out of children's and adolescents' learning needs, for big businesses searching for a new way to make money. The language in NCLB of school takeovers and required reading and mathematics programs is a bonus for companies like McGraw-Hill and Pearson that make the tests, test-preparation materials, reading and mathematics programs, and test-results sheets for parents in each state.

Richard Gibboney, a former state commissioner of education and professor at the University of Pennsylvania, notes, "No Child Left Behind has made public education itself fair game for profiteers, and this can only mean two things: corruption and higher costs. This law turns over huge chunks of public education to those whose overriding goal is to make money, not educate children."[9]

The designers of NCLB had visions of what might happen with a carrot-and-stick approach, but their ignorance of the realities of teaching and learning doomed NCLB from the beginning. NCLB has deadened education in the United States in a way that no other events or plans could have.

A Story That Reveals the Flawed Thinking of NCLB Authors

The following anecdote was written by a school superintendent and has been distributed widely since NCLB was passed by the federal legislature in 2001.[10] The value of this comparison between teachers and dentists is that it demonstrates the lack of control that teachers have over students' overall cognitive growth. This may help noneducators begin to comprehend those factors that really impact a child's overall academic success.

Absolutely the Best Dentists

My dentist is great! He sends me reminders so I don't forget checkups. He uses the latest techniques based on research. He never hurts me, and I've got all my teeth, so when I ran into him the other day, I was eager to see if he'd heard about the new state program. I knew he'd think it was great.

"Did you hear about the new state program to measure the effectiveness of dentists with their young patients?" I said.

"No," he said. He didn't seem too thrilled. "How will they do that?"

"It's quite simple," I said. "They will just count the number of cavities each patient has at age 10, 14 and 18 and average that to determine a dentist's rating. Dentists will be rated as Excellent, Good, Average, Below

Average and Unsatisfactory. That way parents will know which are the best dentists. It will also encourage the less effective dentists to get better," I said. "Poor dentists who don't improve could lose their licenses to practice in South Carolina."

"That's terrible," he said.

"What? That's not a good attitude," I said. "Don't you think we should try to improve children's dental health in this state?"

"Sure I do," he said, "but that's not a fair way to determine who is practicing good dentistry."

"Why not?" I said. "It makes perfect sense to me."

"Well, it's so obvious," he said. "Don't you see that dentists don't all work with the same clientele; so much depends on things we can't control?

"For example," he said, "I work in a rural area with a high percentage of patients from deprived homes, while some of my colleagues work in upper-middle class neighborhoods. Many of the parents I work with don't bring their children to see me until there is some kind of problem and I don't get to do much preventive work.

"Also," he said, "many of the parents I serve let their kids eat way too much candy from a young age, unlike more educated parents who understand the relationship between sugar and decay.

"To top it all off," he added, "so many of my clients have well water which is untreated and has no fluoride in it. Do you have any idea how much difference early use of fluoride can make?"

"It sounds like you're making excuses," I said. I couldn't believe my dentist would be so defensive. He does a great job.

"I am not!" he said. "My best patients are as good as anyone's, my work is as good as anyone's, but my average cavity count is going to be higher than a lot of other dentists because I chose to work where I am needed most."

"Don't get touchy," I said.

"Touchy?" he said. His face had turned red, and from the way he was clenching and unclenching his jaws, I was afraid he was going to damage his teeth. "Try furious. In a system like this, I will end up being rated average, below average or worse.

"My more educated patients who see these ratings may believe this so-called rating actually is a measure of my ability and proficiency as a dentist. They may leave me, and I'll be left with only the most needy patients. And my cavity average score will get even worse.

"On top of that, how will I attract good dental hygienists and other excellent dentists to my practice if it is labeled below average?"

"I think you're over-reacting," I said. "'Complaining, excuse making and stonewalling won't improve dental health' . . . I am quoting that from a leading member of the DOC," I noted.

"What's the DOC?" he said.

"It's the Dental Oversight Committee," I said, "a group made up of mostly lay-persons to make sure dentistry in this state gets improved."

"Spare me," he said. "I can't believe this. Reasonable people won't buy it," he said hopefully.

The program sounded reasonable to me, so I asked, "How else would you measure good dentistry?"

"Come watch me work," he said. "Observe my processes."

"That's too complicated and time consuming," I said. "Cavities are the bottom line, and you can't argue with the bottom line. It's an absolute measure."

"That's what I'm afraid my patients and prospective patients will think. This can't be happening," he said despairingly.

"Now, now," I said, "don't despair. The state will help you some."

"How?" he said.

"If you're rated poorly, they'll send a dentist who is rated excellent to help straighten you out," I said brightly.

"You mean," he said, "they will send a dentist with a wealthy clientele to show me how to work on severe juvenile dental problems with which I have probably had much more experience? Big help."

"There you go again," I said. "You aren't acting professionally at all."

"You don't get it," he said. "Doing this would be like grading schools and teachers on an average score on a test of children's progress without regard to influences outside the school—the home, the community served and stuff like that. Why would they do something so unfair to dentists? No one would ever think of doing that to schools."

I just shook my head sadly, but he had brightened. "I'm going to write my representatives and senator," he said. "I'll use the school analogy—surely they'll see my point."

He walked off with that look of hope mixed with fear and suppressed anger that I see in the mirror so often lately.

This story parallels the details of how the state department of education is required by NCLB to take over a school once the students' test scores on a single test aren't good enough. The author also demonstrates how frustrating it is to educators to be treated as unprofessionally as is humanly possible through NCLB guidelines.

EXTERNAL FACTORS AFFECTING SUCCESSFUL ACADEMIC EXPERIENCES

The factors that affect a child's learning *prior to entering school* are infinite, much more numerous than the factors that affect children's teeth. Factors that positively affect a child's learning *before* kindergarten include the following:

1. Parents' strong educational backgrounds and positive attitudes toward learning/schooling.
2. Healthy dietary habits during infancy and early childhood (e.g., appropriate amount of fat and other nutrients needed for proper brain development and general physical growth).
3. A high number and frequency of varied enriching experiences (e.g., visits to museums, musical experiences, zoos, farms, cities, bodies of water, hills, mountains, bridges).
4. Opportunities for rich language experiences through daily conversations with other children and adults.
5. Regular engagement in fine-motor and large-motor physical activities (e.g., drawing, painting, scribbling, running, jumping, swimming).
6. Exposure to print (e.g., books, magazines, computer text) and other reading material.
7. Healthy interpersonal relationships with and among family members.
8. Limited exposure to or no exposure to carcinogens (e.g., lead paint, poor-quality water, tobacco smoke).
9. A stable family environment (e.g., living in the same house for years, minimal parental conflict or adversity).
10. Financial security that guarantees a safe home, proper diet, appropriate sleeping conditions, opportunities for exercise, access to print materials, and enriching experiences.

11. Freedom from psychological stress.
12. Freedom from physical or sexual abuse.
13. A safe neighborhood.
14. Freedom from parental neglect.
15. Standard English spoken and written at home.
16. 10–20 hours a week of positive "harmonious . . . interactions" between infants and caregivers.[11]

I emphasize that these conditions are necessary *before* children start kindergarten. Researchers insist that from birth to age five is a critical time for proper brain development due to the flexibility of the brain during these first years of life. Ignoring these critical needs has immediate effects on children's abilities to succeed academically during all their years of school.

The list above provides examples of the factors that affect children's abilities to do well in school. There are many more. Many factors on the list above continue to affect children and adolescents throughout their lives. Once school does begin, other factors affect children's abilities to be excited learners every day of the week.

Educators wish they had control over all those factors. If they did, their students would do well in school, and every child would benefit from the daily learning experiences that teachers plan and provide. An added bonus would be that every child would have a better chance to do well on state tests.

Those ideal circumstances do not describe all U.S. children's and adolescents' lives. The reality of what children experience each day in their homes makes a direct hit on teachers each day at school. Teachers know what most of their students' home lives are like in elementary years; but, just as in the case of the dentist, that doesn't provide teachers with the power or authority to change them. Children continue to come to school, and caring teachers dedicate their lives to helping improve the opportunities for their students.

Even if all the students in a school were on grade level, teachers would not be able to control how children or adolescents would act on test day. It's not uncommon for some students to merely fill in the dots on a standardized test in the shape of a Christmas tree. These students have no intention of taking the tests seriously. Fourth-graders are wise enough to understand that these test scores have no impact on their lives, so their actions reflect their beliefs on test day. If fourth-graders are wise enough to comprehend the insignificance and blow the test, you should see high school students who choose not to play the game. Teachers have no control over their actions when this occurs.

The tests aren't motivating, don't have any real significance to children or adolescents, and are seen by many students as a complete waste of their time. Those students who shade in Christmas-tree shapes are wiser than the rest of the educational world that has endured these tests.

THEY WILL NEVER *ALL* BE ON GRADE LEVEL

Each year that NCLB is in effect, the law requires that a higher percentage of students in every school in the United States reach proficiency in mathematics and reading. By 2010, in reading skills, 59 percent of elementary students in each school were to be proficient, 72 percent of middle school students, and 85 percent of 11th-grade high school students. Mathematics minimum levels included 66 percent of elementary students proficient by 2010, 61 percent of middle school students, and 74 percent of 11th-graders.

By 2013, the minimum number of required proficient students will increase again. The percentage of elementary students proficient in reading must be at 79 percent, with percentages of 86 percent for middle schoolers and 92 percent for 11th-graders. Mathematics proficiency levels required for 2013 are 83 percent for elementary students, 80 percent for middle-level students, and 86 percent for 11th-graders.

NCLB requires that *every* student will score on grade level or be proficient on the state reading and mathematics tests by the year 2014. What does NCLB do to ensure that every child has access to the perfect home life before and after school? For every child to be "on grade level" is an impossibility. I haven't lost hope—I simply accept the realities of the diversity of U.S. children's lives.

Think about what it would take for you to become an Olympic swimming champion. What physical factors, primarily based on genetics, would you need to be merely "good" at swimming? What kind of training routine would it take for you to become so fast that you would win local swimming events? How about regional events? How much harder would you have to work to become so good that you might win a national championship? How long, at your current physical condition, would it take for you to be close to an Olympic-quality swimmer? Will you be Olympic quality in one year; two; four; or never? (Be honest.)

Children who enter school having never read a book are perhaps like you—they've never been in the water, so to speak—so they aren't going to be "on grade level" as kindergarteners. As they progress, they become better readers, but many children are never exposed to enough words either in conversations or in their reading experiences to be "on grade level." One reading researcher reports that by kindergarten some children from healthy homes have heard 32 *million* more words than their impoverished counterparts.[12]

If children have heard that many words, they're going to use those words and eventually read them. Kelly Gallagher, who wrote the book *Readicide*, notes that children who enter school considerably behind others are likely to be at least three grade levels below their peers by the time they reach sixth grade.[13] *Proficiency* is not likely for these kids!

One of the factors that clearly influence a child's reading ability is the time he or she spends reading per day. Researchers studied fifth graders and noted the link between minutes of reading per day and students' reading-test-score rankings. Students who read an average of about 90 minutes per day had a test-score percentage rank of 98 percent. Students reading an average of 40 minutes a day ranked at 90 percent; 22-minutes-a-day students scored at the 70-percent range; and less-than-2-minutes-per-day readers scored a 10-percent ranking.[14]

The difference noted in that same study in the *number of words read per year* between the top readers and the lowest readers was 4,682,000. Children aren't going to do all that reading at school—meaning that someone at home has to influence this kind of growth. It is an absurdity to blame teachers for students not working at grade level. Teachers will need many more hours of contact to extend reading opportunities for their lower-performing students. Perhaps teachers can meet with students after school from 3:15 p.m. until 8:00 a.m. the next morning. This is another example of the challenges effective teachers face in getting students to grade level.

THE EFFECTS OF NCLB ON HOW AND WHAT EDUCATORS TEACH

What are teachers supposed to do with students who are below grade level? Give up on them, just because they didn't have a book in their homes when they were children? NCLB has an answer for that question: "drill and kill" reading exercises; scripted curriculum in which teachers read a script to children; and double reading and mathematics periods during the school day.

I frequently work with teachers in a local urban school district. Too many students in one of the middle schools I regularly visit were not proficient in reading and mathematics on their state tests. The district central office mandated scripted reading and mathematics curricula as a response. In a scripted curriculum, teachers read the words from the teacher's edition of the text, while the students often repeat what the teacher has read. Teachers are not permitted to veer from the script. These fifth- to eighth-grade students often moan whenever it's time for reading. They want to be better readers, but they don't want to be lulled to sleep by a teacher reading a script that sounds like someone reading the directions for assembling a recently bought grill.

To add insult to injury, here's the typical daily schedule for fifth- to eighth-grade students at this school:

8:30 a.m.–9:00 a.m.: Test preparation period for reading (M,W,F) and mathematics (T, R).

9:00 a.m.–9:54 a.m.: Corrective reading activities via the SRA scripted reading program developed by the McGraw-Hill Company. (See chapter 6 for the relationship between McGraw-Hill and the presidential Bush Family.)

9:55 a.m.–10:39 a.m.: Corrective scripted mathematics program (also SRA/McGraw-Hill).

10:40 a.m.–12:09 p.m.: Core literacy classes (also SRA materials).

12:09 p.m.–12:54 p.m.: Student lunch. (No reading or mathematics teaching at this time!)

12:55 p.m.–1:39 p.m.: Special classes for students (physical education, music, art, foreign language).

1:40 p.m.–2:10 p.m.: Additional literacy (reading and English curriculum).

2:10 p.m.–2:24 p.m.: Science and social studies. (Notice this is only 14 minutes.)

2:24 p.m.–3:09 p.m.: More mathematics lessons.

You'll notice immediately the amount of time devoted to, and the intensity of, repeated reading and mathematics lessons. Also note how little time is allocated to social studies (history, geography, current events) and science. Many schools in the United States have not made AYP, and the number will increase as the requirements for the percentage of students who must be proficient increases every year until 2014, when all students are expected to be proficient. Will their schedules eventually look like this school's?

Standardized tests used to determine proficiency create instructional suicide because those tests don't measure what counts. State tests measure "the temporary acquisition of facts and skills, including the skill of test-taking itself, more than genuine understanding."[15] Linking this problem to race-related issues, Dorothy Strickland notes, "Skills based instruction, the type to which most children of color are subjected, tends to foster low-level uniformity and subvert academic potential."[16] Once again, this type of learning, if one could call it learning, does the exact opposite of what schools are meant to do for students.

For every child who is curious, scripted reading is not only demeaning, it sends a message that students aren't worthy of teaching that challenges them. The message also is that teachers can't be trusted to act professionally to create lessons that engage students in meaningful learning in the context of improving their literacy or mathematics skills. For instance, some of the faculty in the middle school described above were chastised for teaching novels to their students instead of following the scripted reading curriculum more closely.

These unprofessional expectations explain why many educators are avoiding teaching in urban schools: they do not want to be unable to use their professional judgment and expertise to plan the types of innovative lessons necessary to help students actually learn. In the book *Grading Education: Getting Accountability Right*, the authors provide actual interview transcripts with 14 teachers in urban centers across the United

States who describe how their love and enthusiasm for teaching have diminished since the inception of NCLB.[17] Their stories are laced with the disappointment of not being able to use innovative, research-based teaching practices since NCLB has all but eliminated their professional responsibilities.

No policy and curriculum could more quickly increase the dropout rate than scripted curricula, though their purpose is allegedly to increase reading and mathematics scores. Gallagher describes the deadening process of preparing students for the NCLB tests:

> Readers who are undernourished need good books. Lots of them. Instead, what do many undernourished readers get? They are often placed in remedial classes where the pace is slowed and where the reading focus moves away from books to a steady diet of small chunks of reading. In an effort to "help" prepare them for reading tests, we starve readers. Rather than lift up struggling readers, this approach contributes to widening the achievement gap.[18]

Researchers, teachers, and wise administrators might demonstrate some support for more challenging reading strategies because they know what students need. The NCLB legislation, however, led to a change from listening to the researchers in the field to advocating for business products that lobbied the loudest. McGraw-Hill produces many state tests and just happens to also produce reading and mathematics materials that have been approved by the federal Department of Education for use with children who are not passing the tests.

Eric Jensen summarizes what researchers in the field of cognitive science (how the brain learns) have made clear:

> For those working with kids in poverty, we do know for certain that the following extremes will *not* work [my emphasis]:
> • Focusing only on the basics (drill and kill).
> • Maintaining order through a show of force.
> • Eliminating or reducing time for arts, sports, and physical education.
> • Decreasing interaction among students.
> • Delivering more heavy-handed top-down lectures.[19]

Teachers of students from low-SES circumstances are often required to use these tactics, even though they know these strategies are not supported by the research on effective teaching.

Reading Madness, Not Research-Based Programs

The NCLB legislation includes language regarding the use of research-based teaching and instructional strategies. Unfortunately, the term *research-based* was narrowly defined by the NCLB authors. Some researchers believe that the research language was placed in the law to ensure that some contractors would receive preference when schools across the United States started receiving approval for their reading or mathematics programs. The programs that were approved for use in schools with struggling students were not actually research based.[20]

Further evidence of the lack of credibility for these limited-approach reading programs are the following facts presented by Gallagher:

Intensive focus on state tests has not translated into deeper reading on other assessments [i.e., tests], such as the SAT or National Assessment of Educational Progress . . . Evidence [exists] that this focus [on scripted reading programs] actually decreases college readiness . . . [Since] NCLB began, reading scores have remained flat and . . . the achievement gap has remained wide.[21]

This information was reported in 2009, seven years after NCLB's intrusion on effective teaching. Evidence supporting these findings can be found in the following scores on the "nation's report card": the National Assessment of Educational Progress (NAEP): In 2002, the average reading score for eighth-grade students was 264. The 2003 average was at 263; the 2004 figure was 262; and finally, in 2007, the average was 263 again.[22] Federal Department of Education personnel who suggest test scores are rising as a result of NCLB policies and approved curricula are not to be taken seriously.

Gallagher describes the scenario created by NCLB perfectly:

Let's see whether we have this straight: we immerse students in a curriculum that drives the love of reading out of them, prevents them from developing into deeper thinkers, ensures the achievement gap will remain, reduces their college readiness, and guarantees that the result will be that our schools fail.[23]

Perhaps the worst of the reading madness created by NCLB is the simple fact that children and adolescents in these schools have come to absolutely hate reading. Further damage occurs, as education writer

Alfie Kohn reports that "studies of students of different ages have found a statistical association between high scores on standardized tests and relatively *shallow* thinking" (my emphasis).[24]

NCLB's Impact on Low-Socioeconomic-Status Students

Most teachers realize that states' tests are not designed to promote effective learning or teaching. The most trusted researchers in the field of testing noted this discrepancy years ago. One of those researchers, James Popham, stated, "The standard achievement test makers have *no interest* in selecting test items that will reflect effective instruction."[25] Popham further explained that "anywhere from 15 to 80 percent of questions . . . on norm-referenced standardized achievement tests were SES-linked."[26] In other words, children's low SES levels have a detrimental effect on their ability to score well on the assessment companies' designed tests.

How can teachers have any impact on their students' socioeconomic levels? You know the answer—they can't. But worse than that is the news that the tests students take are especially difficult for students in the low-SES communities in which NCLB is alleged to actually help.

It is wiser to think of low-SES communities and schools in rural areas rather than urban because at any given time the percentage of low-SES families living in rural communities is 5 percent more than those living in urban areas, as has been the case since the 1960s.[27] The public doesn't usually hear about rural-school students' low test scores—just the frequent complaints about urban students' test scores. Schools with many students with low scores, labeled "dropout factories," may be more common in the hinterlands than in the cities.

Effects of NCLB on Schools with Proficient Students

Schools where most students make AYP are also negatively affected by NCLB policies. Educators in every community are always concerned with their students' test scores, no matter how academically well off students are. The effects of a constant "Big Brother is watching" attitude include limitations on subject areas being taught. Social studies and science have taken a big hit in the elementary grades all across the United States.

Special subject areas such as music, band, orchestra, physical education, and art are frequently dropped from a local school for test-preparation time or for additional minutes for more reading and mathematics, as I described earlier in the urban school. When these significant overhauls are made, students suffer in ways that we should all be aware of.

Students identified as not proficient the year before are pulled from other classes to be tutored during the day in elementary, middle, and high schools. Special *test-preparation periods* are common in many schools, replacing the special classes or electives that students used to take.

Teachers respond according to the amount of pressure placed on them by administrators. When the school year begins in August for teachers, before the students arrive, it is common for some principals and superintendents to hold faculty meetings in which students' test scores are magnified on a large screen for the entire school to examine. The message is clear: raising students' test scores is the central mission of the school. It may sound appropriate to some that teachers should be held accountable this way, but the unfortunate result of these tactics is a limited education for the children and adolescents who show up each day looking for excitement, novelty, and imagination in their learning. Some principals make a note of struggling students who have no chance of becoming proficient and advise teachers to not waste time helping these students grow, since passing test scores are unlikely. NCLB was supposed to be advantageous for struggling students; but in this scenario, academically poor students are merely forgotten.

Recesses are often shortened if not completely eliminated, and field trips are discouraged when not actually abolished, in an effort to improve students' test scores. Canceling physical activities has dire consequences for children. Without recess they miss crucial socialization opportunities—ones that can't be learned in formal physical-education classes or in other academic experiences. Children need physical movement to develop large and small motor skills that are essential to becoming better learners.

Researchers from the California Department of Education found a "significant relationship between public school students' academic achievement and their physical fitness" for students who participated in the study from fifth, seventh, and ninth grades.[28] Another set of researchers, at the University of Illinois, discovered that students who were more aerobically fit obtained better scores on reading and mathematics tests, even among low-SES children.[29]

Every elementary teacher can explain the differences in their students following recess. The ability of children to concentrate and focus on academic tasks improves after recess. The sad part is that the children and adolescents who need exercise the most, those from low-SES environments, are often subjected to having recess eliminated with the goal of raising test scores. The effect of eliminating recess is less learning, not more.

The elimination of arts programs (e.g., music, band, drama, dance, art) also takes a toll on students' cognitive growth. A University of California, Los Angeles, professor analyzed data from more than 25,000 students who participated in arts programs. He discovered that "students with high levels of arts participation outperform 'arts-poor' students on virtually every measure," and that "low-SES students who took music lessons in grades 8–12 . . . not only increased their math scores, but also improved their reading, history, and geography scores by 40 percent."[30] Improvements in memory skills, sequencing, manipulation of data, and short-term memory are some of the cognitive advantages for students engaged in the arts.

Many students across the country are forced to lose arts courses when budgets get tight. That's a poor reason for cutting the arts programs, but not as egregious as cutting these programs to improve students' test scores—especially when eliminating them does the opposite.

LET THE CHEATING BEGIN

When teachers hear their leaders complaining about students' test scores at the beginning of each school year, they know what matters to the brass: reading and mathematics test scores. If the superintendent is harping on students' scores, the principal will soon echo the superintendent's concerns at a school faculty meeting. The picture is clear: the principal is being threatened by the superintendent to do something about students' scores; so the principal passes on the stress to teachers, who then feel the pressure to do something—anything—to raise students' scores.

Years before NCLB, Texas principals were rewarded with $5,000 bonuses if their students scored better on state tests. Central-office administrators were promised up to $20,000 for better scores. Texas students did well in these districts. Was it the money that made teachers teach better? No, actually, more creative measures were used by Texas administrators:

- Special-education-student populations doubled because they weren't tested.
- Low-performing high school students were asked to leave school and not return; thus, as dropouts they were not counted, nor tested.
- Many academically low-performing high school students were retained in 9th grade, because students were tested in 10th grade.
- The same low-performing students who had been retained in 9th grade subsequently skipped 10th grade and were placed in 11th, so that they would never be tested.[31]

The Texas game was the model used by the NCLB framers for the new national program to overthrow and replace research-based teaching and learning. The trouble was, the Texas gains weren't actually gains, just fraudulent activities using students as pawns. Other testing "mishaps" occur regularly in places where undue pressure is placed on all stakeholders—whether it's administrators, teachers, parents, or the students themselves.

The former head of the Washington, DC, schools, Michelle Rhee, has been called an educational reformer by pundits who know little about education. Rhee is a lobbyist now, and she promotes the continuation of NCLB and teacher evaluation tied to students' test scores, and she does her share of teacher-union bashing. Her campaign may be useless since her practices as head of the DC schools were questioned by parents and teachers.

USA Today reported that over 3,700 teachers and parents petitioned the U.S. Department of Education and the Government Accountability Office to investigate hundreds of erasures on tests that were then marked with the correct answer.[32] An investigation found that one half of the schools (103) had suspicious erasures over a two-year period from 2008 to 2010. The head of Rhee's lobbying group stated that no evidence existed that Rhee's pressure on teachers in the form of proposing to evaluate them based on students' test scores made cheating any worse in DC than in any other districts. That sounds eerily like an endorsement for cheating.

How can teachers realistically and absolutely ensure that their students will score a *proficient* on state tests? The options are

1. Teach to the test each day of the year until the test date.
2. Provide students who struggle in school with tutors after school.
3. Keep students in school 12 months of the year to ensure a continuous cycle of learning.
4. Sit with and assist students one-on-one with homework daily.
5. Sit with struggling students all day long to help them complete daily school assignments.
6. Ensure that all your students understand academic English.
7. Obtain special services for students who have unidentified learning difficulties (e.g., ADD, dyslexia, dysnomia, auditory-processing difficulties, social and emotional disabilities).
8. Check test questions to be sure that you're teaching the appropriate matching content.
9. Teach and be responsible for only those students who had a passing score in previous years' tests and who regularly demonstrate high academic skills.
10. Stand over students during the test and encourage them to correct their answers when they mark a wrong answer (the Rhee strategy?).

Those are just a few ideas that I know can impact a teacher's ability to help students receive better test scores. Naturally, some of these ideas are considered cheating—numbers 8 and 10—and number 9 is not likely to occur unless a teacher has a favorable relationship with the local administrator.

The other suggestions are not likely to occur either, based on the lack of financial support that exists for urban and rural school districts.

Many children in urban schools don't receive special services and are physically unhealthy, which prevents them from being able to focus on learning. Numbers 4 and 5 above will never happen until student/teacher ratios drop below 10 in urban schools. Few taxpayers are willing to support that kind of expenditure, especially in urban areas.

The odds of teachers having a significant impact on their students' test scores are low because of all the traits mentioned above that children need *before* they begin school. If politicians and business leaders get their way in some states, teachers' worth and futures as professional educators will be based on their students' test scores. The more these high stakes are legalized, the more ways teachers and administrators will find to beat the system, to make their students look good on tests—in short, to cheat.

The problem is, the resulting environment for learning will be destroyed, students will lose any interest in learning, and motivation at school will be a long-lost memory that grandparents will describe when they speak of their childhoods. Unfortunately, this environment already exists.

WHAT ARE THESE TESTS COSTING TAXPAYERS?

So far, we know these tests are limited measures of what students can actually do and what they know. Second, we know that all teachers use daily feedback from students to design instructional strategies and choose curricula that meet their students' needs. Most realize that one test on one day of the year is an extremely limited view of what children know and can do. Educators know that these tests are severely limiting the content teachers deliver and negatively affecting the strategies that teachers choose to motivate children.

It's the costs of the tests that are the most appalling. Each state must first commission a testing company to design the tests. The state department of education then purchases the tests from the test company. Tests are distributed via trucks (probably armored so that teachers will have no idea what students will be tested on) to each school district in the state. The tests are given on the exact same days all across the state, so delivery is time sensitive.

Teachers are paid to waste several perfectly good days of instruction on proctoring the tests—usually three or four days. Following testing days, the trucks return to each school district to collect the tests. State education-department personnel box the tests and send them to the test company for scoring. The state then pays for the test results to be printed by the test companies. The test results are printed on special paper and delivered to the education-department offices.

Test results come in several data formats. Data are separately reported for each student and reported in numerous large-group formats (by grade level, ethnicity, and low-SES results). School districts receive several data sets, including each individual child's scores and the large group reports that are mailed to the schools. Each school district then places each child's test results in an envelope and mails these to the parents.

Who makes more money in this get-rich-scheme: the testing companies or the delivery companies (UPS, USPS, FedEx)? State taxpayers foot most of the bill. Adults without school-age children might not look favorably on these expenditures; having children in school might not make one excited by these costs either.

Indiana's Department of Education reported in 2007 that it cost $557 per student to maintain the state's current level of performance on the graduation tests, and Texas noted that it spent $2 million for personalized study guides for students who did not initially pass parts of their state exit examination. Teachers may need additional training to help students successfully pass these tests; and in Massachusetts, it costs taxpayers an additional $101 per student to train the teachers.[33]

The federal Department of Education is trying to provide your federal taxes in support of all these state costs. In 2010, the Department of Education was appropriating $350 million in federal stimulus funds to help the states buy better tests! I wonder how much better they could be. As part of the 2011 budget, the feds plan to provide $450 million to states to also develop better tests. This money is allocated based on grants, though, so every state doesn't get the funds, only the ones whose state education departments submit proposals for the money.

The testing-company lobbyists were a busy bunch in Washington before and after NCLB passed. Wouldn't it be cheaper to cut out the middleman and just hand the money over directly to McGraw-Hill, Harcourt, NCS Pearson, or Riverside Publishing testing companies, rather than give it to state governments for testing materials? If you think the tests are the only costs, don't forget that if your community schools are not making AYP, the schools are also purchasing test-preparation materials for students to practice on questions that resemble test questions.

There must be a better use of local, state, and federal tax dollars than spending all this money on tests and testing materials. Locally, you'll need to add the dollars you're spending on teacher time used in preparing children for the tests instead of teaching valuable and meaningful content. Researchers estimate that in some schools, teachers spend approximately six to eight weeks just on test-preparation activities. Think of what your children and grandchildren could be learning without such emphasis on the state tests.

What Do State Tests Measure?

The meaning of *content validity* is described in chapter 3. When test items match what you know will be on a test, the education profession considers the test to be *valid*, that is, the test measures what it purports to measure. In the late 1980s and early 1990s, when states began requiring every child to take tests each year, education-department personnel were responsible for ensuring that the tests chosen from the test companies matched the required content or curricula that students were studying at each grade level. If content validity didn't exist, then how could anyone expect students to do well?

Do test companies determine what gets taught—the curriculum for each subject area—or do the textbook companies? What role do teachers, administrators, content-area specialists, child development experts, or professional educational organizations have in determining what students learn? If students are to do well, then a match must exist, and many teachers speak of the match that they believe exists between their content and their state tests. As long as teachers, parents, and administrators can ensure this match, then students have a fighting chance to do well if all of the other circumstances of their lives place them near grade level.

Unfortunately, many students' lives are far from healthy enough to place them near grade level. But beyond that is the idea that some federal Department of Education personnel and some legislators have proposed using the NAEP test as a measure of students' competencies in reading and mathematics. In 2009, national testing experts from the Board on Testing and Assessment warned the education department that using a single test (such as NAEP) is a highly inappropriate method for determining academic student growth. The greatest concern is that NAEP may not be aligned with state content standards.

Federal education-department personnel even suggested using NAEP test scores to evaluate teacher effectiveness. Teachers aren't ever allowed to see the state tests that their students take before, or even after, the tests are given. Any preview of test content is strictly forbidden, despite the fact that teachers administer the tests each spring. Nothing scares testing companies more than teachers knowing what's on the tests before students take it!

The U.S. military is respected for its teaching and training techniques. Imagine that a sergeant is training soldiers to shoot a rocket-propelled grenade. Isn't each soldier permitted to practice over and over on that grenade launcher before the final test? Soldiers know what the test is like, because they are given the questions beforehand. A perfect match exists between what soldiers are supposed to know, what they're taught, and what they're tested on. This scenario seldom occurs in education.

A local middle school mathematics teacher experiencing her first year of teaching explained that she was hired to help the seventh- and eighth-grade students pass the state mathematics test. When asked if she knew what would be on the test, she replied succinctly, "No." How was she going to help students pass a test when she had no knowledge of the content?

It is not as simple as assuming that the school district has chosen a text that is a perfect match with the test. Content validity is never assured. Teachers have no control over that factor, so it's unreasonable and unprofessional to determine teacher effectiveness by looking at their students' test scores for a test that lacks content validity.

Graduation-Test Problems

The beginning of NCLB was not the first time tests were such a high-stakes situation for students. *High stakes* means that failing the test will have a highly negative effect on students and possibly teachers. In the late 1970s, several state departments of education were directed by their state legislatures to administer graduation tests to students. These tests were known as *minimal competency tests* (MCT) because they only tested students on the minimum amount of information that the test companies thought was necessary for functioning well as an adult with a high school diploma.

As an eighth-grade teacher, I recall readying students for the tests. Students took the test initially as ninth-graders; that provided them with three more opportunities to pass before graduation. MCTs were dropped in several states not long after their arrival, perhaps because they were seen as too simplistic. More states, however, developed graduation tests throughout the 1980s and 1990s. As high-stakes graduation tests multiplied, interesting data emerged.

As poor academic students enter high school and discover that no matter how hard they work, their grades don't improve, they start to evaluate their circumstances. Here's the thinking some students might engage in:

I really dislike school. I took the graduation test once already and didn't pass it. I'm 15 years old, and on my next birthday, I can get a job. Because I failed the test the first time, I have to take these remedial reading and math courses every day. I miss out on electives that I have a real interest in—anatomy, carpentry, and modern music—because I have to take the remedials.

My parents don't really care if I graduate because they didn't even finish ninth grade. I think Mom might like it if I contributed to the family budget by bringing home a check once a week. She'll be mad that I quit school, but I know I'll probably never pass that graduation test anyway, so why bother hanging around for another two years?

True to form, data clearly indicate a rise in the dropout rate in several states since the initiation of high-stakes graduation tests. According to the National Board on Educational Testing and Public Policy in 1986, those states with MCTs were more likely to have the highest dropout rates. The board noted that year that 9 of 10 states with the highest dropout rates used an MCT as a requirement for graduation.

In 1996, two researchers and the Florida Department of Education noted that students who failed the Florida MCT were more likely to drop out even though they were receiving passing grades in their classes at the time of the test administration.[34] Pennsylvania State University used the National Educational Longitudinal Study (NELS) data to reveal that the use of an 8th-grade promotion test is strongly associated with increased probability of students dropping out before 10th grade.

Education researchers Kathy Emery and Susan Ohanian reported on the Massachusetts situation in which over 16,000 high school students dropped out once the state tests were used as graduation requirements.[35] An author at a Boston-area website reported that 60 percent of Black and Hispanic 9th-graders were being held back because it was thought that they would not pass the graduation test when given for the first time in 10th grade.[36] You can guess what the majority of those students did upon hearing that they were being retained in 9th grade for another year.

Reviewing these results makes me wonder what would happen if we used a high-stakes test with elementary students, so that they weren't permitted to advance to the next grade without a passing score. Do you suppose they would drop out by fifth grade? When test-score stakes are high, the effects are generally negative.

TEACHER EVALUATION BASED ON STUDENTS' TEST SCORES? DON'T BE ABSURD

As long as proposals exist to evaluate teachers based on their students' test scores, it would be wise for teachers to choose their students carefully! Who's the better teacher in this scenario?

> Ms. Smith's fourth-grade students are all below grade level in reading. In March, the state tests are given and her students have an average gain in reading scores from the 25th percentile all the way to the 40th percentile. None of them will be proficient, though, so the school will not make AYP this year. However, in case you're counting, the students leapt a total of 15 percentage points on the test. Is Ms. Smith an effective teacher?
>
> Ms. Wilson also teaches fourth grade. Her students are all at least near grade level, and most are reading well above grade level. All were proficient last year on their third-grade reading tests. On the state fourth-grade reading test, her students have an average rise in reading scores from the 95th percentile to the 96th percentile—a rise of only one percentile. Is

Ms. Wilson an effective teacher, and does she deserve a raise this year for her students' test-score performance?

I have no idea who the better teacher is due to the limited data provided by test scores, but it's clear that both teachers' students did well on their state tests. Should Ms. Wilson be penalized for her students' paltry gain of only one percentile? Or is she clearly the better teacher since her students scored in the *advanced* category on the state test? Wouldn't you rather reward Ms. Smith for her students' amazing 15-percentage-point gain?

The pressing question is, what will Ms. Smith's students have to endure in fifth grade due to their less than proficient scores on the reading test? Will they lose their opportunities to read novels, have recess, take art, study social studies or science, and go on field trips? This is usually the scenario that occurs in urban schools when students are not proficient. NCLB once again contributes to the dropout rate of both students and teachers, who lose their motivation for learning and teaching based on students' one-day test scores.

The most irritating aspect of state tests is that the scores are released after students have completed the school year—sometime in mid-June or July. What are teachers to do when they discover that the students they taught *last year* weren't proficient, and now they've been promoted to the next grade?

These students' last year's teacher can't use last year's scores to help an entirely new set of students with much different needs from those of last year's group. Plus, the test they took was a fourth-grade test, so the skills they didn't know aren't likely to be taught again in fifth grade. These tests have become worthless to all involved: teachers, students, and parents.

Every teacher knows what students are academically capable of long before the state tests. Effective educators make day-to-day changes in their teaching to meet the needs of their students throughout the school year. Here's a list of some of the information a teacher collects each week on his or her students:

- number of and value of oral responses during class discussions
- performance on homework assignments
- ability to successfully complete classroom assignments

- how often a student asks questions during classes, and the types of questions
- weekly quiz and test scores
- social and emotional behaviors, and how those affect staying on task each day
- number of absences and the impact on growth
- performance (grades) on projects and group assignments
- attitude and effort each day

Through each of these activities, teachers know what their students can do long before the spring state test—they have to, to make a difference in their yearly growth. Waiting until after the state tests to make instructional and curricular decisions for students would mean that the students would have to repeat the grade again. Good teaching is a day-to-day adjustment of strategies, content, and motivational techniques to be sure that the effects of teaching are helping every student grow.

That's how principals currently determine if a teacher is effective: observations of daily instructional and curricular decisions based on what students need. Looking at a set of one-time student test scores is as erroneous as evaluation can possibly be. Imagine if salespersons were evaluated on the effectiveness of one day of sales in a nine-month period—the one day that their cars' engines stopped and they were stranded for two days, several miles from the city they intended to visit. One might suggest, appropriately so, "That's not fair!"

Another U.S. Department of Education reward program, Race to the Top, requires that states use student test scores as an evaluative instrument for teachers in order for states to receive more federal funds. This is a competitive grant program. Notice the theme emanating from the feds: you can't have the people's money until you play the education game our way. *Our way* means evaluating teachers based on student test scores.

Educational researchers, administrators, and teachers clearly know that *our way* is the wrong way to evaluate effective teaching. Educational-policy decisions made by politicians, federal education-department personnel with no teaching experience, a secretary of education with a bachelor's degree in sociology, and NCLB: these are some of the reasons that teachers and school administrators have no respect for the current education climate and political leadership in America. Teachers know that students suffer the most from these inappropriate education ideas and policies led by NCLB legislation.

Most educators are now suggesting that the federal government keep their money in exchange for states dropping NCLB requirements. Virginia's Fairfax County Schools, with more students than the entire state of Connecticut, did just that when they told the federal Department of Education that they wouldn't follow NCLB guidelines for testing students because they had so many immigrant students who would fail miserably on state tests. The district eventually backed down due to the fact that they would lose $17 million in federal revenue needed for many of those students.

It is time, though, for schools to "just say no" to NCLB. Teachers will gladly forego the rewards of following poor, unresearched practices unleashed by NCLB, so that children can receive an education guided by quality educational research; delivered by experienced, certified teachers; and informed by the excitement of what motivates children and adolescents, instead of the teachers having to worry about students' test scores.

THE BOTTOM LINE: NCLB IS A TOTAL FAILURE

The fact that the federal legislature or the president would have any voice in the state's rights to determine education issues has long been controversial, but it has been even more so since the inception of NCLB. This federal intrusion by the most conservative members of the U.S. Congress and the Bush administration was a far cry from the hands-off philosophies and legislation usually promoted by conservatives.

Every educational researcher who has studied the effects of NCLB has proclaimed it disaster. Even conservative pundits from earlier Republican administrations have begun bashing NCLB—people like Diane Ravitch and Chester Finn, who denounced the narrowing of curriculum caused by NCLB due to the focus on only mathematics and literacy skills.

Robert Schwartz, a businessperson and one of the first supporters of, and an influential member of, a group advocating standards and accompanying testing during the early 1990s, wrote in 2004,

> The goal of equipping all students with a solid foundation of academic knowledge and skills is leading to an undue narrowing of curricular choices and a reduction in the kinds of learning opportunities for academically at-risk students that are most likely to engage and motivate them to take school seriously. This is a painful acknowledgment from someone who considers himself a charter member of the standards movement.[37]

Even the general public is beginning to note the problems with NCLB. In the *Phi Delta Kappan* poll of 2008, 67 percent of adults wanted the law changed significantly or wanted to let it completely expire.[38] People who responded to that *Kappan* survey also made it clear that the president should rely on education leaders to develop policies for schools—not businesspersons or politicians. One more notable finding from that survey is that four of five people believe that "examples of student work, teacher grades, or teacher observations are the most accurate measures of students' academic progress *rather than test scores*" (my emphasis).[39]

Two respected educational researchers, Sharon Nichols and David Berliner, clearly explain why NCLB is inappropriately designed:

> If a person volunteers to take exams for the medical boards, the bar, or a pilot's license, that individual should be encouraged to follow a dream. But not all of us should be forced to take and fail such exams. In the current high-stakes environment, teachers, students, parents, and American education are being hurt by required high-stakes testing.[40]

NCLB is certainly responsible for fewer teachers seeking professional positions in urban or rural districts. How can the specter of losing one's job based on factors beyond a teacher's control—students' test scores—entice anyone to take a position in a district in which most students are immigrants who struggle with English at every grade level? Effective educators want to help every student grow and succeed, but basing their worth on students' test scores demeans the pride that accompanies successful teaching.

Why would educators place themselves in a teaching position in which they have no opportunities to be creative teachers, but instead are required to follow scripted curricula? Teaching provides many intrinsic rewards, but the sanctions and punitive actions that accompany NCLB cancel any good feelings associated with helping children learn.

Often politicians, pundits, and businesspersons suggest that NCLB helps keep teachers accountable for their efforts and successes. Accountability is always on teachers' minds because every day those to whom teachers are accountable sit in front of them waiting to be engaged in the excitement of learning. Accountability for teachers is

- discovering what students' academic backgrounds are, so that lessons can be planned that match their developmental levels;
- establishing a physically and psychologically safe learning environment where students can focus on learning;
- finding grade- and developmental-level materials for each student to learn and succeed with;
- watching students closely enough during lessons to know when they don't understand, even when they don't say so (they seldom tell you);
- stopping lessons when students don't understand and starting in a different place so they can understand;
- providing students with appropriate feedback on their schoolwork, so they grow from their mistakes;
- finding ways to motivate students every day of the school year.

Teachers who are accountable

- help struggling immigrant students learn to speak conversational English before the year ends;
- identify students who have special learning needs, so that they receive the help they need to succeed academically;
- contact parents regularly when parental help is needed;
- tie children's shoes, button their coats, and put their hats on them when they need it;
- administer first aid whenever the situation arises;
- help soothe emotionally upset students;

- challenge academically advanced students to grow more;
- protect all their students from harm (bullying) during the day.

This is merely a beginning, because everyone remembers a teacher who did something special for him or her that's not on this list. No other accountability measures, imagined in the vacuum that exists for legislators or pundits who have never taught, are needed. There is no simple scale, real or imaginary, that one can create that identifies, labels, and measures the value of a teacher's accountability.

Politicians, pundits, and businesspersons often cite economic professors' studies as a reasonable process for measuring whether smaller classes matter, the value of more years of teaching experience, or if a master's degree leads to better teaching. Economists are not educators. It is not likely they have ever been with 20 kindergarten students versus 30 at one time and been able to determine the differences in interactions between teacher and students based on adding 10 more to the mix.

An economist has never experienced the joy of finally developing a classroom-management technique that works with most students after three years of teaching. Bean counters have never received an advanced degree in teaching/pedagogy and realized how the additional classes positively affect the influence teachers have on students.

NCLB's rules requiring the measuring of every event at schools, from the number of suspensions to each child's test score, have eroded volumes of educational research the profession has produced for years promoting innovative teaching practices. From medical research on how the brain works to newfound knowledge on motivation and learning, teachers are reluctant to use any of what recent science has produced, as they try to ensure that their students will score well on a two-hour test given once a year. Imagine if the medical profession had to endure such archaic rules, thus preventing the development and use of recent science or new drugs to cure certain illnesses.

Herbert Kohl has written much on what learning is supposed to look like in classrooms across America. In his most recent book, *Stupidity and Tears*, he describes the problem with the "magic bullet curricula" (scripted reading and mathematics programs) that are alleged to help make any teacher effective no matter how poor he or she was before:

Many public school districts these days have adopted a single curriculum tied to an expensive, so-called teacher-proof program such as Open Court or Success for All . . . . They are intended to ensure that even the worst teachers will be able to deliver adequate teaching. The goal is admirable though foolish, since a terrible teacher will be terrible with whatever he or she is required to do . . . . It is an attempt to take the "human factor" out of teaching, when that factor is at the heart of all good teaching.[41]

Teaching is a science and an art, and those who believe in measuring the effects of superior pedagogy through students' test scores have poisoned the profession in irreparable ways. The pain created by NCLB is insidious. Nothing short of dismantling it will begin to heal the wounds it's created.

10

URBAN SCHOOLS

More Successful Than We Hear

The spirit of NCLB also denies the real cause of education inequality—poverty, funding gaps, and psychological damages caused by racial discrimination—by placing all responsibilities on schools and teachers. While schools can definitely do a lot to help children overcome certain difficulties, their influence has limits.[1]

Faced with a future of low-wage work with little opportunity for advancement in the service sector, many [poor urban youth] have little incentive to come to class or stay in school.[2]

Most low SES kids' brains have adapted to survive their circumstances, not to get As in school. Their brains may lack the attention, sequencing, and processing systems for successful learning.[3]

Some of my university teacher education students were placed in an urban school for their first experiences with teaching. Some often expressed fear about stepping into an urban school and becoming responsible for working with small groups of students. The fear was unnecessary, because for the several years my students attended that school, most returned after a semester with a love for the students they encountered and a much better understanding of the challenges urban teachers faced. At the end of each semester, a few students told me they wanted to teach in an urban environment, even though they never would have considered it prior to that semester.

After two semesters of my frequent visits to the school, one of the secretaries in the school office made a habit of giving hugs to each of my students and to me whenever we came in each Tuesday and Thursday. I wondered if any suburban-school secretary would hug people she barely knew each day when they entered the building. That urban middle school was the friendliest school I'd ever been in. There was no reason for fear.

INACCURACIES ABOUT URBAN SCHOOLS

Whenever politicians, news broadcasters, and pundits complain about America's public schools, they are usually referring to those schools in the cities—schools *their* children will never attend. Most people have never visited an urban public school. If one were to ask, "What is it that is so bad about our city schools?" the response would probably be, "They're just terrible; you know they are!"

My experiences with urban schools have revealed a highly dedicated set of teachers—perhaps more dedicated than in any other schools. When people speak of a "bad" school, they're generally referring to urban schools. The fear and loathing for urban schools is unfounded and based primarily on people's complete lack of knowledge about them.

The effectiveness of a place of learning is partially determined by how it nurtures those who attend it each day. Urban schools must be more nurturing than any other schools because urban teachers support children more frequently and in deeper ways than most teachers in other communities need to. Several urban teachers have told me that their students have asked them to be their mothers. I know this happens in other communities, but not with the same frequency with which it occurs in city schools.

Most urban schools match all of the research-based criteria noted in the chapter 2 description of what makes a school a "good" school. To mention a few, urban schools have caring teachers, many academically successful students, effective teachers in many classrooms, and many extracurricular opportunities available.

The rumors that are foolishly believed by much of the public are that there are few successful students and few effective teachers, and that urban schools are not safe places. The percentage of graduates for urban schools doesn't match many suburban and rural schools; but urban schools graduate millions of successful citizens each year.

Safety at Urban Schools

Many factors influence whether a school should be labeled as *safe*. Factors that matter include both psychological safety and physical safety. Students should be safe from psychological bullying and physical danger while anywhere near their school. Records of school suspensions as a result of fighting, or office referrals, would clarify the safety record of schools.

It may be interesting to note that in school shootings around the country from 1996 to 2010, of a total of 41 reported K–12 school shootings, 11 of them took place at large urban schools, while the majority of shootings were at rural schools.[4] It is common for security guards to exist in urban schools, and their presence may make them safer than some rural or suburban schools that do not have security available.

Urban Schools in Poor Physical Condition

Many U.S. public schools in most communities are in disrepair. A 2000 report revealed that one third of America's 80,000 public schools needed substantial physical repair, from new ventilation systems to roofs, with particularly high rates of problems with heating and cooling, plumbing, and lighting.[5] The Government Accountability Office reported that "30% of rural, 38% of urban and 29% of suburban schools have at least one building needing extensive repair or total replacement."[6] It appears that urban environments have the most schools in need of repair—but suburban and rural schools are close behind.

The low level of funding for many urban schools, due to a limited tax base, prevents new construction or remodeling of buildings. A higher commitment to urban schools is required for students to enter healthy, well-constructed buildings in many U.S. cities. It is also common for rural and suburban schools to ignore building-infrastructure needs due to reluctance by communities to support such projects.

WHO ATTENDS URBAN SCHOOLS?

Recent History of Changing Demographics in U.S. Cities

Schools are defined as *urban* based on their location—huge metropolitan areas with a high percentage of people living in a limited geographic space. Urban areas dot the U.S. landscape, but most Americans don't live in urban areas. They live in rural areas or in suburbs miles from cities. If you've ever flown across the United States and looked out the window of the plane, you've noticed how much land you pass where it appears no one lives. But there are homes out there, far from large cities.

Those who were born in cities between 1900 and 1950 were likely to spend their entire K–12 schooling experiences in the city. After World War II, many middle- and upper-middle-class families began to leave the cities for the suburbs, thus leaving an entirely different population of families in cities. One researcher explains the change in demographics:

> What changed so dramatically with the suburbanization of the American population was not just the relative proportion of the population living in cities and suburbs, but the racial and economic distribution of the population within the metropolitan areas . . . . During the 1940s, 1.6 million African Americans migrated from the south to northern and western cities, and another 1.5 million followed in the 1950s. By 1970, 47 percent of all African Americans lived outside the South and three-quarters lived in metropolitan areas.[7]

It's difficult to comprehend the changes that occurred during this migration. The socioeconomic-status (SES) changes were the most critical; and with new immigration patterns also occurring, the SES of the cities began to drop significantly. After 1970, although African American urban migration slowed, many Hispanic families from Mexico, Central America, and Puerto Rico began moving into cities at a much faster rate. By 1980, Spanish was the primary language of one fifth of the population in New York City, and the population of the metropolitan areas of the Midwest and Northeast were 77 percent African American.[8]

Although immigrant and African American families had the financial means to move into the suburbs, discrimination in the housing market prevented many Blacks and immigrants from obtaining housing anywhere outside of the cities. The poverty rate in cities had risen from 27 percent in 1959 to 43 percent by 1985—almost one of every two families living in U.S. cites was poverty stricken. These circumstances had a significant impact on students' academic performance.

It is likely that graduation rates in cities were higher during the 1950s because African American and immigrant students were graduating at much higher percentages in the northeastern and midwestern cities than in the South. African Americans and Hispanics had greater academic success because prior to the 1960s, 1970s, and 1980s students from these families weren't afforded an effective education in their previous locations: African Americans in the South, and immigrants in their native lands.

Some previously all-White public schools in southern states completely closed their schools during the early 1960s rather than permit Blacks to attend them as required by the landmark *Brown v. Board of Education* U.S. Supreme Court Case of 1954. These public school closings occurred a full decade after the decision. So one may completely understand why many African Americans fled their rural communities during the 1950s–1960s.

The promise of gainful employment, less discrimination, and an opportunity for their children to experience a better life than they had are the reasons that White European American immigrants left northern Europe during the late 19th and early 20th centuries. These are the same reasons that African American families left the South and more recent immigrants from Mexico, South America, and the Caribbean islands migrated to U.S. cities. Who can blame them for seeking better lives, as did millions of European Americans?

Results of Moving into Northern Cities

Graduation rates rose for African Americans, Hispanics, and immigrant populations from the end of World War II until the 1960s. The

National Assessment of Educational Progress (NAEP) test scores in reading and mathematics rose among African American and Hispanic students in the late 1970s and during the 1980s.[9]

Other successes were evident for African Americans as a result of migrating to the cities after World War II. Federal statistics revealed that "average educational attainment among African Americans age 25 to 34 increased from eight years to eleven years between 1960 and 1970 and to slightly over twelve years by the early 1980s."[10] Hispanic graduation rates also rose during this same time period.

These are success stories that one never hears about from the media. Good news about public schools never sees the light of day, even on 24/7 news stations. Those urban schools that had the lowest graduation rates and test scores during the 1970s and 1980s also had students from the lowest-SES communities. Low-scoring students likely struggled with learning a new language as immigrants. They came from families whose parents couldn't find decent jobs, didn't have access to health care, and couldn't afford purchasing enough food for their children.

When businesses and factories left the cities, the types of jobs that were available to high school graduates left the cities. After the 1970s, some corporations moved their headquarters back into cities, but those jobs required college educations, and many low-SES families couldn't afford college. The result was a considerable rise in the unemployment rate.

The greatest impact of these financial circumstances landed on adolescents' hopes. If receiving a high school diploma didn't have any positive effect on finding gainful employment, why bother? As two educational researchers note,

> To be effective, urban school reform must be linked to programs and policies that attack the social and economic effects of inner-city isolation and that expand educational and economic opportunities for poor and minority youth once they finish high school. For the problems that afflict urban schools today extend well beyond the classroom, not only to the new ecology of American cities but also to labor market changes that have eroded the rewards for work and altered the relationship between education and income.[11]

Despite many efforts to alter the educational opportunities for children and adolescents living in urban centers, few resources have been put into repairing the economic circumstances that afflict the lives of so many living in cities.

Why Some Urban Youth Aren't Interested in Receiving an Education

During the 1970s and 1980s, the Great Society legislation passed during the 1960s didn't play out the way legislators predicted for many low-SES families. Much of the ineffectiveness of the federal programs was due to the declining financial situation of the U.S. economy. Many of the difficulties were compounded due to the social unrest of the late 1960s and early 1970s.

The need for a civil-rights movement was surely an indication of the mistrust between African Americans and the White leadership of the day, especially in southern cities. The fact that entire public school districts shuttered their doors to prevent Blacks from entering their schools years after *Brown v. Board of Education* was just one example of a multitude of reasons for Blacks to believe that genuine opportunities for equality would *never* exist.

Trust in public figures in the government eroded quickly due to the assassinations of John and Bobby Kennedy and Martin Luther King, Jr., during the 1960s. The Vietnam War certainly didn't inspire trust in the government. These societal events cannot be downplayed as essential aspects affecting the hopes and aspirations of low-SES students, particularly some African American adolescents and adults whose mistrust in the government led to further strained relationships with all Whites. The feelings of hopelessness among some ethnic minorities during these challenging times perhaps enhanced the *oppositional identity* that may have already been evident in some communities.

Oppositional identity is a term coined by John Ogbu to describe the feelings and beliefs associated with being an *involuntary minority* in the United States.[12] Involuntary minorities didn't choose to come to the United States—in the case of African Americans, they were forced during the slavery era. African Americans cannot return to their native lands. They are centuries removed from their ancestors. The only option is to remain in the United States for the rest of their lives.

When the possibility of a better life is hopeless—a fighting chance for equality and happiness an impossibility in the minds of the many—the result is an attitude of "I won't play your game (in a majority-White society), because there is no chance that I will ever receive the respect I deserve." That attitude of despair—oppositional identity—plays out in the lives of a considerably high percentage of urban youth who feel like involuntary minorities.

Oppositional identity is demonstrated in several ways, as students refuse to:

- come to school prepared to learn;
- do assignments during the school day;
- act cooperatively at school;
- complete any homework;
- accept help from teachers;
- complete high school.

It's challenging enough for teachers to address the oppositional identity of students, but when parents share negative views of the value of education with their children, teachers' jobs are even more difficult.

African Americans aren't the only population of students to demonstrate the uncooperative characteristics of oppositional identity. Immigrants from other countries are apt to act similarly if their circumstances mirror the unhappiness of being in America that African Americans may feel. Teachers in some U.S. communities experience Mexican immigrant students who demonstrate oppositional identity.

In one particular western-state school district I visited, teachers complained that after three generations of immigrant families living in the community, many students refused to acknowledge that they knew enough English to speak it at school. A drive around the district revealed a huge socioeconomic divide between higher-SES Whites and the low-SES Hispanic community.

The dividing line between the communities happened to be the river that ran through the city. On one side of the river were many three-story homes with large properties. On the other side, where the immigrants lived, were many one-story brick buildings that looked like military barracks. Many of those immigrant families never saw themselves as having an opportunity to cross the river to live on the other side. Their economic circumstances seemed dire to them.

Oppositional identity isn't a factor that is ever added to the explanation for urban students refusing to do school work, being suspended frequently, and doing poorly on state tests. Yet how much control do teachers have over this attitude toward academic success, which can permeate the nature of an adolescent's entire schooling career? When teachers understand this attitude, they can certainly attempt to help change the student. But when economic circumstances prevent minority families from moving out of poverty, all the hope from teachers is often not enough to make a difference in students' academic performances or successes.

Other Factors Affecting Urban Students' Opportunities for Academic Success

Academic success for those urban youth whose parents want them to succeed and whose attitudes are positive can also be elusive, due to uncontrollable circumstances that no children should ever endure. Effective educators don't make excuses for why their students don't do well in school because it will do nothing to help them teach better or help their students learn more. But when politicians and business leaders attack urban public schools, some reality about these students' lives is critical to understanding the challenges teachers experience each day.

Crystal England noted some of the problems that affect the success of urban educators:

> Latchkey children. Teen Parents. Children living on the streets. Non-English-speaking learners. Poverty levels. Schools are reflections of society as a whole . . . . When we speak of school failure, we must take a hard look at the failures in the greater American society and seek solutions that reflect a comprehensive effort on behalf of all people.[13]

Effects of Poverty

As cognitive scientists learn more about how the brain works, their revelations explain much about what children and adolescents in low-SES communities experience and the problems that they encounter due to physical issues. Poverty is a critical factor affecting children's chances for academic success.

The effects begin in utero, during those first nine months, and researchers claim they influence a child's IQ score.[14] Those factors include access to quality prenatal care, exposure to carcinogens in the air or water supply, and the level of stress the mother experiences.

Environmental Risks   Once children are born, these same factors continue to affect their cognitive opportunities. Continued exposure to poor air and water quality through lead paint peeling from old walls, noisy neighborhoods, air polluted by constant auto traffic, and a water supply affected by years of pollution from previous industries all negatively affect children's brain development. They experience developmental delays due to exposure to constant unhealthy environments that alter their brains.

As recently as 2003, one of every five children who entered kindergarten in Providence, RI, was diagnosed as having lead in the bloodstream. The state of Ohio noted in 2007 that approximately 150,000 of Ohio's children lived within two miles of medical-waste incinerators.[15]

Even in higher-SES families, children's health issues affect their learning abilities. We all know of children who endured ear problems that eventually led to tubes being placed in their ears, or upper-respiratory difficulties that led to treatment for asthma. In upper- and middle-class neighborhoods, access to health care means that these maladies will be addressed and children will have few reasons to do poorly on academic tasks.

When health care doesn't exist for families, children lose their hearing and suffer from asthma, resulting in much poorer academic performances. Although brains are quite capable of bouncing back from temporary circumstances, low-SES families' situations are not temporary.

Inadequate Diet   My visits to urban schools reveal a surprising missing component in most urban neighborhoods across the United States: large grocery-store chains. As urban populations changed from the 1950s to the 1970s, the traditional small, family-owned grocery stores began to close, as the owners either became too old to continue them or sold their properties. No new grocery chains moved into the cities, as they did in the suburbs.

When the old stores closed, some were reopened as convenience stores, selling snacks rather than fresh produce, grains, dairy products, meats, and other essentials for preparing full, healthy meals. The result in many urban communities is limited access to healthy foods. Plus, due to low-paying jobs, families steer away from expensive proteins and settle for cheaper choices, which usually include high-calorie carbohydrates.

Even if there are possibilities for healthy foods, time limitations for two-job parents prevent children from receiving healthy meals. Many urban youth prepare their own dinners each evening starting at the age of eight or nine. When this occurs, urban children frequently miss their required daily allowances of protein and healthy fruits and vegetables. Without appropriate amounts of protein, children and adolescents turn to carbohydrates as a substitute.

Sugar also becomes a staple that is consumed by children as soon as they begin receiving allowances from caregivers to obtain their meals and snacks for the afternoon and evening. An unbalanced diet presents difficulties for urban youth and compounds their challenges in focusing on learning while in school. School is often the only place where many urban children can depend on receiving a meal each day.

Many teachers recognize the difficulty they have with low-SES students on Mondays, often due to inadequate calorie intake on the weekends—in other words, hunger. This occurs in both rural and urban communities, and teachers often seek strategies for combating it, such as providing children with Friday backpacks filled with food for the weekends. Teachers in some schools studied the effects of loading their low-SES children with extra food during state test time, with gains of 4–7 percent as a result.[16] A greater advantage for urban youth would be to spend less money on tests and more on providing for students' dietary needs!

Effects of Stress   Studies associated with the effects of stress on brain development contribute to low-SES-children's lack of academic success. Eric Jensen describes both *acute* and *chronic* stress that affect children's healthy brain development.[17] Acute stress is associated with abuse or violence, whereas chronic stress is daily and sustained over long periods of time. Stress affects all aspects of a child's growth, from physical to psychological to cognitive processes.

Low-SES children experience stress related to overcrowded living conditions, malnutrition, exposure to poor water quality, family unrest, frequent relocations to new communities, and living in dangerous neighborhoods. These constant pressures cause the brain's neurons to shrink, thereby causing a chain reaction of preventing children from exercising appropriate emotional judgment and preventing them from learning as well.[18]

Stress affects children's learning, as it

- Is linked to over 50 percent of all absences . . . .
- Impairs attention and concentration . . . .
- Reduces cognition, creativity, and memory . . . .
- Diminishes social skills and social judgment . . . .
- Reduces motivation, determination, and effort . . . .
- Increases the likelihood of depression . . . .
- Reduces neurogenesis (growth of new brain cells) . . . .[19]

Accumulated stress also affects students' attitudes about the value of education to their futures. Most victims of gun violence in the United States are from poverty. In 2009, David Berliner reported that 15 percent of adolescents surveyed, most of whom were from low-SES neighborhoods, thought that they would die before the age of 30.[20] Why would 15-year-olds look forward to and strive for high academic achievement if they believed they only had a few years to live?

The effects of stress are overwhelming for poor families. Urban public schools don't have the option of telling these parents to go away when they register their children for school. Recent immigrants frequently flock to cities in America where they might find reasonable housing costs to match their meager hourly wages. With two jobs, the parents can together afford to stay in the states, but the challenges for their children are risky ones.

Modeling the Learning Game: Lagging Language Development

For many children, nothing compares to the joy of being read to by parents. The opportunity to sit alone in a parent's lap and have undivided parental attention as part of the bedtime routine creates more academic success than researchers may ever comprehend. Yet it is not unusual for many low-SES children to have never held a book in their hands prior to entering school.

When children miss that opportunity, they lose access to thousands of minutes of academic preparation. The social exchange, the questions asked by parent and child, and the way questions are asked all contribute to a preparation for reading success. When parents ask their children, "What do you think the character is going to do next?" or "What do you think is going to happen?" before they turn the page, children begin to "play school." If children begin "play reading," that is, retelling the story before they can actually read the words, they begin to develop an understanding of the reading process.

More than that, children who have access to books begin to build a vocabulary—both a listening and speaking vocabulary—that prepares them for schooling. Low-SES children's vocabularies start at an alarmingly lower rate than those of children from higher-SES families. Two educational researchers found in comparing children from diverse SES backgrounds that "by age 3 the children of professional parents were adding words to their vocabularies at about twice the rate of children from welfare families."[21]

Social Difficulties   Beyond physical factors are social factors— whether children receive social support or gain knowledge of, and guidance from parents on, appropriate socialization processes. For decades, researchers have been identifying the link between healthy attachment to the adults in children's lives and their use of appropriate socialization skills. Social relationships are always a factor influencing children's success at school.

Some of the underdeveloped social and academic skills of low-SES children are due to child neglect and abuse. These two factors can result in cognitive delays, language difficulties, obvious psychological problems, high-risk behaviors, depression, and anxiety among urban youth.[22]

How much time can parents and caregivers provide to their children when their lives are consumed by working two or three jobs to make ends meet? Poverty-stricken families frequently face the issue of never having enough time for their children. Jensen, an educational researcher who writes about poverty and its effects on learning, reports,

In many poor households, parental education is substandard, time is short, and warm emotions are at a premium—all factors that put the attunement process [i.e., nurturing children] at risk . . . . Caregivers tend to be overworked, overstressed, and authoritarian with children, using the same harsh disciplinary strategies used by their own parents. They often lack warmth and sensitivity . . . and fail to form solid, healthy relationships with their children.[23]

Jensen's explanation might remind some of their own childhoods, and perhaps some would admit they "turned out all right" despite missing out on warm, caring relationships with parents. But nurturing children impacts their chances for educational success, and nothing is as power-ful as the message that parents send about the daily responsibilities a child has for completing homework, acting appropriately at school, and being conscientious about academics.

Researchers have discovered that family economic challenges often translate into behavioral problems for children at school.[24] Jensen notes the following behaviors that children in poverty may commonly display:

- "Acting out" behaviors.
- Impatience and impulsivity.
- Gaps in politeness and social graces.
- A more limited range of behavioral responses.
- Inappropriate emotional responses.
- Less empathy for others' misfortunes.[25]

When children demonstrate these behaviors, learning doesn't occur until teachers address the social and emotional problems that detract from learning. The more time students need for social and emotional training, the less time they have to focus on the cognitive tasks required for real academic growth. The effects of low SES on children's and ado-lescents' abilities to start school on grade level or ever reach grade level are immense and possibly insurmountable.

MONEY DOES MATTER

Politicians, economists, and businesspersons like to make public state-ments proclaiming that the amount of money available for schools just doesn't make any difference. The morning news broadcasters on CNN frequently mention how much more money schools have received in the past three decades with no positive results to show for it. That comment, sadly, is another sweeping statement with no accurate data to support it.

What businesses won't operate better when their profits provide investments in more innovative machines, greater numbers of employees, or better managers? No businesspersons would deny that the more money available for their operating budgets, the more likely the products they create will be better sellers.

Most urban schools across each state receive the lowest percentage of per-pupil expenditures of all the districts in the state. *Per-pupil expenditure* is the amount of money the school district receives from state and local taxes for each student who attends the district's schools. The per-pupil rate in one suburban district is approximately $22,000, compared to a rate of approximately $12,000 in the neighboring Philadelphia School District. Does a $10,000 difference for each child sound like a great deal of money?

The following are some of the differences between one local suburban school district and Philadelphia:

- Every high school student in the suburban district receives a laptop computer from the school to use at home as well as at school, whereas many of the Philadelphia schools have two or three computers per classroom.
- The suburban district recently completed the construction of two new high schools within a year of one another, whereas only a handful of new schools have been built in Philadelphia, a district with approximately 300 schools, in the past 20 years.
- Middle schools in the suburban district have numerous after-school athletic-team opportunities, whereas the recently proposed state budget has prompted the Philadelphia School District to eliminate all after-school athletics at the middle schools.

Does it appear that money makes a difference in this scenario? A 2008 Title I report to Congress revealed, "In the highest poverty schools, Title I funding per low-income student has not changed since 1997–98, after adjusting for inflation."[26] It may be more money than was provided 10 years ago, but like your paycheck, that money doesn't go as far as it did in 1997!

Recent changes in gubernatorial seats in several states have accelerated the loss in state revenues for many urban districts. In Pennsylvania, for instance, the governor's proposed 2012 education budget would cut the per-pupil expenditures in Philadelphia by over $1,400. Proposed cuts for New York City schools would leap to over $1,500 per student. Other low-SES communities' schools are also facing significant cuts to their per-pupil expenditures. Nothing could be more devastating to educators and parents in those low-SES communities, where every dollar adds to improving opportunities for many needy students.

These cuts will have significant impacts on students' abilities to get closer to becoming proficient on their state tests. Cuts mean larger class sizes, fewer services for students with special needs, less technology, and fewer teachers. Anyone who has ever taught would agree that money has an enormous impact in providing for the learning needs of students and the teaching needs of educators.

The greatest impact that money makes on effective teaching and learning is when it is used to provide more teachers to handle the needs of fewer students. Every school that alters the ratio of teacher to students such that teachers must handle more students compromises the effectiveness of the teacher and decreases the opportunities for learning among students.

An Educational Testing Services researcher found that state education spending positively affected students' test scores. *A Harvard University professor discovered that districts that reduced class size had improved test scores*, as did the Finn and Achilles study called the Student Teacher Achievement Ratio study.[27]

One particular economist, Eric Hanushek, has tried to uphold the theory that class size doesn't matter in student achievement. His studies and theories have been cited by many, and he does speaking engagements across the United States in support of his findings. Educational researchers and several other economists, however, have found significant flaws in Hanushek's research techniques.[28]

If Hanushek's promoting a point of view based on faulty research to purposely prevent children in every community from receiving the funding they deserve to improve their chances for school success, then he should feel great shame. How will his offspring fare when they land in a class of 30 students instead of 22?

NOTHING IS MORE POWERFUL THAN PARENTAL INFLUENCE

CNN aired a documentary in the spring of 2011 titled *Education in America: Don't Fail Me.*[29] The lives of three high school students were followed throughout the hour-long program. They were chosen based on the distinct socioeconomic differences among them: a male from a high-SES neighborhood in New Jersey, another male from a middle-class town in eastern Tennessee, and a female student from a low-SES urban school district in Phoenix, Arizona.

All three high school students were members of their schools' technology-challenge teams, charged with using robotics kits to design machines that would perform elaborate physical tasks. It was a national competition, and the stakes were high as winning teams would likely also garner college scholarships for their efforts. These high school students were required to be in advanced mathematics and science classes for the opportunity to participate in the challenge.

One part of their interview with CNN correspondent Soledad O'Brien included questions about their educational interests, and they were asked to explain why they had such high academic expectations for themselves. The two male students admitted that their parents were the driving force behind their decisions to perform well academically, and that without their parents' influence they wouldn't have been so successful. Both sets of parents agreed that they expected academic excellence from their children.

O'Brien asked the New Jersey student, who was of Asian descent, why there were so many Asian American students in his advanced mathematics classes at school. He stated, without hesitation, that parents were the reason for such academic success, no matter what a student's ethnic background.

The student from Phoenix admitted that her father had expected her to drop out of school, based on the record of her older sisters getting pregnant prior to graduation and dropping out. Her mother, though, had pushed for her to become more engaged in science and technology, pleading with local school officials to place her in advanced classes.

Without the driving force of parental support and expectations of college, these students might never have chosen an opportunity to achieve such high academic success. They recognized the overwhelming power of parental influence, as do researchers and teachers. Teachers from all communities have a fairly accurate idea of which parents have established a set of high expectations for their children. As much effort as urban teachers put into pushing their students to excel, they all know that in almost every situation, parents have a greater impact than they do.

WHO TEACHES IN URBAN SCHOOLS?

Teacher Dropouts

A set of seventh- and eighth-graders in inner-city Philadelphia explained in interviews that they had just met their ninth new teacher of the year for their mathematics class. The other eight had left, one by one, at some point between September and January. The students were highly disappointed. They explained that they wanted to learn, but the teaching changes made it difficult for them to make progress in a continuous manner.

Urban public schools paid the highest teacher salaries in the United States prior to the late 1960s, when the tax base of corporations and factories left the cities. Drawing effective educators into urban schools was easier from the 1930s to the early 1960s because many high- to middle-income families lived in the cities. The suburbs changed the demographics of cities as corporations left, middle- and high-income families moved out, and the tax base was ripped away from urban centers.

The thought of becoming an urban teacher no longer held the prestige that it had previously. Teacher compensation also dropped, and the best-paying education jobs moved into suburban districts. The districts that were drawing the most profitable big businesses were also hiring the best teachers, as higher salaries were available. Following graduation from college, the best teaching candidates often took jobs far from the big cities, and experienced teachers also moved into the higher-paying districts, some leaving urban teaching positions.

Who, then, signs a contract with an urban school district? Recent graduates and other novice educators who aren't hired in the suburbs often reluctantly take positions in urban schools. The money isn't great, and the students' lives that they encounter in cities don't reflect their childhoods.

The Danger of Uncertified Teachers

By the early 1990s, finding enough teachers for urban districts was so difficult that schools started hiring many highly unqualified, uncertified teachers through the Teach for America program. These uncertified teachers have a considerable failure rate due to the fact that they lack the training and certification to be professional educators. They also enter urban schools, where the most experienced, certified teachers are needed.

Urban districts hire many teachers who receive temporary certification for a year or two while they take education courses at local universities to become certified. That can be a long two years, though, to place someone's child or adolescent with an unqualified and untrained educator. But the allure of entering the profession via an urban school is unappealing to many certified graduates.

As they begin their teaching careers around the United States, as many as 20 to 30 percent of urban teachers are initially *uncertified*. Urban districts are making some progress in retaining more certified teachers as a result of NCLB legislation, but recent attacks by business leaders and proposals by some state legislatures and governors are beginning to erode the teaching force in urban centers, as more *uncertified* teachers are permitted to enter the schools. Charter schools that hire uncertified teachers also damage the opportunities for urban youth.

I have met many dedicated, certified, and well-prepared teachers in my experiences working with and visiting several urban schools over the past 20 years. It takes strong-willed and determined people to teach in urban schools. It also requires a dedication to helping children and adolescents grow from the often low academic levels with which they enter school. Effective urban teachers focus on students' abilities to develop better academic abilities, attitudes, motivation, and confidence as learners, no matter how low students' abilities are when they enter classrooms each year.

Not every teacher education candidate, even when certified, is the best choice for an urban teaching position. Certified teachers have a much better opportunity for success, but the learning curve is often slow and long due to the realization that these students aren't like the kids that most teachers grew up with. Teachers who use the "these kids sure are different" excuse are useless as professional educators.

NCLB: Turning Away Effective Teachers

Research reveals that effective urban teachers use genuine care for their students each day in making learning a more motivating experience. Care for students can't be faked, because all children know when and to what extent their teachers care. Urban students also need teachers who do much more than read a script from one of the publishing companies, approved by the federal Department of Education.

Urban students want and need content that addresses their questions about the world; reflects their ethnic backgrounds; honors their families and their heritage; respects the challenges they experience in their poverty; and addresses their searches for identity in their ethnic diversity. NCLB has ruined the possibility for urban students' academic motivation for learning through its negative impact on the delivery of meaningful curricula.

Urban youth can begin to enjoy school as soon as publishing companies, charter schools, scripted curricula, and NCLB regulations are eliminated from their lives. Until that time, educators won't find valid reasons to apply for or accept teaching positions in urban centers. Even if proposals to pay bonuses to urban teachers go into effect, urban teaching will continue to be demeaning to certified teachers who are trained to listen to students and provide motivating experiences based on their needs—something scripted reading programs don't provide.

Many highly qualified certified teachers continue to drive into the cities every day across the United States because they have held on to hope despite the negative influence of NCLB. They are effective educators because their students make progress each day. Their growth may not match the bar set by NCLB, but urban educators' teaching inspires children and adolescents, and that's what these youth need.

It is too convenient and inaccurate to cast aspersions on urban teachers. They deserve as much respect, if not more, as teachers in places where parents meet most of their children's needs. Urban teachers have daily battles with students that suburban teachers seldom experience. The lack of respect for urban educators leads to policy and personnel decisions that are disrespectful to the teaching profession.

Lack of Leadership

When you hear the term *CEO* (i.e., chief executive officer) of a school district, be warned—a noneducator has stepped into a role for which he or she is unprepared. Several education CEOs exist, usually hired by urban school boards to do a job previously reserved for former teachers who have received their master's degrees and been trained via certification as viable administrators—principals and superintendents. Anyone with the CEO label is *not* an educator.

Another demeaning component of urban schools is the hiring of noneducators to be school superintendents. Among the questionable hires for superintendents' positions are Michelle Rhee, Paul Vallas, and Roy Romer. There are many others, but these three are more well known. Rhee has a bachelor's degree in government and a master's in public policy, but no education courses that might improve her vision of the research in the field. Her experiences as a Teach for America candidate hardly qualify her as an effective candidate for a superintendency.

Paul Vallas has made the rounds visiting famous cities—Chicago, Philadelphia, New Orleans—while masquerading as an educational leader along the way. He attempted to become the governor of Illinois, but lost in the primary, so he headed to Philadelphia to make hundreds of thousands of dollars as the CEO of schools there.

Vallas was asked to speak at the opening session of the 2005 National Middle School Association meeting in Philadelphia, since he was the CEO there at the time. A year or so prior to the meeting, Vallas had begun dismantling several middle schools in Philadelphia, claiming that they weren't good for kids. His speech wasn't particularly supportive of the middle school concept because he wasn't aware of the research on middle schools.

How did Roy Romer suddenly become the superintendent of the Los Angeles Schools, with his bachelor's degree in agricultural economics and a law degree? His role as a governor in Colorado did not provide him with the necessary knowledge to comprehend a day in the life of an urban teacher. Urban superintendents tend to rotate from city to city, as has been the situation with Vallas and the former superintendent of the Philadelphia schools, Arlene Ackerman, who was previously the super in San Francisco and in Washington, DC.

These appointments to urban educational-leadership positions are like whirlwind tours of hip-hop musical artists. These urban superintendents and CEOs are well paid, too. Ackerman was recently relieved of her duties, and her remaining contract was bought out by taxpayers for $905,000. Ackerman's close associations with educational management organizations were frequently questioned, as she continued to court charter school companies such as Mosaica to take over another of Philly's public high schools. Ackerman's purchasing of scripted curricula in mathematics and science put elementary and middle school students through several hours of mind-numbing learning each day of the week. Teachers describe it as torturous for them and their students (see chapter 9).

Some urban school-leadership appointments ignore the critical information needed by a leader in education—information associated with seeing the lives of children living in poverty, and seeing urban teachers living the day-to-day challenges they face and experiencing the frustration of being treated with disrespect by parents, the press, and politicians who dismiss their significance. CEOs are not educators: lacking the education profession's credentials and experience, they cannot represent the profession. This trend of hiring noneducators to head the schools is hurting children—it's a terrible injustice to their chances for successful educational experiences.

THE FALLACIES OF "FAILING SCHOOLS" AND "DROPOUT FACTORIES"

If one listens to the news often, one will hear the recently coined phrases *dropout factory* and *failing school*. Why would someone choose these labels when the dropout rate has decreased every decade for the past century? As mentioned before, during the 1950s the dropout rate was near 50 percent. Where were the "dropout factories" then?

They may have been in your neighborhood, or your parents' or grandparents' neighborhoods, somewhere west of Dallas; or just south of Boston; or perhaps 100 miles north of Minneapolis. Or maybe the failing school was in Peoria, Illinois, miles away from urban centers. How many students dropped out of your high school? Usually *dropout factory* is applied to urban high schools in places like Houston, New Orleans, Chicago, and Wichita. The fact that a considerable percentage of those who drop out live in urban areas should not be a surprise considering the circumstances in many of these students' lives.

But dropouts are everywhere. My second year of teaching was in the middle of Iowa. One of my sixth-grade students that year was determined to become a cowboy. He already had a circle-shaped outline in his back pants pocket, caused by his habit of placing his smokeless-tobacco can in his pants. I guessed his future plan was as good as anyone else's—even those who planned to graduate from high school. Plus, who hasn't dreamed of becoming a cowboy or cowgirl? I didn't see any reason to disrupt his future plans—as if I had any influence anyway.

One year I taught in Wisconsin, in the community where the state prison was located. I know several students I taught dropped out of school. One of them didn't have running water in his house, and another lived in a house that was shot at one evening—unfortunate circumstances that had an impact on their attitudes about the value of a high school degree.

I knew friends during my high school years who dropped out of school—and they were some of the smartest students at school. Some immigrant students drop out because receiving an education runs afoul of their plans for a happy adulthood, that is, they don't perceive a high school diploma as necessary to successful adult lives. Some African American students drop out because they feel the pain of oppositional identity in their mistrust for Whites. The likelihood of dropping out of school is certainly much greater when graduating seems pointless.

The uselessness of a high school diploma can easily be justified by many adolescents, students whose lives are so very different from those of students in higher-SES neighborhoods who have greater motivation and hope to graduate. The "American dream" is often the driving force behind students' academic success and perceived happiness. The northern European influence on what *happiness* is in the United States causes those in power to believe that no other description of *success* can be substituted for it.

The White European American perspective on what success means is:

1. Work hard—it'll lead to a wonderful life.
2. Find a way to make as much money as is possible—because success can only be measured by how much money one makes.
3. Once you find a high-paying job, buy expensive items—a big house, expensive cars, furniture, and a big-screen, three-dimensional TV.
4. If you have to move away from your family to get a higher paying job, then do it.
5. Always take the highest-paying job offered—that's what successful people do, even if it means competing with and stepping on your colleagues in the process, or taking a job you may highly dislike.
6. The order of priorities in your life should be as follows: (1) making money; (2) work; (3) family.
7. Don't share your monetary gain with those less fortunate than you—they can work hard enough to get their own needs met.
8. Everyone can become as financially successful as every other person in the United States—if he or she just works hard enough.
9. Those who don't have what I have in life financially don't need any help to reach the heights I have, because they have every opportunity that I did to get to the top.

Not every person buys into these philosophies, but these perspectives drive the current education policy in America. NCLB is based on these premises, among many other flawed theories of human behavior. The idea that the purpose of education is to enter the workforce to provide labor for the richest people in the United States is motivation enough for some to drop out of school.

Many people's ideas about being successful in life aren't defined by the standards mentioned above. Success doesn't have to be associated with making money; moving away from family; living in a large house or the "right" neighborhood; or taking the highest-paying job. Success may be defined as having your first child at the age of 17; becoming an apprentice to a plumber at the age of 15; starting a rap group and performing in the neighborhood at 17; or becoming a cowboy at the age of 14. Life is a journey, and the purpose of education is to help others find their own joy in living their lives, rather than pushing them into someone else's dream.

There are plenty of valid reasons to leave school before graduating, and many suburban students choose to do so, just as do urban and rural students. *Students drop out—teachers don't make them drop out.* It's senseless to blame urban teachers for the dropout rate in cities. The dropout rate is not the fault of urban teachers, any more than it is suburban teachers' fault when their students drop out. Was I to blame for my sixth-grader's becoming a cowboy instead of receiving his high school diploma? Why isn't his dream as significant as those dreams of other, more academically successful, students?

The label *failing school* is a misnomer because students either grow or don't grow while at school. Entire schools are not filled with poor teachers ruining students' lives every day. Teachers can't afford to be lazy, because of the real accountability described in chapter 9—an accountability based on helping each student grow some every day. Knowing what low-SES students' lives are like should help us all to recognize the fallibility of NCLB policies that penalize schools and teachers for factors beyond their control. No rationale exists for the blame game from politicians, pundits, and businesspersons who skewer teachers, teacher unions, and colleges of education for allegedly failing schools.

ACHIEVEMENT GAP? JUST ANOTHER BLAME GAME

A terminology shift with the effect of placing blame on public schools was the introduction and eventual institutionalization of the term *achievement gap.* "Achievement gap" is supposed to represent the idea that students from high-SES communities do well in school, whereas students from low-SES communities don't do as well—thus a gap exists. The purpose of such a term may be to reinforce any legislation or policies that promote business takeovers of schools. Such language may encourage the idea of dismantling urban public schools in favor of reducing taxes, as they are replaced by charter schools.

Renowned educational researcher Berliner repeated a journalist's observation that both the *New York Times* and *Education Week* had more frequently used the label *a lack of equal educational opportunity* to describe educational differences from the early 1980s until around 2000. Following that time period, there was a sharp rise in the frequency with which both papers switched to the term *achievement gap*.[30] By 2002, few in the media were writing about the realization that the lack of educational opportunities was the cause of many discrepancies in students' academic performance. Instead, they were labeling the differences as a *gap*.

The label *achievement gap* is absurd terminology. When African Americans were slaves, would anyone have imagined mentioning that an "achievement gap" in educational attainment existed between them and those who were not slaves at the time? When southern public school districts refused to open their doors to African Americans who were by law permitted to attend previously all-White schools, did anyone suggest that an achievement gap existed? When only wealthy families sent their children to school during the 1800s, did anyone suggest a *gap* between children of the wealthy and lower-class citizens? Every one of these situations describes an *inability to provide equal opportunities* to those who are entitled to the same chances as all others.

Performance gaps among children have always been obvious when it comes to educational success. An achievement gap has always existed between students studying to enter professions such as carpentry or hair styling and college-bound students. How about the gap between women who were discouraged from attending college during the early part of the 20th century and men of the same era? When these gaps occurred, concerned citizens identified the problem as one of a lack of equal educational opportunities, and used that premise to equalize the opportunities.

A gap between and among students has always existed and will always exist. Each time a gap is discovered, citizens have a responsibility to address it in moral ways, rather than labeling it, perhaps in part, with the goal of disparaging teachers. When these inequities are identified as *a lack of equal educational opportunity*, a better chance of finding solutions exists.

It is appropriate to stop using *achievement gap* to compare differences among children, and to choose instead to discuss how every community in each state is going to erase the *funding gap* between children in cities and those from the higher-SES suburban neighborhoods. A genuine conversation is needed about *equal opportunities* before using *achievement gap* to blame the education profession. When taxpayers begin to address this *opportunity gap*, then educators might have a fighting chance to erase the achievement gap.

As *gaps* go, it's time to begin studying the *salary gap* between teachers and other college graduates. Many politicians aren't interested in that conversation because it may mean raising taxes to move education spending into the 21st-century economy—something a majority of politicians seem averse to. In examining serious gaps, will someone ever address the *millionaires gap* between Bill Gates, Eli Broad, and the Waltons, and millions of people in this country?

WHAT URBAN SCHOOLS MEAN TO THOSE WHO LIVE THERE

This entire book is about defining *good* schools. The students in urban centers are home. This is where their families live and where they play. Their neighbors live here. Their existence is in the cities they call home: Chicago, New York, Wichita, Las Vegas, Minneapolis, Philadelphia, Los Angeles, San Francisco, and Portland. The lives of some residents of American cities are considerably better than their previous existence in other countries.

Their public schools are urban schools—providing the services, content, effective teaching, and care that gives these children the same hope that children all over America receive each day in their schools. Diane Ravitch notes,

> Our schools will not improve if we continue to close neighborhood schools in the name of reform. Neighborhood schools are often the anchors of their communities, a steady presence that helps to cement the bonds of community among neighbors. Most are places with a history, laden with traditions and memories that help individuals resist fragmentation in their lives.
>
> Their graduates return and want to see their old classrooms; they want to see the trophy cases and the old photographs, to hear the echoes in the gymnasium and walk on the playing fields. To close these schools serves no purpose other than to destroy those memories, to sever the building from the culture of its neighborhood, and to erode a sense of community that was decades in the making.[31]

Urban families aren't ashamed of their schools; neither are urban teachers. Learning takes personal pride. The urban students I've met and interviewed over the past 10 years feel this pride and want their schooling experiences to be meaningful and to take them somewhere. The politicians, businesspersons, and press who use the bully pulpit to continually dismiss the efforts of educators in urban schools do nothing to help the students who attend those schools.

All parents care about their children, and although some don't have the means to give children everything they need to succeed academically, they certainly expect their urban schools to help their children grow—just as others expect the schools in their neighborhoods to help their children grow. Support from outside of the cities would help the parents and children who reside in the cities. When can urban children and educators expect support from the rest of the United States?

AFTERWORD

Americans' commitment to public schools should never be compromised. The act of building public schools in or near every community of all 50 states is a testament to the significance Americans place on the value of equal educational opportunities for all citizens.

The past and current success of America's public schools is the reason that immigrants still flock to U.S. shores—to share the dreams that are fulfilled through the unending possibilities provided via a public education. Many immigrant families don't take their public-education opportunities for granted—they comprehend the meaning of the power of education to their children's lives.

Most Americans' ancestors shared the same dreams as current immigrant families. The gains achieved by their families over several generations as a result of their public school experiences create great pride for current grandparents, who comprehend the relationship of more educational opportunities to families' improved social and economic circumstances.

Families' academic successes are only possible due to the education professionals who dedicate their lives to improving the academic abilities of every child and adolescent they encounter. That mission defines *American public education*. America's public education system has evolved through time; it is an evolutionary process often driven by societal forces beyond the control of the professionals who strive to meet students' needs in more areas than is humanly possible.

Yet public educators have weathered America's past and current challenging times, always attempting to meet society's expectations for improving all citizens' lives. The very fact that Americans place the responsibility for improving lives on educators is a sign of the constant faith that persists in public education. Continued support is also a recognition by citizens of the past successes that public education has produced.

This is no time for Americans to abandon this hallowed system that has opened so many doors for the country as a whole and for each individual who has benefited from a public education. May the facts within this book provide the populace with the evidence for an explicit and definitive, continued support for teachers, administrators, and support personnel who do their best to ensure the success of every child through their daily interactions in America's public schools.

NOTES

FOREWORD

1. Gerald W. Bracey, *On the Death of Childhood and the Destruction of Public Schools* (Portsmouth, NH: Heinemann, 2003), 59.

2. Ann McGill-Franzen and Richard L. Allington, "Got Books?" Educational Leadership 65, no. 7 (April 2008): 20–23.

CHAPTER 1. PUBLIC SCHOOLS: SUCCESSFUL GRADUATES

1. Richard A. Gibboney, "Why an Undemocratic Capitalism Has Brought Public Education to Its Knees: A Manifesto," *Phi Delta Kappan* 90, no. 1 (September 2008): 21–31.

2. William J. Bushaw and John A. McNee, "Americans Speak Out—Are Educators and Policy Makers Listening? The 41st Annual Phi Delta Kappa/Gallup Poll of the Public's Attitudes toward the Public Schools," *Phi Delta Kappan* 91, no. 1 (September 2009): 9–23.

3. Words written on the inside walls of the Jefferson Memorial in Washington, DC.

4. Kathleen Bennett DeMarrais and Margaret D. LeCompte, *The Way Schools Work: A Sociological Analysis of Education*, 3rd ed. (New York: Addison Wesley Longman, 1999), 8.

5. Retrieved on March 5, 2006 from Japan.guide.com and www.hyperstudy.com/institutions_ courses/ukeducationsystem.asp.

6. This federal law (PL 94-142) was originally passed in 1975 and subsequently amended five times, most recently in 2004.

7. At www.nces.ed.gov/ (accessed February 2, 2008).

8. At www.nces.ed.gov/.

9. Retrieved either through direct telephone calls to admissions offices, or through university websites.

10. William J. Bushaw and Alec M. Gallup, "Americans Speak Out—Are Educators and Policy Makers Listening? The 40th Annual Phi Delta Kappa/Gallup Poll of the Public's Attitudes toward the Public Schools," *Phi Delta Kappan* 90, no. 1 (September 2008): 8–20.

11. William J. Bushaw and Shane J. Lopez, "A Time for Change: The 42nd Annual Phi Delta Kappa/Gallup Poll of the Public's Attitudes toward the Public Schools," *Phi Delta Kappan* 92, no. 1 (September 2010): 9–26.

12. Lowell C. Rose and Alec M Gallup, "The 39th Annual Phi Delta Kappa/Gallup Poll of the Public's Attitudes toward the Public Schools," *Phi Delta Kappan* 89, no. 1 (September 2007): 33–45. (Quotation on 37.)

13. Lowell C. Rose and Alec M. Gallup, "The 38th Annual Phi Delta Kappa/Gallup Poll of the Public's Attitudes toward the Public Schools," *Phi Delta Kappan* 88, no. 1 (September 2006): 41–56.

14. Bushaw and Gallup, "Americans Speak Out."

CHAPTER 2. IS THE PUBLIC SCHOOL IN YOUR COMMUNITY A "GOOD" SCHOOL?

1. Lowell C. Rose and Alec M Gallup, "The 39th Annual Phi Delta Kappa/Gallup Poll of the Public's Attitudes toward the Public Schools," *Phi Delta Kappan* 89, no. 1 (September 2007): 33–45.

2. Robert J. Marzano, *What Works in Schools: Translating Research into Action* (Alexandria, VA: Association for Supervision and Curriculum Development, 2003), 16–19.

3. Jan L. Goodman, Virginia Sutton, and Ira Harkevy, "The Effectiveness of Family Workshops in a Middle School Setting: Respect and Caring Make a Difference," *Phi Delta Kappan* 76, no. 9 (May 1995): 694–700.

4. Kris Bosworth, "Caring for Others and Being Cared For: Students Talk about Caring in School," *Phi Delta Kappan* 76, no. 9 (May 1995): 686–93.

5. William J. Bushaw and Shane J. Lopez, "A Time for Change: The 42nd Annual Phi Delta Kappa/Gallup Poll of the Public's Attitudes toward the Public Schools," *Phi Delta Kappan* 92, no. 1 (September 2010): 9–26.

6. James H. Strong, *Qualities of Effective Teachers* (Alexandria, VA: Association of Supervision and Curriculum Development, 2002), 16.

7. Susan M. Brookhart, *How to Give Effective Feedback to Your Students* (Alexandria, VA: Association for Supervision and Curriculum Development, 2008).

8. Robert J. Marzano, *The Art and Science of Teaching* (Alexandria, VA: Association for Supervision and Curriculum Development, 2007), 1.

9. Retrieved on 3 March 2006 from educators.state university.com/pages/2003/guidance-Counselors-School.html and www.usatoday.com/new/health/ 2009-08-10 -school-nurses-Nhtm.

10. Alfie Kohn, *The Case against Standardized Testing: Raising the Scores, Ruining the Schools* (Portsmouth, NH: Heinemann, 2000). See also Deborah Meier and George Wood, eds., *Many Children Left Behind: How the No Child Left Behind Act Is Damaging Our Children and Our Schools* (Boston: Beacon Press, 2004).

11. A. T. Henderson and Nancy Berla, *A New Generation of Evidence: The Family Is Critical to Student Achievement* (Washington, DC: Center for Law and Education, 1995), 14–16.

12. Angela Duckworth and Martin Seligman, "Self-Discipline Outdoes I.Q. in Predicting Academic Performance of Adolescents," 2005. At www.blackwell-synergy.com/doi/ abs/10.1111/ j.1467-9280.2005.01641.x. Cited in Kathy Christie, "Stateline: Innovations and Other Findings," *Phi Delta Kappan* 87, no. 8 (April 2006): 566.

13. Kathy Christie, "Stateline: Innovations and Other Findings," 566.

CHAPTER 3. HOW AMERICA'S SCHOOLS OUTSHINE OTHER NATIONS' SCHOOLS

1. Yong Zhao, *Catching Up or Leading the Way: American Education in the Age of Globalization* (Alexandria, VA: Association for Supervision and Curriculum Development, 2009), vii.

2. Rana Foroohar, "The Best Countries in the World," *Newsweek*, August 23–30, 2010, 30–38.

3. Gerald W. Bracey, *Education Hell: Rhetoric vs. Reality: Transforming the Fire Consuming America's Schools* (Alexandria, VA: Educational Research Service, 2009).

4. Bracey, *Education Hell*, 6.

5. Bracey, *Education Hell*, 130–31.

6. Bracey, *Education Hell*, 132.

7. Bracey, *Education Hell*, 181.

8. Alfie Kohn, *What to Look for in a Classroom, and Other Essays* (San Francisco: Jossey-Bass, 1998), 101.

9. Po Bronson and Ashley Merryman, "The Creativity Crisis," *Newsweek*, July 19, 2010, 44–50.

10. Zhao, *Catching Up or Leading the Way*, vii.

11. Bracey, *Education Hell*, 107.

12. Bronson and Merryman, "The Creativity Crisis."

13. See Dave F. Brown and Trudy Knowles, *What Every Middle School Teacher Should Know*, 2nd ed. (Portsmouth, NH: Heinemann, 2007). See also Mark Springer, *Soundings: A Democratic Student-Centered Education* (Westerville, OH: National Middle School Association, 2006).

14. Robert L. Canady and Michael D. Rettig, *Block Scheduling: A Catalyst for Change in High Schools* (Princeton: Eye on Education, 1995).

15. Zhao, *Catching Up or Leading the Way*, vi.

16. Ali Velshi (correspondent on *Live CNN*), May 11, 2010.

17. Bracey, *Education Hell*, 5; Fareed Zakaria, "We All Have a Lot to Learn," *Newsweek*, January 9, 2006, at fareedzakaria.com/articles/newsweek/010906.html.

18. Bracey, *Education Hell*, 66.

19. Linda Darling-Hammond and Robert Rothman, eds., *Teacher and Leader Effectiveness in High Performing Education Systems* (Washington, DC: Alliance for Excellent Education, 2011), 5.

20. Darling-Hammond and Rothman, *Teacher and Leader Effectiveness in High Performing Education Systems*, 6.

21. Darling-Hammond and Rothman, *Teacher and Leader Effectiveness in High Performing Education Systems*, 16.

22. Thomas L. Friedman, *Hot, Flat, and Crowded: Why We Need A Green Revolution—And How It Can Be Done* (New York: Farrar, Straus and Giroux, 2008).

23. Friedman, *Hot, Flat, and Crowded*, 11.

24. Eric Jensen, *Teaching with Poverty in Mind: What Being Poor Does to Kids' Brains and What Schools Can Do about It* (Alexandria, VA: Association for Supervision and Curriculum Development, 2009), 31–32.

25. Bracey, *Education Hell*, 64–65.

26. Keith Baker, "Are International Tests Worth Anything?" *Phi Delta Kappan* 89, no. 2 (October 2007): 101–4. (Quotation from 102.)

27. Zhao, *Catching Up or Leading the Way*, 17.

28. At nces.ed.gov/programs/coe/2010/section4/ indicator38.asp (accessed January 13, 2011).

29. David C. Berliner and Bruce J. Biddle, *The Manufactured Crisis: Myths, Fraud, and the Attack on America's Public Schools* (Reading, MA: Addison-Wesley, 1995).

30. Deborah Meier, *In Schools We Trust: Creating Communities of Learning in an Era of Testing and Standardization* (Boston: Beacon Press, 2002), 11.

31. Lawrence A. Cremin, *Popular Education and Its Discontents* (New York: Harper and Row, 1989).

32. Cremin, *Popular Education and Its Discontents*.

33. David Tyack, *The One Best System: A History of American Urban Education* (Cambridge, MA: Harvard University Press, 1974).

34. Tom Brokaw, *The Greatest Generation* (New York: Random House, 1998).

35. Brokaw, *The Greatest Generation*, inside front-cover material.

36. Lawrence Mishel and Richard Rothstein, "Improper Diagnosis, Reckless Treatment," *Phi Delta Kappan* 89, no. 1 (September 2007): 31–32, 49–51.

CHAPTER 4. THE VALUE OF PUBLIC SCHOOL TEACHERS

1. Gaea Leinhardt, quoted in Daniel Moulthrop, Ninive Clements Calegari, and Dave Eggers, *Teachers Have It Easy: The Big Sacrifices and Small Salaries of America's Teachers* (New York: New Press, 2005), 101–2.

2. Martin Carnoy et al., *The Charter School Dust-Up: Examining the Evidence on Enrollment and Achievement* (Washington, DC: Economic Policy Institute, 2005), 3.

3. Jayne Boyd-Zaharias and Helen Pate-Bain, "Class Matters—In and Out of School," *Phi Delta Kappan* 90, no. 1 (September 2008): 40–44.

4. Kenneth D. Kastle, "Educators Must Rally for Reform," *Phi Delta Kappan* 90, no. 1 (September 2008): 38–39.

5. Moulthrop, Calegari, and Eggers, *Teachers Have It Easy*, 2.

6. Reg Weaver, "President's Viewpoint," *NEA Today*, January 2008, 9.

7. Weaver, "President's Viewpoint," 17.

8. Mary Ellen Flannery, *NEA Today*, November 2006, 34.

9. Moulthrop, Calegari, and Eggers, *Teachers Have It Easy*.

10. Charles Murray, *Real Education: Four Simple Truths for Bringing America's Schools Back to Reality* (New York: Three Rivers Press, 2008), 47.

11. Moulthrop, Calegari, and Eggers, *Teachers Have It Easy*, 102.

12. Moulthrop, Calegari, and Eggers, *Teachers Have It Easy*, 103.

13. Moulthrop, Calegari, and Eggers, *Teachers Have It Easy*, 6.

14. Gerald Bracey, *Setting the Record Straight: Responses to Misconceptions about Public Education in the United States*, 2nd ed. (Portsmouth, NH: Heinemann, 2004), 4.

15. Frank Schwartz, "Why Many New Teachers Are Unprepared to Teach in Most New York City Schools," *Phi Delta Kappan* 78, no. 1 (September 1996): 82–84.

16. Moulthrop, Calegari, and Eggers, *Teachers Have It Easy*, 10.

17. Moulthrop, Calegari, and Eggers, *Teachers Have It Easy*, 49.

18. Moulthrop, Calegari, and Eggers, *Teachers Have It Easy*, 83.

19. Moulthrop, Calegari, and Eggers, *Teachers Have It Easy*, 90.

20. Rick Allen, *Education Update* 50, no. 3 (March 2008): 4.

21. Linda Darling-Hammond, "Teacher Quality and Student Achievement: A Review of State Policy Evidence," *Education Policy Analysis ARCHIVES* 8, no. 1, at epaa. asu.edu/epaa/v8n1.

22. Ildiko Laczko-Kerr and David Berliner, "In Harm's Way: How Uncertified Teachers Hurt Their Students," *Educational Leadership* 60, no. 8 (May 2003): 34–39.

23. Laczko-Kerr and Berliner, "In Harm's Way," 36.

24. Laczko-Kerr and Berliner, "In Harm's Way"; citing from S. M. Wilson, R. E. Floden, and J. Ferrini-Mundy, "Teacher Preparation and Research: An Insider's View from the Outside," *Journal of Teacher Education* 53, no. 3 (2002): 190–204.

25. Laczko-Kerr and Berliner, "In Harm's Way," 37; from Wilson, Floden, and Ferrini-Mundy, "Teacher Preparation and Research."

26. Jay Matthews, "Jay vs. Valerie: Who Needs Teach for America?" December 10, 2010, at voices.washingtonpost.com/class-struggle/2010/12/jay_vs_valerie.html.

27. Julian Vasquez Heilig and Su Jin Jez, *Teach for America: A Review of the Evidence*, Boulder and Tempe: Education and the Public Interest Center & Education Policy Research Unit, June 9, 2010, at http://epicpolicy.org/publication/teach-for-america (accessed September 13, 2011); Jodi Wilgoren, "Wendy Kopp, Leader of Teach for America," November 12, 2000, at partners.nytimes.com/library/national/111200edlife-kopp-edu.html (accessed September 13, 2011).

28. Steven Farr, "Leadership, Not Magic," *Educational Leadership* 68, no. 4 (2010): 28–33.

29. James Stronge, *Qualities of Effective Teachers* (Alexandria, VA: Association for Supervision and Curriculum Development, 2002), 7.

30. Kathy Emery and Susan Ohanian, *Why Is Corporate America Bashing Our Public Schools?* (Portsmouth, NH: Heinemann, 2004).

31. James H. Stronge, *Qualities of Effective Teachers* (Alexandria, VA: Association for Supervision and Curriculum Development, 2002).

32. Stronge, *Qualities of Effective Teachers*, 5.

33. Bracey, *Setting the Record Straight*, 144.

34. Sean Corcoran, William N. Evans, and Robert M. Schwab, "Teacher Quality: Changing Labor Market Opportunities for Women and the Quality of Teachers, 1957–2000," *AEA Papers and Proceedings, American Economic Review*, May 2004, 230–35.

35. Laczko-Kerr and Berliner, "In Harm's Way"; citing from D. Gitomer, A. S. Latham, and R. Ziomek, *The Academic Quality of Prospective Teachers: The Impact of Admissions and Licensure Testing* (Princeton: Educational Testing Service, 1999), at www.ets.org/teachingandlearning /rschnews.html#impact.

36. Found on the websites of each school district listed.

37. Center for Education Reform, "Charter School Laws Across the States: Ranking Scorecard and Legislative Profiles" (Washington, DC: Author, 2006).

38. Russell W. Rumberger, "Why Students Drop Out of School," in *Dropouts in America: Confronting the Graduation Rate Crisis*, ed. Gary Orfield (Cambridge, MA: Harvard Educational Press, 2004), 131–55. (Quotation on 142.)

39. At www.ncate.org/public/aboutNCATE.asp?ch=1 (accessed September 15, 2009).

40. Stronge, *Qualities of Effective Teachers*, vii.

41. Stronge, *Qualities of Effective Teachers*, vii.

42. Moulthrop, Calegari, and Eggers, *Teachers Have It Easy*, 283.

43. Stanley Pogrow, "The Bermuda Triangle of American Education: Pure Traditionalism, Pure Progressivism, and Good Intentions," *Phi Delta Kappan*, 88, no. 2 (October 2006): 142–50.

44. Moulthrop, Calegari, and Eggers, *Teachers Have It Easy*, 14.

45. Bureau of Labor Statistics, *Occupational Outlook Handbook*, 2008–2009, at www.bis.gov/oco/ocos069.htm#earnings (accessed October 17, 2009).

46. Moulthrop, Calegari, and Eggers, *Teachers Have It Easy*, 295.

47. Bobby Anne Starnes, "John L. Lewis, Jesus, and President Bush," *Phi Delta Kappan* 85, no. 6 (February 2004): 475–76.

48. Diane Ravitch, *The Death and Life of the Great American School System: How Testing and Choice Are Undermining Education* (New York: Basic Books, 2010), 174.

49. Starnes, "John L. Lewis, Jesus, and President Bush," 476.

50. Starnes, "John L. Lewis, Jesus, and President Bush," 476.

51. Michael Simpson, "L.A. Story: How the *Los Angeles Times* Used Junk Science to Malign an Entire City of Teachers," *NEA Today* 29, no.3 (January 2011): 18–19.

52. Simpson, "L.A. Story."

53. Al Ramirez, "Merit Pay Misfires," *Educational Leadership* 68, no. 4 (2010–2011): 55–58.

54. Ramirez, "Merit Pay Misfires," 57.

55. Stephen Sawchuk, "Study Casts Cold Water on Bonus Pay: Lasting Achievement Gains Absent," *Education Week* 30, no. 5 (September 29, 2010): 1, 12–13.

56. Sawchuk, "Study Casts Cold Water on Bonus Pay," 13.

57. Ronald F. Ferguson, "Paying for Public Education: New Evidence on How and Why Money Matters," *Harvard Journal on Legislation* 28, no. 2, (1991): 465–98; cited in Linda Darling-Hammond, "The Flat Earth and Education: How America's Commitment to Equity Will Determine Our Future," *Educational Researcher* 36, no. 6 (2007): 318–34. (Quotation on 323.)

58. Darling-Hammond, "The Flat Earth and Education," 323.

CHAPTER 5. INACCURACIES AND ABSURDITIES DELIVERED BY THE PRESS, PUNDITS, AND POLITICIANS

1. Gerald W. Bracey, *Setting the Record Straight: Responses to Misconceptions about Public Education in the United States*, 2nd ed. (Portsmouth, NH: Heinemann, 2004), xiii.

2. John D. Draper, quoted in Gerald W. Bracey, *Education Hell: Rhetoric vs. Reality; Transforming the Fire Consuming America's Schools* (Alexandria, VA: Educational Research Service, 2009), viii.

3. In January 2005, *USA Today* reported that documents obtained under the Freedom of Information Act revealed that Williams had been paid $240,000 to promote the controversial No Child Left Behind Act.

4. Diane Ravitch, *The Death and Life of the Great American School System: How Testing and Choice Are Undermining Education* (New York: Basic Books, 2010), 202.

5. Lou Dobbs, *Lou Dobbs Tonight*, CNN News, November 9, 2006.

6. Harry Spence, interview by Marty Moss-Coane, *Radio Times*, NPR, January 31, 2007.

7. Michael Lewis, interview by Terry Gross, *Fresh Air*, NPR, October 24, 2006.

8. At en.wikipedia.org/wiki/Michael_Lewis_(author) (accessed January 9, 2011).

9. Comment by Sarah Palin during vice-presidential debate aired on ABC, October 2, 2008, at www.cnn.com/ELECTION/2008/issues/issues.education.html.

10. Cited in Association for Supervision and Curriculum Development, *SmartBrief*, January 29, 2010.

11. At www.nctq.org/p/about/funders.jsp (accessed January 10, 2011).

12. Gary Thompson, *Philadelphia Daily News*, September 30, 2010, at www.philly .com/philly/entertainment/movies/20100930_The_schools_debate__adorable-student_ edition.html.

13. Karl Weber, ed., *Waiting for "Superman"* (New York: Public Affairs, 2010), 15.

14. U.S. Bureau of the Census, *U.S. Census of the Population, U.S. Summary*, PC80-1-C1; and *Current Population Reports*, P20-455, P20-462, P20-465RV, P20-475.

15. At nces.ed.gov/pubsearch/pubsinfo.asp?pubid=2011034 (accessed September 15, 2011).

16. *American Morning AM Fix*, CNN, September 29, 2010.

17. Yong Zhao, *Catching Up or Leading the Way: American Education in the Age of Globalization* (Association for Supervision and Curriculum Development: Alexandria, VA, 2009), 11.

18. Jonathan Alter, "A Case of Senioritis: Gates Tackles Education's Two-Headed Monster," *Newsweek*, December 6, 2010, 20.

19. Linda Darling-Hammond and Robert Rothman, eds., *Teacher and Leader Effectiveness in High-Performing Education Systems* (Washington, DC: Alliance for Excellent Education, 2011).

20. James B. Starkey, *ASCD Education Brief*, January 29, 2010. This was written in response to a *Denver Post* article describing Gates's project.

21. Stephanie Banchero, "Bill Gates Seeks Formula for Better Teachers," *Wall Street Journal*, March 22, 2011.

22. Evan Thomas and Pat Wingert, "Why We Can't Get Rid of Failing Teachers," *Newsweek*, March 15, 2010, 24–33.

23. Thomas and Wingert, "Why We Can't Get Rid of Failing Teachers." (Quotations on 25.)

24. Adapted from James Stronge, *Qualities of Effective Teachers* (Alexandria, VA: Association of Supervision and Curriculum Development, 2002).

25. Gerald Bracey, *Setting the Record Straight: Responses to Misconceptions about Public Education in the United States*, 2nd ed. (Portsmouth, NH: Heinemann, 2004), 4.

26. Sean Corcoran, William N. Evans, and Robert M Schwab, "Teacher Quality: Changing Labor Market Opportunities for Women and the Quality of Teachers, 1957–2000," *Phi Delta Kappan* 85, no. 9 (May 2004): 50.

27. Corcoran, Evans, and Schwab, "Teacher Quality," 50.

28. Ildiko Laczko-Kerr and David Berliner, "In Harm's Way: How Uncertified Teachers Hurt Their Students," *Educational Leadership* 60, no. 8 (May 2003): 34–39; citing from D. Gitomer, A. S. Latham, and R. Ziomek, *The Academic Quality of Prospective Teachers: The Impact of Admissions and Licensure Testing* (Princeton: Educational Testing Service, 1999), at www.ets.org/teachingandlearning /rschnews.html#impact.

29. Thomas and Wingert, "Why We Can't Get Rid of Failing Teachers," 25.

30. At www.msta.org/faq/default.aspx?CAT_ID=119&Section=services #ID=112 (accessed October 10, 2010).

31. Amanda Ripley, "A Call to Action for Public Schools," *Time*, September 20, 2010, 32–42. (Quotation on 32.)

32. Ripley, "A Call to Action for Public Schools," 34.

33. See the following studies: Dave F. Brown, "The Effects of State Mandated Tests on Elementary Classroom Instruction" (Ed.D. diss., University of Tennessee, Knoxville, 1990); Donald H. Graves, *Testing Is Not Teaching* (Portsmouth, NH: Heinemann, 2002); T. Kellaghan, G. F. Madaus, and P. W. Airasian, *The Effects of Standardized Testing* (Boston: Kluwer Nijhoff, 1982); S. B. Nolan, T. M. Haladyna, and N. S. Haas, "A Survey of Actual and Perceived Uses, Test Preparation Activities, and Effects of Standardized Achievement Tests" (paper presented at the annual meeting of the American Educational Research Association and the annual meeting of the National Council for Measurement in Education, April 1990); James Popham, *The Truth about Testing: An Educator's Call to Action* (Alexandria, VA: Association for Supervision and Curriculum Development, 2001).

34. Ripley, "A Call to Action for Public Schools," 35.

35. Ripley, "A Call to Action for Public Schools," 36.

36. Chang, Soojung, "Statistics Show Only Few Hispanics Attend College," *Michigan Daily*, February 13, 2003, at www.michigandaily.com/content/statistics-show-only-few -hispanics-attend-college (accessed October 9, 2010).

37. "This Year's Freshmen at Four-Year Colleges: Highlights of a Survey," *Chronicle of Higher Education*, January 21, 2010, at chronicle.com/article/This-Years-Freshmen -at-4-Year/63672/ (accessed October 9, 2010).

38. Ripley, "A Call to Action for Public Schools," 38.

39. John Cloud, "How to Recruit Better Teachers," *Time*, September 20, 2010, 48.

40. Gerald W. Bracey, *The War against America's Public Schools: Privatizing Schools, Commercializing Education* (Boston: Allyn and Bacon, 2002), 53.

CHAPTER 6. WHEN GOVERNMENT AND BIG BUSINESS GET COZY

1. Herbert Kohl, foreword to *The Public School and the Private Vision*, by Maxine Green (New York: New Press, 2007), xii.

2. Susan Ohanian, *One Size Fits Few: The Folly of Educational Standards* (Portsmouth, NH: Heinemann, 1999), 6.

3. Gerald W. Bracey, quoted in William E. Smith, *Restoring Honor to Public Schools: A Teacher's Vision for American Education* (Lanham, MD: Rowman and Littlefield Education, 2009), vi. Also found at www.susanohanian.org/outrage_fetch.php?id=351.

4. David C. Berliner and Bruce J. Biddle, *The Manufactured Crisis: Myths, Fraud, and the Attack on America's Public Schools* (Reading, MA: Addison-Wesley, 1995), xi.

5. At en.wikipedia.org/wiki/A_Nation_at_Risk (accessed October 11, 2010).

6. U.S. Department of Education, *A Nation at Risk*, 1983, at www2.ed.gov/pubs/NatAtRisk/risk.html (accessed October 12, 2010).

7. Yong Zhao, *Catching Up or Leading the Way* (Alexandria, VA: Association for Supervision and Curriculum Development, 2009), 30.

8. Berliner and Biddle, *The Manufactured Crisis*, 3.

9. Kenneth J. Saltman, *The Edison Schools* (New York: Routledge, 2005), 7.

10. Kathy Emery and Susan Ohanian, *Why Is Corporate America Bashing Our Public Schools?* (Portsmouth, NH: Heinemann, 2004), 32.

11. Gerald W. Bracey, *Education Hell: Rhetoric vs. Reality; Transforming the Fire Consuming America's Schools* (Alexandria, VA: Educational Research Service, 2009) 216.

12. Samuel I. Meisels, "Doing Harm by Doing Good: Iatrogenic Effects of Early Enrollment and Promotion Policies," *Early Childhood Education Quarterly* 7 (1992): 155–74.

13. Emery and Ohanian, *Why Is Corporate America Bashing Our Public Schools?* 4.

14. Diane Ravitch, *The Death and Life of the Great American School System: How Testing and Choice Are Undermining Education* (New York: Basic Books, 2010), 200.

15. Louis V. Gerstner, Jr., "Lessons from Forty Years of Education 'Reform': Let's Abolish Local School Districts and Finally Adopt National Standards," *Wall Street Journal*, December 1, 2008, at online.wsj.com/article/SB122809533452168067.html (accessed November 20, 2010).

16. Gerald W. Bracey, *The War against America's Public Schools: Privatizing Schools, Commercializing Education* (Boston: Allyn and Bacon, 2002) 42.

17. *Education in America: Don't Fail Me*, produced by Soledad O'Brien, CNN, May 15, 2011.

18. Ravitch, *The Death and Life of the Great American School System*, 199.

19. Rita Beamish, "Back to School for the Billionaires," *Newsweek*, May 9, 2011, 38–43.

20. Ravitch, *The Death and Life of the Great American School System*, 203.

21. *The Detroit News*, at detnews.com/article/20101013/POLITICS02 /10130419/Bernero-unveils-plan-to-waive-taxes-for-new-job-creating-firms#ixzz16 (accessed November 23, 2010).

22. Ravitch, *The Death and Life of the Great American School System*, 200.

23. William E. Smith, *Restoring Honor to Public Schools* (Lanham, MD: Rowman and Littlefield, 2009), 35; quoting Mary McClellan, *Why Blame Schools*, Research Bulletin 12 (Bloomington, IN: Phi Delta Kappa Center for Evaluation, Development, and Research, 1994).

24. From the Sandia Report. Quoted in Bracey, *The War against America's Public Schools*, 53.

25. Bracey, *Education Hell*, 53.

26. Bracey, *Education Hell*, 74–78.

27. Bracey, *Education Hell*, 82–87.

28. Smith, *Restoring Honor to Public Schools*.

29. Smith, *Restoring Honor to Public Schools*, 45.

30. Rachel Anne Levy, "Is Michelle Rhee Truly Putting Students First?" So Educated, posted December 17, 2010, www.soeducated.com/2010/12/is-michelle-rhee -truly-putting-students.html (accessed March 23, 2011).

CHAPTER 7. ADVANTAGES OF ATTENDING PUBLIC SCHOOLS

1. At www.jbhe.com/preview/winter07preview.html (accessed January 21, 2011).

2. National Center for Education Statistics data, at nces.ed.gov/fastfacts/display. asp?id=16 (accessed January 21, 2011).

3. At www.friendscentral.org/admission/welcome (accessed January 23, 2011).

4. At www.episcopalacademy.org/admission/admission-process-and-timeline/index.

5. National Center for Education Statistics data, at nces.ed.gov/fastfacts/display. asp?id=16 (accessed January 21, 2011).

6. Diane Ravitch, *The Death and Life of the Great American School System: How Testing and Choice Are Undermining Education* (New York: Basic Books, 2010).

7. Ravitch, *The Death and Life of the Great American School System*, 205.

8. Dennis Cauchon, "Americans Pay Less Taxes," *USA Today*, May 6, 2011.

9. Patricia Rice, "Haiti, One Year Later: St Louis–Based Groups Growing, Helping More," part 1, *St. Louis Beacon*, January 11, 2011, at www.stlbeacon.org/issues-politics/112-region/107377-anniversary-of-the-haitian-earthquake.

10. American Association of School Administrators, "School Budgets 101," at www. aasa.org/uploadedFiles/Policy_and.../SchoolBudgetBriefFINAL.pdf (accessed May 25, 2011).

11. Robert B. Everhart, "Why Are Schools Always Begging for Money?" *Phi Delta Kappan* 88, no. 1 (September 2006): 70–75. (Quotation on 72.)

12. Everhart, "Why Are Schools Always Begging for Money?"

CHAPTER 8. CHARTER SCHOOLS AND VOUCHERS

1. Martin Carnoy, Rebecca Jacobsen, Lawrence Mishel, and Richard Rothstein, *The Charter School Dust-Up: Examining the Evidence on Enrollment and Achievement* (Washington, DC: Economic Policy Institute, 2005), 2.

2. Diane Ravitch, *The Death and Life of the Great American School System: How Testing and Choice Are Undermining Education* (New York: Basic Books, 2010), 221.

3. At en.wikipedia.org/wiki/School_voucher (accessed April 2, 2011).

4. Gerald W. Bracey, "Schools-Are-Awful Bloc Still Busy in 2008," *Phi Delta Kappan* 90, no. 2 (October 2008): 103–14.

5. Rita Beamish, "Back to School for the Billionaires," *Newsweek*, May 9, 2011, 38–43.

6. Bracey, "Schools-Are-Awful Bloc Still Busy in 2008," 111.

7. "D.C. Abortion Funding Banned in 2011 Federal Budget Deal," at www.tbd .com/articles/2011/04/government-shutown-deal-includes-d-c-abortion-school-voucher -riders-58244.html (accessed April 9, 2011).

8. "Vouchers' Failed Record," *PSEA Voice*, April 2011, 18.

9. Christy Gullfoyle, "Examining Charter Schools," *ASCD EDge Brief* 16, no. 1 (2011).

10. At www.uscharterschools.org/pub/uscs_docs/o/faq.html#2.

11. At www.uscharterschools.org/pub/uscs_docs/o/faq.html#2.

12. Kenneth Saltman, *The Edison Schools: Corporate Schooling and the Assault on Public Education* (New York: Routledge, 2005), 2.

13. Beamish, "Back to School for the Billionaires," 42.

14. Ravitch, *The Death and Life of the Great American School System*, 55.

15. Ravitch, *The Death and Life of the Great American School System*, 15.

16. At www.plunderbund.com/2011/04/03/ohios-for-profit-charter-schools-make -great-business-lousy-educators (accessed April 20, 2011).

17. Saltman, *The Edison Schools*, 2.

18. Daarel Burnette II, "Magnet Schools Lose Pull" (St. Paul) *Star Tribune*, updated April 12, 2011, at www.startribune.com/local/stpaul/119667429.html (accessed April 15, 2011).

19. Saltman, *The Edison Schools*, 5.

20. Saltman, *The Edison Schools*, 40.

21. At en.wikipedia.org/wiki/Edison_Schools_TitlePlan_would_bolster_trouble (accessed March 18, 2011).

22. Saltman, *The Edison Schools*, 74.

23. Jon Marcus, "Going Private—The U.S. Experience," (London) *Independent*, June 18, 1998.

24. Saltman, *The Edison Schools*, 144.

25. John O'Neil, "Who Profits When For-Profits Run Schools?" *NEA Today* 21 no.1, (September 2002): 31.

26. Saltman, *The Edison Schools*, 169.

27. Christopher Lubienski and Sarah Theule Lubienski, *Charter, Private, Public Schools and Academic Achievement: New Evidence From NAEP Mathematics Data* (New York: National Center for the Study of Privatization in Education, 2006).

28. At www.plunderbund.com/2011/04/03/ohios-for-profit-charter-schools-make -great-business-lousy-educators (accessed March 25, 2011).

29. Lubienski and Lubienski, *Charter, Private, Public Schools and Academic Achievement*, 40.

30. Gullfoyle, "Examining Charter Schools."

CHAPTER 9. NO CHILD LEFT BEHIND

1. Mark Twain, *The Adventures of Tom Sawyer* (New York: Aladdin Paperbacks, 2001), 154.

2. Yong Zhao, *Catching Up or Leading the Way: American Education in the Age of Globalization* (Alexandria, VA: Association for Supervision and Curriculum Development, 2009), xi.

3. Alfie Kohn, *The Case against Standardized Testing: Raising the Scores, Ruining the Schools* (Portsmouth, NH: Heinemann, 2000), 7.

4. Gerald Bracey, *Setting the Record Straight: Responses to Misconceptions about Public Education in the U.S.*, 2nd ed. (Portsmouth, NH: Heinemann, 2004), 69.

5. Bracey, *Setting the Record Straight*, xv.

6. U.S. Department of Education, *A Nation at Risk*, 1983, at www2.ed.gov/pubs/NatAtRisk/risk.html (accessed October 12, 2010).

7. David T. Kearns and Denis P. Doyle, *Winning the Brain Race: A Bold Plan to Make Our Schools Competitive* (San Francisco: Institute for Contemporary Study, 1991).

8. Bracey, *Setting the Record Straight*, 75.

9. Richard Gibboney, "Why an Undemocratic Capitalism Has Brought Public Education to Its Knees: A Manifesto," *Phi Delta Kappan* 90, no. 1 (September 2008): 21–31. (Quotation on 22.)

10. John Taylor, "Absolutely the Best Dentist," 2002, at www.trelease-on-reading.com/no-dentist.html (accessed May 11, 2011).

11. Eric Jensen, *Teaching with Poverty in Mind: What Being Poor Does to Kids' Brains and What Schools Can Do about It* (Alexandria, VA: Association for Supervision and Curriculum Development, 2009) 15.

12. Maryanne Wolf, *Proust and the Squid: The Story and Science of the Reading Brain* (New York: Harper Collins, 2007).

13. Kelly Gallagher, *Readicide: How Schools Are Killing Reading and What You Can Do About It* (Portland, ME: Stenhouse, 2009).

14. Richard C. Anderson, Paul T. Wilson, and Linda G. Fielding, "Growth in Reading and How Children Spend Their Time Outside of School," *Reading Research Quarterly* 23 (1998): 285–303.

15. Kohn, *The Case against Standardized Testing*, 37.

16. Regie Routman, *Literacy at the Crossroads: Crucial Talk about Reading, Writing, and Other Teaching Dilemmas* (Portsmouth, NH: Heinemann, 1996); cited in Kohn, *The Case against Standardized Testing*.

17. Richard Rothstein, Rebecca Jacobson, and Tamara Wilder, *Grading Education: Getting Accountability Right* (Washington, DC: Economic Policy Institute, 2008).

18. Gallagher, *Readicide*, 32–33.

19. Jensen, *Teaching with Poverty in Mind*, 64.

20. Richard L. Allington, *Big Brother and the National Reading Curriculum: How Ideology Trumped Evidence* (Portsmouth, NH: Heinemann, 2002).

21. Gallagher, *Readicide*, 25.

22. Gallagher, *Readicide*, 21.

23. Gallagher, *Readicide*, 23.

24. Kohn, *The Case against Standardized Testing*, 10.

25. W. James Popham, "A Game without Winners," *Educational Leadership* 62, no. 3 (2004): 46; cited in Jensen, *Teaching with Poverty in Mind*, 108.

26. Jensen, *Teaching with Poverty in Mind*, 108.

27. D. Jolliffe, *Rural Poverty at a Glance*, Rural Development Research Report 100 (Washington, DC: Economic Research Service, U.S. Department of Agriculture, 2004).

28. Jensen, *Teaching with Poverty in Mind*, 120.

29. Jensen, *Teaching with Poverty in Mind*, 121.

30. Jensen, *Teaching with Poverty in Mind*, 119.

31. Gallagher, *Readicide*, 19.

32. Marisol Bello and Jack Gillum, "Inquiry Sought into D.C. Tests: High Erasure Rate Puts Cloud over Rhee, Students' Improved Performance," *USA Today*, May 5, 2011, sec. A.

33. "High School Exit Exams: Issues to Consider," 2008, at www.greatschools .org/students/academic-skills/587-high-school-exit-exams-issues.gs (accessed March 5, 2008).

34. B. W. Griffin, M. H. Heidorn, and Florida Department of Education, "An Examination of the Relationship between Minimum Competency Test Performance and Dropping Out of High School," *Educational Evaluation and Policy Analysis*, Fall 1996.

35. Kathy Emery and Susan Ohanian, *Why Is Corporate America Bashing Our Public Schools?* (Portsmouth, NH: Heinemann, 2004), 23.

36. Emery and Ohanian, *Why Is Corporate America Bashing Our Public Schools?* 23.

37. Robert Schwartz, "Multiple Pathways—And How to Get There," in *Double the Numbers: Increasing Postsecondary Credentials for Underrepresented Youth*, ed. by Richard Kazis, Joel Vargas, and Nancy Hoffman (Cambridge, MA: Harvard Education Press, 2004), 26; cited in Rothstein et al., *Grading Education*, 51.

38. William J. Bushaw and Alec M. Gallup, "Americans Speak Out—Are Educators and Policy Makers Listening? The 40th Annual Phi Delta Kappa/Gallup Poll of the Public's Attitudes toward the Public Schools," *Phi Delta Kappan* 90, no. 1 (September 2008): 8–20.

39. Linda Darling-Hammond's comments, quoted in Bushaw and Gallup, "Americans Speak Out," 11.

40. Sharon L. Nichols and David C. Berliner, "Why Has High-Stakes Testing So Easily Slipped into Contemporary American Life?" *Phi Delta Kappan* 89, no. 9 (May 2008): 672–76.

41. Herbert Kohl, *Stupidity and Tears: Teaching and Learning in Troubled Times* (New York: New Press, 2003), 23–24.

CHAPTER 10. URBAN SCHOOLS

1. Yong Zhao, *Catching Up or Leading the Way: American Education in the Age of Globalization* (Alexandria, VA: Association for Supervision and Curriculum Development, 2009), xi.

2. Harvey Kantor and Barbara Brenzel, "Urban Education and the 'Truly Disadvantaged': The Historical Roots of the Contemporary Crisis, 1945–1990," *Teachers College Record* 94, no. 2 (Winter 1992): 278–314. (Quotation on 304.)

3. Eric Jensen, *Teaching with Poverty in Mind: What Being Poor Does to Kids' Brains and What Schools Can Do about It* (Alexandria, VA: Association for Supervision and Curriculum Development, 2009), 57.

4. "Time Line of Worldwide School Shootings," at www.infoplease.com/ipn/AO777958.html (accessed May 21, 2011).

5. "Schools in Need," at www.rebuildamericasschools.org/Need.html (accessed May 21, 2011).

6. "Schools in Need."

7. Kantor and Brenzel, "Urban Education and the 'Truly Disadvantaged,'" 281.

8. Kantor and Brenzel, "Urban Education and the 'Truly Disadvantaged,'" 282.

9. Office of Educational Research and Improvement, *Youth Indicators, 1988* (Washington, DC: Government Printing Office, 1988), 58–59, 62–63.

10. Kantor and Brenzel, "Urban Education and the 'Truly Disadvantaged,'" 289.

11. Kantor and Brenzel, "Urban Education and the 'Truly Disadvantaged,'" 297.

12. John U. Ogbu, "Cultural Diversity and School Experience," in *Literacy as Praxis: Culture, Language, and Pedagogy*, ed. Catherine E. Walsh (Norwood, NJ: Ablex, 1991).

13. Crystal M. England, *None of Our Business: Why Business Models Don't Work in Schools* (Portsmouth, NH: Heinemann, 2003), 53–54.

14. B. Devlin, Michael Daniels, and Kathryn Roeder, "The Heritability of IQ," *Nature* 388, no. 6641 (1997): 468–71.

15. David C. Berliner, *Poverty and Potential: Out-of-School Factors and School Success*, 2009, at epicpolicy.org/files/PB-Berliner-NON-SCHOOL.pdf (accessed May 22, 2011).

16. A. Orr, "Hunger Pangs: The Empty Stomach Problem," *Edutopia*, December 2008, at www.edutopia.org/student-hunger-nutrition-food-banks; cited in Berliner, *Poverty and Potential*, 18 (and accessed by Berliner on February 27, 2009).

17. Jensen, *Teaching with Poverty in Mind*.

18. Jensen, *Teaching with Poverty in Mind*.

19. Jensen, *Teaching with Poverty in Mind*, 26.

20. Berliner, *Poverty and Potential*.

21. Betty Hart and Todd R. Risley, *Meaningful Differences in the Everyday Experiences of Young American Children* (Baltimore: Brookes Publishing, 1995); cited in Jensen, *Teaching with Poverty in Mind*, 35.

22. Ruby K. Payne and Paul D. Slocumb, *Boys in Poverty: A Framework for Understanding Dropout* (Bloomington, IN: Solution Tree Press, 2011), 33.

23. Jensen, *Teaching with Poverty in Mind*, 16.

24. Kenneth A. Dodge, Gregory S. Pettit, and John E. Bates, "Socialization Mediators of the Relation between Socioeconomic Status and Child Conduct Problems," *Child Development* 65, no. 2 (1994): 649–65.

25. Jensen, *Teaching with Poverty in Mind*, 19.

26. Payne and Slocumb, *Boys in Poverty*, 15.

27. Gerald W. Bracey, *The War against America's Public Schools: Privatizing Schools, Commercializing Education* (Boston: Allyn and Bacon, 2002), 32–33.

28. Bracey, *The War against America's Public Schools*, 21–33.

29. *Education in America: Don't Fail Me*, produced by Soledad O'Brien, CNN, May 15, 2011.

30. Berliner, *Poverty and Potential*, 8–9.

31. Diane Ravitch, *The Death and Life of the Great American School System: How Testing and Choice Are Undermining Education* (New York: Basic Books, 2010), 227.

INDEX

achievement gap, 241–42

adequate yearly progress (AYP), 184. *See also* No Child Left Behind

Allington, Richard L., ix–xi, 137

American Association of Colleges for Teacher Education (AACTE), 111

A Nation at Risk (ANAR): effects on drop in creativity scores, 35; inaccuracies of, 116; introductory statements, 115

Berliner, David C., ix, 63, 114, 116, 136

Biddle, Bruce J., 114, 116

Bill and Melinda Gates Foundation. *See* Gates Foundation, Bill and Melinda

Bracey, Gerald W., ix, xi, 1, 26, 89, 104, 106, 111, 117, 132, 137, 166, 180

Broad Foundation, Eli and Edythe: money spent to influence education policies, 123, 125; money spent to influence school board elections, 170; money spent to support charter schools, 125, 170; training noneducators to be administrators, 124

career paths, 31

caring for students, 13

certified teachers: definition of, 62; effects on student test scores, 63, 65; requirements for, 62, 103–4, 141; value of, 15, 62, 63, 65, 140, 235–36

Chamber of Commerce, 117

charter schools: billionaires' contributions to, 170; definition of, 160, 168; as EMOs, 122, 169; failed/closed schools, 177; for-profit schools, 172; governing boards, 169; history of, 169–71; initiation of, 159–60; poor student

test score performance, 159,
176–77; purposes of, 168; student
populations, 173; uncertified
teachers, 69–70, 169. *See also*
Edison Learning Incorporated

China's educational system, 25,
34–37

class size, 232

content standards, 117–18

content validity: definition of, 44;
ensuring it, 205

cream-skimming, 164, 175. *See also*
charter schools; Edison Learning
Incorporated; private schools;
vouchers

creative thinking: U.S. ranking in, 26;
value of, 28

critical thinking, 26, 32

Darling-Hammond, Linda, 38–39,
63, 136–37

developmentally appropriate practice
(DAP), 119

diversity of students, 153

dropouts: past decades' rates, 48;
reasons for, 51–52, 239–40

Duncan, Arne, 92, 124

Edison Learning Incorporated:
contracting nonunionized
services, 171; cream-skimming,
175; description of, 122, 170;
difficulties, 173–76; for-profit
schools, 172; inexperienced
teachers, 174; standardizing
curricula, 171; student
populations, 173; urban schools,
173; use of nonprofessional
administrators, 171

educational management
organizations (EMO): definition
of, 122; initiation of, 170. *See also*
Edison Learning Incorporated;
Knowledge Is Power Program

education journals, 106

education majors, 64, 104

Eli and Edythe Broad Foundation.
See Broad Foundation, Eli and
Edythe

Emery, Kathy, 117

external factors affecting learning,
190–92

extracurricular activities: importance
of, 30–31; opportunities for, 16–
17; public school offerings, 145

Finland's educational system, 38–39,
101

Friedman, Thomas L., 40

funding schools, 230–32

Gates Foundation, Bill and Melinda:
college dropout, 47; ignorance
of educational issues, 100–102;
inaccuracies on value of master's
degrees, 87, 100–101; influence on
education policies, 91–92; money
spent to influence education
policies, 101–2, 123; money spent
to support charter schools, 125,
170; small school initiative, 146

good school, 13–18

grade level performance, 192–93

graduation rates, 99

immigrant students, 110, 220–21

Individuals with Disabilities Act
(IDEA), 3

intelligence quotient (IQ), 21–22, 143
international test score comparisons,
    41–44
Ivy League schools, 6

Japanese educational system, 37
Jefferson, Thomas, 1, 2, 109, 129
Jensen, Eric, 42

Knowledge Is Power Program
    (KIPP), 122
Kohn, Alfie, 20, 27, 136–37

Marzano, Robert, 12
master's degrees, 86–88, 101
McGraw-Hill Testing Company:
    money garnered from NCLB, 204;
    relationship to Bush family, 128;
    test preparation materials, 128
merit pay, 85–86
Moulthrop, Daniel, 73, 75

narrowing the curriculum, 35
National Assessment of Educational
    Progress (NAEP), x, 63, 132, 206,
    222
National Center for Education
    Statistics (NCES): bachelor's
    degrees awarded, 99; graduation
    rates, 48; international test
    comparisons, 44; number of
    public schools, 140; public school
    enrollment figures, 4; U.S.
    education expenditures, 46
National Council for Accreditation of
    Teacher Education (NCATE), 63,
    66, 71, 97
National Education Association
    (NEA), 77–78, 95

Nobel Prize, 5, 25, 29
No Child Left Behind (NCLB):
    adequate yearly progress, 185;
    costs of testing requirements,
    203–5; costs to the public, 151;
    description of policy, "best
    dentists" scenario, 187–89;
    destruction of local and state
    control of education issues, 179;
    effects on teachers, 199, 236;
    encouraging business intervention
    in educational matters, 123, 175,
    187; encouraging cheating, 201–2;
    encouraging EMOs, 122–23,
    175, 185–87; failure of, 211–12;
    history of, 180–82; impact on
    certification, 62; lack of research
    support for, 197–98; negative
    effects on learning, 183; negative
    effects on low socioeconomic-
    status students, 198; negative
    effects on proficient students,
    198–99; negative effects on school
    day design, 194, 199–200; negative
    effects on specials, 200; negative
    effects on students' reading
    progress, 183, 194–99; negative
    effects on teaching, 183, 194–96;
    negative impact on creativeness,
    34; opposition to, 212;
    politicization of, 20; proficiency,
    43–44, 183–84; reauthorization
    of, 181; rewarding principals,
    201; seizing control of schools
    not making AYP, 185; seizing
    state and local control of school
    policies, 157; testing costs, 151;
    transfer policy, 185–86
norm-referenced tests, 131

Ohanian, Susan, 117, 122, 137
Ontario's educational system, 39
opportunity gaps, 242–43
oppositional identity, 223–25

parental influence, 233–34
parochial schools: cream-skimming,
164; loss of local control, 165;
teacher compensation compared
to public school teachers, 147–48;
uncertified teachers, 69–70
pedagogy: courses related to, 103–4;
definition of, 66–67; impact on
teacher effectiveness, 72; value to
certification, 62
performance standards, 121
per-pupil expenditures, 70
Phi Delta Kappan: survey results,
7–8, 13, 212; value to teaching
profession, 106
poverty: effects on children's
learning, 225–30; effects on stress,
227–28; environmental effects,
226; impact on IQ, 42; inadequate
diet, 226–27; politicians' efforts,
43. *See also* socioeconomic status
private schools: cream-skimming,
164; entry requirements, 143–44;
loss of local control, 165; services
offered, 23; teacher compensation
compared to public school
teachers, 147–48; tuition costs,
145, 162; uncertified teachers,
68–69
proficiency: definition of, 43–44, 184;
ensuring it, 202–3
prospective teachers' grade point
averages, 68
Pulitzer Prize, 5

retention of students, 120

Sandia Report on Education:
description of, 130; release of,
182; suppressed from the public,
130–31
Scholastic Aptitude Test (SAT),
131–32
school boards: local control, 154;
reflect community values, 155–56;
requirements for membership, 154
self-discipline, 21
Singapore's educational system, 38
socioeconomic status, low: effects on
learning, 225–30; impact on IQ,
42. *See also* poverty
Sputnik, 1
Stronge, James, 14, 65–67, 71–72
student evaluation, 209–10

taxes: breaks for corporations,
46, 126–27, 152–53; breaks
for the wealthy, 152; lowest
rates in decades, 148, 150;
personal property, 150; school
expenditures, 150
teacher evaluation: research-based
process, 82, 209–10; using
students' test scores, 84, 208–9;
value-added models, 83–84
teachers: accountability, 213–14;
attrition rate, 60; compensation
compared to international
teachers, 45; compensation
compared to other professions,
55–56; compensation compared to
private school teachers, 147–48;
compensation effects on quality,
74–76; effective characteristics,

71–72, 82–83; increases in salary, 56; influence on test scores, 72–74

Teach for America candidates: cost to taxpayers, 64–65; effects of being uncertified, 64; attrition rate, 64. *See also* uncertified teachers

teaching, challenges of, 58–61

teacher unions: attacks on, 135; effects on tenure, 105; value of unionized teachers to student test scores, 77–79

tenure: definition of, 79–80; need for, 80–81; violation of, 105

tests: costs of international, 45; costs of NCLB requirements, 203–4; for graduation, 207; high stakes, 206–7; increasing dropout rate, 207–8; time spent preparing for, 205; used to evaluate teachers, 208. *See also* merit pay

uncertified teachers: in charter schools, 69–70; in parochial schools, 69–70; in private schools, 68–39; in urban schools, 70, 235–36

urban schools: history of, 220–22; inaccuracies, 218–19; inequitable funding, 231–32; physical condition, 219; poor leadership, 237–38; teachers, 234–35; uncertified teachers, 70, 235–36. *See also* poverty

vouchers: costs to tax payers, 161, 166; DC Opportunity Scholarship Program, 162, 166; definition of, 161; history of, 161–62; legality of, 162–63; loss of local control, 165; lower student test scores, 165–67; organizations opposed to, 167; public's opinions of, 8, 163; uncertified teachers, 166; voted down, 163

Walton Foundation (Walmart): influencing education policy, 92, 123, 125; money spent to influence school board elections, 170; money spent to support charter schools, 92, 125, 170; money spent to support vouchers, 92, 125; opposing unions, 126

Zhao, Yong, 25, 29, 36, 45, 180

ABOUT THE AUTHOR

Dave F. Brown, Ed D, is a professor in the College of Education at West Chester University in Pennsylvania. After he received his bachelor's degree in elementary education from Northern Illinois University, he taught as an elementary- and middle-level educator. Following 13 years as a public school teacher in the Midwest and Virginia, Dave attended the University of Tennessee and received his doctorate in curriculum and instruction.

He is an educational researcher and national consultant, providing in-services on urban-education issues, young adolescent development, appropriate middle school design, and cultural responsiveness. Dave served on a U.S. representative's educational advisory board and has provided research analyses to state and federal legislators.

Dr. Brown has authored several book chapters and numerous research articles published in journals such as *Phi Delta Kappan, Educational Leadership, Middle School Journal, Action in Teacher Education,* and *Urban Education*; and he serves on the editorial advisory and review boards of three educational journals. Dave is coauthor of the book *What Every Middle School Teacher Should Know* and the author of *Becoming a Successful Urban Teacher*.

CPSIA information can be obtained at www.ICGtesting.com
Printed in the USA
BVOW061502290212

284035BV00002BA/1/P